— A LIFE UNRAVELED —

PAULA VAN ZYL

WINGS ON MY HEELS: A LIFE UNRAVELED

COPYRIGHT 2021 by Paula Van Zyl

ISBN: 9798543527320

All rights reserved. No part of this publication may be reproduced or distributed in any form or by any means, electronic or mechanical, without prior written permission from the publisher.

Requests for permission to make copies of any part of this work should be emailed to the author (wingonmyheel@gmail.com), subject line "permissions." The author hereby grants permission to reviewers to quote up to 100 words from up to three chapters in their reviews, and requests that hyperlinks to said reviews be emailed to the address above.

All proceeds from the sale of this book are donated
to Compass Zambia, a 501-c3 charity for community
development and education in Africa.
CompassZambia.com

Front cover design ©2021 by Lynnette Bonner of Indie Cover Design
Back cover artwork ©2021 by Taylor Durick

Printed in United States of America

To my late mother,
Evie-Irene Petty

and my daughter,
Amelia McFarland

*You never gave up on me
and loved me in spite of myself
and all my bone-headed adventures.*

Contents

1	Introduction
2	Grand Jury Indictment
3	Normal Childhood?
9	Move and I'll Shoot You
18	Drugs, Sex and…
25	Wear What?
41	Busted
48	Gone, Baby, Gone
68	Life Anew
78	Party and Crash
102	Sucked Back In
110	Spit Out
117	On the Road Again
126	Wild Life and Heaven
136	Piranhas and Pot
142	On the Edge
146	Winds of Change
149	Storm Warnings
154	Uninvited Guests
165	Strange World
176	The Blue Code
185	Mom
192	Letting Go
194	Freedom
202	Baboons and Me
216	What Tree
226	Long Drops
232	Life Worth Living
238	Epilogue
240	Acknowledgments
241	About the Author

Introduction

"Paula you were born with wings on your heels."

From my earliest memories, Mom told me this often.

"Sure. Whatever," I retorted while continuing on my merry little way.

All of my life I have felt this urgency to go, to experience it all—everything that was out there. I was never satisfied with staying put. The wings on my heels were too strong to resist.

I have lived through a lot and had quite a few experiences. Sometimes I had great fun and other time's great pain and darkness. But I was never bored.

Everyone experiences life differently, but there are moments in everyone's life that define us, help us, hurt us, and even shame us. But they are never wasted on us.

God uses all of our moments to shape us into the person He created us to be. I am who I am today because of the life I lived. The moments have become my story. I thank God for giving me wings on my heels and allowing me to share this extraordinary story with you.

This book is not just about my life; rather, it's a book about all of us and how God doesn't waste any of our moments, using all of the good, the bad, the big, and the small to connect us. We are not alone; our lives are connected like pixels making up the larger picture that can be seen only when we step back and look at the whole.

May *Wings on My Heels* be a blessing and encouragement to you in your own life and the life hereafter. Until we meet again.

Grand Jury Indictment
Filed May 23, 1974

COUNT ONE

Beginning at a date unknown to the Grand Jury and continuing up to and including January 12, 1974, in the Southern District of California, and elsewhere, defendants Dale Weaton, Jerome Wonders, Larry Means, Katie Mero, Frank Cost, Dina Weaton and Paula Petty, along with un-indicted co-conspirators Felix Change, SharonChange, Nellie Hanson, Mike Fell and Sue Wonders, did knowingly and intentionally combine, conspire, and agree together and with each other and with diverse other persons unknown to the Grand Jury to knowingly and intentionally import and attempt to import approximately 141 pounds of cocaine, a Schedule II Controlled Substance into the United States from a place outside thereof: in violation of Title 21, United States Code, Section 952, 960 and 963.

The indictment missed a few trips, but I wasn't about to correct them. They also missed all the misadventures of these participants, and I should know. I am Paula, and this is my story.

1

Normal Childhood?

That I even have a story to tell is a miracle. After the birth of my mother's first child from a previous marriage, the doctors told her that she should never have another child and she was RH negative. At that time, the second child from a mother with RH negative blood would have what is called blue baby syndrome. These children had a life expectancy of about thirteen years, and they were usually deformed, some unable to walk, and mentally challenged.

Seventeen years later, in 1951, when Mom learned she was pregnant with me, her first concern was about the effects on her baby because of her being RH negative. Some experimental drugs had just become available to correct this problem. Though she received no assurances that they would work, Mom agreed to try them.

Thankfully, the treatment worked. I was born with a head full of red fuzz. My dad, Paul, took one look at me and fell in love with his baby girl. They named me Paula after him. I was blessed with my mom's brown eyes instead of my dad's blue ones, and for that I have always been grateful. The red hair, however, would curse me for years.

When I was around six months old, a fire broke out in our home. I was with the babysitter. She rescued me from the burning, smoke-filled house that was destroyed. It was discovered that a fault in an electrical appliance had caused the fire. The insurance was enough for Mom and Dad to buy a lovely home in San Fernando.

In 1954 they opened the first drive-in restaurant in Los Angeles and named it after my dad: Paul's Drive-In. It was a huge success. A child's menu was on the back of the main menu, featuring my photo.

It took years for my hair to grow. My mom taped little bows on my fuzzy head so that people would know I was a girl. Despite the frilly dresses I wore, some people would still say, "Oh, what a cute little boy." My dad rubbed lanolin on my head every night for years to promote growth. Finally, hair came in—thick, coarse, heavy red hair.

I was a lively child and, I admit, very spoiled. Most of my cousins on Dad's side of the family were grown or in their teens by the time I was born. My brother from Mom's previous marriage was seventeen, and I was the apple of his eye. My aunts and uncles from my dad's side of the family, who nearly all worked for him, did their share of giving me whatever I wanted whenever I wanted it. My dad could never say no to me. I had every toy a child could desire. I even had a nanny since my parents worked. My dog was my playmate. I often dressed up my little poodle and arranged my dolls around the table for tea parties with my "friends." Truthfully, I had very few friends, only my cousins when they came to visit. With only myself and my dogs to play with, I developed a vivid imagination. I was always up to something and did many little projects and experiments that ended in messes. My dad would not allow me to be punished; he called it a good sign of my inventiveness and imagination. One of my nannies told my mom, right before she quit, "Your child! I don't know where she comes up with all the things she does. She is more than a full-time job. I quit!"

Ah well. There were others. When in need of someone to babysit me, it fell to my older cousins. They hated the job because I loved to play pranks on them. When they told my dad about my misbehaver, he only laughed.

When I was three, my mom promised me a baby sister or brother. Unfortunately, my baby brother lived only a few hours after birth. He had a lung-heart issue that could not be corrected. When Mom and Dad returned from the hospital with no baby, I was inconsolable. I refused to eat, flung myself onto the floor; beat my little fists on the ground—I excelled at tantrums. Not knowing what to do with me, my parents enrolled me in several activities to distract me from the missing baby. I took ballet, tap, and soft-shoe lessons. I demonstrated talent and was in ballet toe shoes by age five or six. My dance teacher was a well-known dancer and had several movie connections. She urged my parents to put me in films. They declined, wanting me to have a normal childhood.

At five I was informed that I would have to go to something called "school," where I would be with other children all day. This did not suit me at all, especially when I learned that my dog could not attend with me. Mom and Dad enrolled me in Villa Cabrini Academy, an all-girls Catholic school in the Los Angeles area, assuring me that it would be wonderful to have other kids to play with. They lied! I fought with all that was within me…and that was just getting into the car to go to school. It was an uphill battle for my parents from day one. I hadn't lost my skill at throwing a temper tantrum, but this time I was fighting for my life, as school was out of the question to me. I kicked and screamed, saying that I was never going to grow up, I was happy being a five-year-old, and I was not going to school.

After much bribing on my dad's part, they got me to school. Sure enough, I hated it. From my memories, the teasing and torment started on the first day of school. I was a five-year-old with wild red hair, unlike any of the other kids. The nuns in their head-to-toe black habits scared me to death. Praying and going to church were not for me.

Mom enrolled me in piano class at the school, which was also a failure. The nuns finally told my mom, "Don't waste any more money on these lessons. Unless we are here all the time and watching her, she disappears into the olive grove around the school, making us hunt for her." Thus ended my budding piano career.

My parents sold Paul's Drive-In and built a classy bar and restaurant called Paul's Bonanza. The waitresses wore long dresses in the Old West style; female bartenders and servers wore cool dance-hall outfits. Overall, this venture turned into another big success for my dad. The high-class clientele included some minor TV stars from popular TV shows at the time, such as *'77 Sunset Strip*, whose stars were regular customers. I was about seven or eight and wanted to be a waitress. Of course, I was too young, so I worked in the kitchen washing dishes as I stood on a Coca-Cola bottle crate so I could reach the big dish washing machine.

My parents also built a full-size bar at the house as well as two apartments in the back, one for their top waitress, who had become a very good friend of Mom, and her daughter Linda, and a crash pad for customers who were too drunk to drive home after the parties. My niece, the only daughter of my brother, Linda and I had devised several schemes to spy on the grownups at these parties. Whenever the parties got loud and woke us up, we would sneak up to the top of my big playhouse. From there we had a great view into the sliding glass windows that opened up to the yard. My brother, who was twenty-four and worked as a cook in the restaurant, was always the life of the party. We saw some pretty wicked dirty dancing from our little perch until someone went into the bedroom to check on us and discovered we were not there. The first time this happened all hell broke loose as they had no idea what had happened to us. The search was on. We knew what was going on, and after a while, we surrendered ourselves. We were soundly put back to bed. But that didn't stop us; we did it time and time again. And we always got caught. But we had a jolly time watching through the curtain of smoke the partiers having a grand time.

But all was not well with Mom and Dad. They had met shortly after Mom's first marriage ended in divorce. Paul took one look at the raven-haired, petite, big-breasted beauty and fell head over heels in love with her. She, however, swore she would never love another man and informed him of this fact. He told her he loved her and promised to take care of her. She considered her limited prospects and knew this suitor to be a hard worker, so she decided to marry him, telling him it was a business partnership, pure and simple. They had married for the first time in 1946 in Yuma, Arizona.

My mom refused to tell my dad she loved him. She reminded him time and time again that she had told him from the start she would never love another man because she would never again be hurt the way my brother's father had hurt her. So the fights between Mom and Dad grew increasingly worse and more frequent. My dad had a temper and was extremely jealous of anyone who even looked at my mom, as beautiful as ever. During their fights, Dad yelled and called Mom names; she tried to calm him down.

I got expelled from the Catholic school a time or two, but my dad gave them a donation. Bingo! I was back in, much to my displeasure.

When I was twelve, my parents sold the Bonanza and our beautiful house, and we moved to a horrible place, a hick town called Calimesa. My dad bought another restaurant, Hills Halfway House, named because it was almost halfway from Los Angeles to Palm Springs. It sat on the highway, so business was very good.

I was put back into a Catholic school. I still hated it—school, the nuns in their habits, and all the rules. I finally managed to get myself expelled for the last time.

I had this nice gig going where I could get into the storm drain and walk to town quickly. There I acted like a sweet young kid while I shoplifted makeup and candy. One day I took with me a blabbermouth who had no expertise in shoplifting. Sure enough, she got us caught. Naturally, with my history at the school, the only choice was expulsion.

I finally got my wish to go to a public school. I thought life would be instantly better. But I quickly discovered that I was still the freak with my wild flaming red hair that frizzed at the slightest moisture. I thought it was only the kids at Catholic school who were mean to me, but I learned the hard way that I was the problem. I was not like the other kids who called me names and flung insults at me. Their favorites were "Red Red wet the bed" and "Rather be dead than red in the head."

Things at home were heating up with my parents fighting almost every night. My dad had bought another fancy bar and restaurant that had a small hotel attached to it. Shortly after, he bought the rights to the Palm Springs airport restaurant. The new freeway cut the access to Hills Halfway House, so he sold it. My parents were working long hours and traveled often between Redlands and Palm Springs, about a ninety-mile round trip. I was left on my own most of the time and had no friends. I was a lost soul. Who needed those kids? Not me, I had my dog—my best friend!

Then my mom and dad had one heck of a fight. I had learned to tune out the name-calling and my dad's yelling and was used to waking up in the morning and finding my dad's bureau drawers missing. The morning after this horrific fight, my mom got a call from the police. My dad had run off the road in his convertible Cadillac and was in bad shape. We hurried to the hospital. He looked a mess with numerous cuts and bruises, but nothing was broken, and he suffered no life-threatening injuries. We took him home, and he recovered quickly. My mom bought new bureaus, as half of my dad's drawers were smashed, lying in the ditch where they'd flown out of the convertible during the wreck.

One memorable fight scared me like none other. I was in bed, and as usual, the fighting started. When it escalated, I got out of bed to have a look. Bad timing. I watched in horror as my dad pulled a big cook's knife out of the drawer and jumped on my mom's lap. Just as he brought the knife down to plunge into my mom's neck, she raised her hand in defense. The knife sliced her hand, almost cutting off her thumb. My dad leaped up, ran out the door, jumped into his car, and tore off. Mom calmly tended to her injury. I ran and hid in my closet. Fearing that my mom was going to die, I didn't know what to do. I believe she drove herself to the hospital that night because when I saw her the next morning, her hand was wrapped in a large bandage. When I asked her what happened, she said, "Oh, I cut myself." It was years before I finally told her that I had seen the attempted stabbing. But by that time, so many more battles had been fought that it was no longer a big deal.

It wasn't long after this incident that my dad was caught selling, or trying to sell, illegal drugs to an undercover cop. It turned into a muddle when my brother, who was there when dad made the deal, took the blame and went to jail. He said he did it to protect me so that I would not find out about it. Unfortunately, it was in the papers, which made it a hundred times worse. The kids at school stared at me as they pointed and whispered.

Could this torture camp get any worse?

2

MOVE AND I'LL SHOOT YOU

Life went on. Cocooned in my own little world—just me and my dog—I was safe there with just the two of us. My dog loved me, and no one called me or my mom names.

My parents' divorce was in progress. One day I found myself living with my mom at my aunt's house in Norwalk. How we got to my aunt's is still a mystery as I was so closed off. I have no memories of packing up or moving. Nothing.

What I do vividly remember is living with my aunt and her horrible fat husband, whom I hated…with good cause. We had been there only for a few weeks when I was alone with my uncle. As I walked past his room, he called for me to come in. Like a dope I did. He was lying on his bed like a beached whale, naked from the bottom down and playing with himself. "I'll give you some money if you do this to me," he said.

He messed with the wrong niece, the one who had built up such rage and hurt inside. I was like a pressure cooker about to burst. And burst I did, right on top of his little plaything. With every bit of strength in my twelve-year-old body, I jumped onto his package. He squealed like the pig he was. From that day forward, he never looked me in the eye or even came near me. Naturally, no one noticed, for everyone had their own problems.

My dad was a major problem for my mom. He was fighting for custody of me. Anything he could do to smear her reputation, he did. During the divorce hearing, the judge had me removed from the courtroom. Since I was twelve and able to express whom I wanted to live with, he took me into his chambers. "Which is it, Paula, your mom, or your dad?"

"If you make me live with my dad, I will be gone before the ink dries on the divorce papers."

He awarded my mom custody.

My father was so mad at my mom's attorney; he tried to attack the man right there in court, all the while calling my mom everything but a human being. The bailiffs hustled Mom and me out of the courthouse while others dealt with my dad.

Mom decided to lay low. The next thing I know, we were on a bus to Texas, me in a brown wig. Finally, I had real hair! I thought being on the run with Mom was a cool adventure. We stayed with my mom's older sister until things died down a bit; then we quietly returned to California. Mom and I moved into an apartment on the outskirts of Long Beach in a town called Lakewood.

Although Mom had a restraining order against my dad, it did not stop him from finding us. One night he broke into our apartment and ripped out the wires from the downstairs phone. The bedrooms were upstairs, where there was an extension phone. Mom told me to stay put. She went downstairs, and the fighting ensued. It quickly escalated. The slaps and distinct sound of flesh pounding flesh told me that Dad was beating Mom. I ran downstairs and found my parents locked in battle. My mom was bent over with my dad on her back, beating her in the face with his horseshoe diamond ring.

"If you hit me again, I will shoot you!" Mom screamed.

Well, he did, and she did! She used a little .22 handgun. She had taken lessons and was a good shot. The bullet hit a silver dollar in my dad's pants pocket and did very little damage to his leg.

He yelled. I ran upstairs and called the police. By the time I went back downstairs, my mom's face was a mass of blood, and my dad was hopping around, yelling, "You shot me!"

Mom remained cool-headed as she handed me her gun. "Don't let him out of your sights." Then she went to the sink and washed some of the blood running down her face.

I glanced at her. She looked bad, and I was worried about her. Shifting my gaze back to Dad, I said, "One move and I'll shoot you!"

The police arrived, pried the gun from my hand, and arrested my dad for battery and for violating the restraining order. The officers talked to me and mom separately. Since our stories were the same, they let my mom go. For some reason, my dad was never taken to court. To this day I don't know if anything ever came of it.

We moved to Norwalk, a suburb of Los Angeles, to be closer to my mom's family. I started junior high school with my cousins, who were close in age to me. Now thirteen, I'd had enough of the red hair and the angst it caused. I dyed it…behind Mom's back. I tried to go blonde. But it seemed my coarse red hair would not budge beyond a rather ugly orange, which only made the teasing worse than before. My mom was mad at me, but what could she do? Since I could not go blonde, I would try going black. Now that took. But I looked awful with ebony hair, ultra-fair skin, and red eyebrows. My only recourse was to go dark with my makeup. Too bad Goth was not in fashion; I would have fit right in. So back to trying for at least a brown color. It lightened up a bit, but I couldn't alter the frizzy curls, not to mention that the numerous colorings had damaged my hair. But I was determined to conquer my cursed hair. "I know! I'll try Curl Free!" This hair straightening solution might have worked if my hair had not been so damaged, but I'll never know because my hair broke off and fell out. Almost bald and in tears, I ran home. I had really done it this time. Mom took one look and shook her head. Then she took me out and bought me an expensive wig. I wore it for over a year. My ninth-grade graduation picture was taken with me wearing my wig.

When enough new hair had come in, my mom had a professional stylist dye my hair, matching the new hair with what hadn't fallen out. But my hair was super short. Lucky for me, Twiggy, a supermodel from the '60s, was all the rage. She wore her hair short. But hers was blonde and straight. Every night I taped my hair down, forcing it to straighten. In the morning it would be okay…for a couple of hours. Then the frizzing and curling took over. But at least my hair was finally growing.

I turned fourteen and started high school. I also started smoking cigarettes and pot.

I don't remember how or who introduced me to "reds," a barbiturate, but before long I was using them regularly. They made me no longer care what I was called or by whom. I was into my own little world. But the drugs proved to be a problem with school because I nodded off during class. One day I fell asleep in French class. I told the teacher I was sick. She sent me to the school nurse, who put me to bed in the back room to keep an eye on me. I promptly went to sleep. But she got busy and forgot about me. A janitor woke me up at about 5:30 p.m. When I realized the time, I jumped out of the bed and made a beeline for the exit, managing to get home just before my mom did.

The school finally caught on that I was up to no good. I received the "bad one" label and the "good kids" avoided me. Not one counselor, teacher, or staff member at the school bothered to find out what my problem was. No one cared. My mom was busy trying to make a living for the two of us, not easy for a single mom in 1967. She never dreamed what I was up to because by the time she arrived home from work, I was there, her perfect kid wide awake and doing homework. How I passed tenth grade remains a mystery because I don't have much memory of that school year.

That summer of 1967, the hippie movement was budding in my world. It had blossomed in San Francisco, where most of the hippies hung out. My mom found one of her long-lost cousins living up in the Bay Area. She and I drove up with my cousin Rhonda to meet her and her two sons, who were a bit older than Rhonda and me. For most of the trip, Rhonda and I slept, thanks to our love of reds. By then Mom had caught on to my use of drugs. While my cousin and I slept, Mom went through my stuff and found the pills. She did not say a word to me about them but continued driving. When we woke up and looked for our stash, my mom said as calmly as if she were noting the time, "I found your pills and flushed them all down the toilet at the last gas station."

Rhonda and I went bug-eyed. Then Mom gave us a dressing down, after which she assumed the problem was solved since the pills were gone. My cousin and I were not pleased, but what could we do but make the most of our trip and meet these unknown cousins. We were in for a very happy surprise.

Our newly discovered cousins were seventeen and eighteen and had longish hair. As we got to know them better, we found out they were kind of hippies and had something they thought we would like much better than reds: LSD. We had heard of it but never knew anyone who had used it.

As my mom and her long-lost cousin chatted, they left us kids to our own devices. We waited until Mom and her cousin went to bed, then we four sneaked out and drove to the top of a mountain. There my cousin and I took our first hit of LSD. We loved it! It was like nothing else on the planet. We laughed all night at nothing and had a ball. As we watched the sun come up over the mountains, I thought, *This is the best morning ever.* Everything was so bright and wonderful. We got back to the house before anyone woke up and quickly dressed in our pajamas. The grownups were none the wiser about our all-night LSD experience.

We missed our reds, but driving back home without them was not so bad. Now we were smoking pot and had taken LSD. We were just so very cool.

The long summer stretched before me, and I wanted to know more about this hippie thing. Other than San Francisco, the only hippies in Southern California were hanging out in the beach areas, like Huntington Beach. People described them as freaks with long hair. The freak part I got—that's what the kids at school said I was. I wondered if the hippies were like me. I decided I should have a look. I sneaked out of my bedroom window and hitchhiked to Huntington Beach where I ran smack into a group of them. They welcomed me with open arms. As I meandered among the hippies, I discovered that they were doing more than just LSD. They were shooting up reds. Naturally, I wanted to try this as well. I could not do it myself, so the guys helped and "shot me up."

I stayed with them for the rest of the summer, only going back home in time to start school. We typically shot up in the bathroom, and more than once I found myself lying in the bathtub. But, hey, I was having a ball! I was so in love with a twenty-year-old guy with long black hair. All I had to do was sleep with him and I got all the drugs I wanted. No problem there. I lost my virginity months before to some guy I don't even remember, but I do recall that it was not so good. I have no idea why I did it in the first place. Sex for me was not enjoyable but a means to get what I wanted.

When I was fifteen, my seventeen-year-old friend had a car. Anytime I could sneak out, which was often, we went to Hollywood. The Hollywood Palladium was going strong in those days with lots of rock 'n' roll. The Aquarius Theater, which was almost across the street, showed all-night movies. Stoned after the concerts, we went there to watch Betty Boop cartoons all night, or we crashed with the rest of the hippies. One night we had just parked the car near the Palladium when the reds hit us both at the same time. We must've fallen asleep leaning against the doors of the car. All of a sudden, I was awakened. I was laying half in and half out of the car, staring up into the face of a police officer. The police hauled my friend and me to jail and called our parents. I was such an idiot. I took off my granny shoes and hit the woman police officer over the head with one of them. That did not help my case any, but as I was just fifteen, all she could do was take my shoes away from me and leave me until my dad came to get me.

I was given probation and told to keep out of trouble. The next week I was back in Hollywood having a ball. I met and became the girlfriend of a now well-known Hollywood personality. He was much older than I was, but I was smitten with him. After the concerts we would go to the International House of Pancakes, take reds, drink coffee, in which they dissolved faster and we got higher faster. Then we'd go back to his place not far from Sunset and Vine and either pass out or have sex, depending on how high we were. Sometimes he had sex with me as I slept. But who cared? It wasn't long before he dropped me for an up-and-coming movie star, a young woman about eighteen. But it was fun while it lasted.

We also had another place where we'd gather: the Shrine Auditorium in Los Angeles, where big bands played. There I saw Janis Joplin, my hero! She had hair like mine. I loved her and started drinking Southern Comfort because she did. I saw all the top rock bands of the time, including Jimmy Hendrix, and loved them all. I was a rocker, loving everything rock 'n' roll, and was a confirmed Stones fan.

We moved to another LA suburb, where I was enrolled in eleventh grade at Gardena High School. I immersed myself in the hippie mind-set. I wore hippie clothing, and my shoulder-length wild hair fit nicely into that lifestyle. But Gardena High School was located in a Hispanic area, so I did not fit in at all. Once again I was a freak to my classmates. The girls wore their hair ratted up, and some tucked razor blades into their big hair. One look at the kids in that school and I was out the back door and back at home. I called my mom. "No way am I going back to that school. I wouldn't live beyond a day, two at most." I was 5'2" and weighed about ninety-five pounds. The girls in that school did not like the way their boys looked at me. I had no intention of finding out what they would do to me. After about three or four days of my constant whining, Mom visited the school counselor and asked to be shown around the school. On seeing the girls I had told her about, even she was scared of them. She saw for herself that this school was not for her daughter. She decided that I would spend the weekdays with my cousin who lived in Redondo Beach, a surfer kids' area. I was able to attend Aviation High School. The school was a bit better; the kids still called me names, but I did not fear for my life. I did try to fit in and even took up surfing. Big mistake. Coarse frizzy hair and salty ocean water equal wild hair on steroids. Mind you, surfer girls had straight, long, blonde hair. But I was not going down the hair-falling-out routine again. It was better to have frizzy red hair than no hair at all. My light fair skin that turned bright red with too much sun stood out among all the golden-tanned bodies. But I made the effort to fit in.

In 1968 I was working part-time after school as a waitress at a restaurant in Torrance, not far from Redondo Beach. I bought an old Toyota Corolla from my uncle who was in the car business. It did not matter if at times I had to push it to start it or that hitting a bump would turn on the heater. It ran, more or less, and I was mobile. As soon as I had paid off the car, I quit my job and started running away on the weekends. My mom eventually gave up trying to find me. Back then, the police did not do much to find runaway hippies—there were too many of us.

I met a girl named Chris at one of Griffith Park's love-ins. She lived near Los Angeles in a part of town called Silver Lake, which was a low- to medium-income area. Her mom was also a single mom. Since her mom was there, it was okay for me to spend some weekends with her. Her mom worked the night shift at the post office. Chris and I hung out with some older hippie guys. I fell in love with one of them, Guy;

this time it was the real deal, I just knew it. He had two awesome dogs. One was part wolf and part German shepherd; the female was a full-blooded, police-trained German shepherd. The boys had some really good pot, and with my friend's mom gone all night, we had some wonderful parties.

I was going to school, staying with my cousins all week, hanging out with Chris and the guys on the weekends, going to a few love-ins in Griffith Park, and smoking lots of pot and cigarettes. Guy eventually got busted for pot and went to jail. He had friends to take care of the dogs, but the female was only weeks away from giving birth, so I took her. My dog from childhood had passed away years before, so it didn't take much to convince my mom that I needed this dog. The dog gave birth to ten pups. Mom and I had to bottle feed the runt or she would have died. Part of the deal for taking care of them was that I could keep one of the pups. I decided it would be the runt and named her JR. When the puppies were six weeks old, the guy who was taking care of the male picked up the mom and her pups.

One fateful Sunday when I was supposed to be at my cousin's house in Redondo Beach, I was at Chris's with the guys. We had been listening to the Rolling Stones' "2000 Light Years from Home" from *Their Satanic Majesties Request* album and smoking some strong pot. I was so high I couldn't get off the floor, let alone drive home. We played the song over and over again. When I did not show up at my cousin's house or my home, Mom called Chris's house. The moment Mom heard my voice, she knew something was wrong. I told her I was sick and needed someone to come get me. I had been acting out for so many years; she was at her wit's end about what to do with me. She called my dad, and they both came. By the time they got there, all the guys had gone, leaving just Chris and me. Mom drove my Corolla, while I rode with Dad, who yelled at me all the way home. I was so high I did not hear a word he said. He thought I was drunk, so I let him think that. After all, to his thinking, drinking was a normal thing for a teenager to try, but pot…that was not in my dad's reality at all.

I caught contagious hepatitis while in eleventh grade and did my schoolwork at home. It was quite the ordeal. My cousin had to get the lessons from my teachers and take them to my mom in Gardena. Once

I did the work, I had to get them back to school within a week. This went on for eight long weeks. When I returned to school and the name-calling, I was now the "weird hippie girl."

My breasts developed quickly and were large for my small frame; however, my pubic hairs refused to grow. Even at age sixteen, they were few. PE was a nightmare because the girls always had something to say about that: they made fun of my sparse pubic hair and said I had fake boobs. The final straw was when my PE class was swimming, my first period of the day. No way was I going to go through the whole school day with frizzed hair. I flatly refused to attend. The school told me I would not pass PE unless I did the swimming class. I didn't care. Mom went to the school and explained the situation. The PE teacher gave me a swimming test, which I passed. So instead of PE, I took an extra study period, which would certainly not hurt me, if I had attended.

I met some long-haired guys in Hermosa Beach. Of course, one of them became the next love of my life. He would pick me up in front of Aviation High School in his Jag. I felt so cool having this long-haired man—at twenty-one he was a man, not a boy—pick me up.

I ran away to San Francisco every chance I got. To fly from LA to San Francisco cost between $12.00 and 15.00 on the midnight flight. It was always full of people who looked just like me. I'd make my way to the corner of Haight and Ashbury streets and join the many hippies, ready and willing to take in a young teen. Drugs freely flowed, everything from heroin to LSD and magic mushrooms. I was never into heroin, for that I consider myself lucky; however, anything that was mind-altering, such as LSD, was my drug of choice.

When I wasn't in San Francisco, I was in Hermosa Beach with the hippies, my friends. I have no idea how I made it through the eleventh grade since I was not there that much. I had to go to summer school that year for Biology, which I passed, thanks to my mom, who did most of the work for me.

3

Drugs, Sex and...

At a love-in at Griffith Park, I met a cousin I didn't know I had. It was really strange because in those days, I would not even look at a guy who did not have long hair. But I was talking to this sailor. He told me his name, which was my mother's maiden name, and not that common a name. "Hey, my mom's maiden name is the same as yours."

He got an odd look on his face. "What's her name?"

I told him.

His eyes grew wide. "That's my aunt!"

We checked stories, and, sure enough, he was my cousin. I invited him to come home. When he walked in and mom saw him, she went pale, immediately recognizing him.

He was getting out of the Navy soon, and we became close friends. I introduced him to my hippie friends, and they all got on well.

Also at the Griffith Park love-in, I had met Jim, a long-haired cool guy who lived in a hippie commune in Echo Park, a suburb of LA. During the second semester of my senior year, I'd had enough of school. I had way more important things to do. So I more or less moved in with Jim and the hippies at the commune. We had a big old school bus that we named The Family. When Charles Manson and his group went on their murderous campaign, the cops only knew that they went by the name The Family. So the police checked us out. We were all stoned on PCP, which was legal then. When the cops arrived, they found most of us naked, unable to walk or talk. All I remember is crawling to the bathroom to find something to put on. The interview did not last long because the cops quickly realized that we were not who they were looking for. By the time I crawled out of the bathroom, they were gone. We had no idea what was up until the Manson horror came out. Like everyone else, we were appalled. I mean, we were hippies—love and peace, not violence.

We went down to Hollywood all the time, and we girls sold the *Free Press* to tourists who did not know that the *Free Press* was just that, free. We made quite a bit of money. Anyone of us who weighed more than 100 pounds gave blood. In those days, the Red Cross paid for your blood. Most of the guys and some of the girls sold theirs. I still did not weigh enough and had had hepatitis, so I was happy that I was unable to give blood.

The year 1969 was *big*. Woodstock was a blast, but we were very high most of the time. Too bad I remember only parts of it. The summer offered several three-day rock concerts.

In December, I saw the Stones live at Altamont Festival with Jefferson Airplane and a host of other groups. The concert ended in a big mess with trouble from the Hell's Angels, who were supposed to be handling the security. Instead, they became aggressive with the audience and the performers, causing near riots, several injuries, and, subsequently, at least one death. High as I was, I was unaware this was taking place. We only learned later what had happened. It was so sad. The Stones were doing a good deed by giving a free concert, but it back-fired.

Jim and I, as well as our friends whom we lived with at the commune, were to work at the second International Atlanta Pop Festival in Macon, Georgia, in July 1970. A couple of months before we were to report for work, we moved to Memphis and rented an old house that was in probate. The guys who were living there were devil worshippers and were being evicted because they couldn't pay rent. They visited us often and became friends. They were a bit strange, but, then again, so were we. The house was large with all kinds of rooms and secret passages. It was a spooky place, with old slave quarters on the back of the property, even the cells were still in good condition and a pet graveyard with headstones naming the dogs.

We stayed high most of the time. June 5, 1970, I got busted by the Memphis Sheriff's Office for possession of pot. They booked me but released me quickly. In the Freedom of Information Act paperwork I obtained in 1999, it states "Charge Investigation Vice with no disposition." Whatever that means I have no idea, but I do know nothing ever came of my arrest, except that the FBI opened what would become a rather long file on me. I have no idea why they did not lock me up since I had turned eighteen in April and was an adult in the eyes of the law.

We finally got to Macon, Georgia, and worked at the festival. The girls cooked for the guys who were building the stage and putting up towers for the large speakers, the fences, and everything else that goes into putting on a three-day rock festival. JR quickly became the watchdog, and it was a good thing because we were in redneck county. We had a few problems with the locals trying to vandalize the site in the middle of the night. JR scared them off. She became a favorite of everyone.

The festival was just great. It was my first time being backstage. I met a lot of entertainers and fell in love with Lee Michaels, a hot performer at the time. I have long forgotten many of the bands that were there, but I do remember the group Mountain singing their hit song "Mississippi Queen." Every time I hear that song, it brings back memories of those carefree hippie days.

I loved being with all these people and being at the heart of the music and activities. We loved cooking the massive amount of food. Drugs were flowing, including lots of LSD along with everything else. We stayed after and helped with the cleanup. Then our job was done all too quickly, although we had spent about three months at the site.

Jim and I then drove in our old car to Ohio to stay with his family. We arrived just about the time the first snow started. We stayed in a hotel room, where JR promptly birthed seven puppies. We moved in with Jim's mom and sisters, where we stayed part of the winter. I went to work at a burger joint. I almost broke my neck many times trying to walk on the snow and ice. It didn't take long before I'd had enough of Ohio and the snow.

We returned to Los Angeles in late 1970. My mom was glad to have me back. She had a duplex, so we moved into the one next to her. Soon after, I found out that I was pregnant. Abortions had just become legal. I was an eighteen-year-old who could not take care of herself, let alone a child. Looking back, having an abortion was the worst thing I have ever done, but at the time, it did not seem so. I was young, I wanted my life, and I wanted to party.

I went to night school in Redondo Beach to finish high school. I saw some of the guys I had known when I was a junior in high school. But now that I was an adult, I was no longer jail bait, so I could party with them.

It wasn't long before Jim and I went our separate ways. I moved in with a cousin who had just gotten divorced. While she worked, I watched her kids. I was on welfare, so I had a bit of money and an old car.

I met a guy named Craig, who was and still is the most fantastic person in the world. He fell in love with me. He was such a nice guy, and I liked him a lot, but I was not into nice guys—I went for the rebels. Craig treated me like a queen. My mom loved him, and he was so very good to her. I regret that I was horrible to him.

I would take his van and go out for the night, leaving him to sit with the kids. He always forgave me. We had many happy times going to Mexico. He was into Motocross and bought me my first and only motorcycle, a small one he taught me how to ride. Every time I hear "Maggie May" by Rod Stewart, I think of Craig with love. He was the *only* man I have really loved and the only one who had truly loved me for me. Love is so elusive and I threw it away. I would suffer from tremendous guilt during my life, many times over my treatment of Craig and never thought I would be able to tell him how sorry I was for the way I treated him. But as you will come to understand as you read my life story, I have learned never to say *never*!

We hung with the same crowd, more or less, but Craig was always the nice guy. The time came for me to move out of my cousin's house. I started working for a photographer in Redondo Beach who had a friend with a baby and needed a place to live. The two of us got along well. As luck would have it, a house was for rent across the street from where I worked. We moved in and started to party. Everyone hung out at the Flying Jib in Redondo Beach. I met a couple of gals, Anna and Molly, who knew everyone. I wanted so much to be with the in crowd.

By this time, 1971, I had learned to control my hair, which was easy enough: put it in big rollers and dry it. What a transformation! My hair was long and wavy but beautiful, no frizz unless it got wet, so I made a point never to get it wet. Even though I still had an ugly-duckling complex, I wasn't at all ugly—I just couldn't accept anything different.

Anna, Molly, and I became friends. They still lived at home and both had babies. We partied with the gang at Hermosa Beach and did the whole drugs, sex, and rock 'n' roll thing. Anna and Molly were getting their feet wet in the Hollywood scene, so they took me along backstage. My first time at the Whiskey A Go Go they introduced me to the lead singer from a then very popular up-and-coming band from Arkansas. The lead singer loved red-haired girls, so I was his date. Wow! I was in heaven. I was backstage and with the lead singer. They had just signed a record deal and rented a big house with a pool outside of LA. We partied with them there. Although the band members looked hip with their long hair and cool clothing, they had strong Southern accents and were naïve, especially about drugs. We girls made it our mission to instruct them in the ways of our culture. On one occasion, Molly, Anna, and I dosed the band members with LSD. We told them after the fact and before they came on to it so they would not freak out. They didn't care. We were the locals and everyone else was doing it, so it was cool.

I should point out when we were going to Hollywood or any concert, our clothing, or rather the lack of it, was very revealing. It was my generation who invented the mini skirt, hip huggers, and bell bottom pants. We wore as little as we dared while not getting arrested for indecent exposure. We wore the shortest skirts or cutoff jeans, scarves for tops, and to the knee or over-the-knee boots. We were young and had great bodies. And we did flaunt them. We could not leave home dressed like this, so we would change in the car when we arrived where we were going.

I went to concerts, and we always got backstage passes because Anna and Molly knew several roadies and guys who worked security at the concerts. They knew what to do and say, so we were able to talk our way in. For this "privilege," we had to sleep with the guys at some point, whether we wanted to or not. But as time went by, we got to know many of the big-name artists of that time, among them The Who, Deep Purple, Black Sabbath, and more.

After the concerts, we partied with the band members, either at rented houses or hotels. The bands had money and drugs and were not shy about sharing with us young eighteen- and nineteen-year-old girls. I was still seeing Craig, making his life miserable, but he always forgave me no matter what I did.

You have to realize that this behavior was normal for us in the early '70s. There was no HIV/AIDS; the "clap" was easily cured with a dose of penicillin obtained from free clinics. I never caught any STDs. Sex was nice, clean fun. We were free spirits having a good time. Sex was neither special nor held meaning; rather, it was always a means to an end: belonging to the in group and getting free drugs. I got what I wanted. Period.

Jenny, my roommate, and I had met some other girls who needed a place to live. We banded together and rented a house in Redondo, almost on the beach. It was a big house, so the five of us girls moved in, including my precious JR. Between the five of us, we knew every cool guy within twenty-five miles. And, as usual, we partied hard! We were a hit because we were all into the same thing: drugs, sex, and rock 'n' roll. The house became known as the "cat" house for obvious reasons. I was still working for the photographer in Redondo, being paid under the table while receiving welfare checks. So I was okay for money.

I was popular and up for anything. My friends and I kept going to concerts and parties in Hollywood or Malibu while continuing to screw our brains out. Life in 1971 was all about guys, drugs, and, of course, rock 'n' roll—it was all we knew. We functioned and we all worked, except for Dina and Jenny, who had babies and received welfare.

One of the gals knew a photographer who paid her well to take nude photos of her. They got to be friends, and when he learned she lived with four other young girls, he asked to meet us and maybe a few of our guy friends who looked young but were over eighteen. We met with him at his studio in Hollywood. His idea was to shoot a series of photos of all of us sprawled, intertwined with one another, no sex and nothing crude such as is available today. The photos were innocent and tastefully done. It didn't hurt that it paid very well. He sold the pictures to *Playboy* but not for the USA markets, only overseas. After that session he wanted me and another of our guy friends to do another project with him—a series of photos compiled into a little book and available for order through *Playboy* overseas. It was an innocent little bit of photography shot through a crystal ball with the two of us young-looking kids, our faces showing awe during our lovemaking. No close-ups and G-rated compared with what's in magazines and online now. The money was good, and I figured I'd never see the book. Little did I know that in a few years I would be living in another country halfway around the world and that my boyfriend at the time would order it.

In December 1971, my boss took some marketing photos he placed in his store window for a time. It was one of the best photos ever taken of me. Craig loved it and made a wood frame for it.

4

WEAR WHAT?

Early 1972, all of us girls were still living in the big house in Redondo Beach when a phone call came in for one of my roommates, Dina. That call would forever change my life.

Her estranged husband, Dale, needed a ride to Tijuana, the town right over the California-Mexico border, and back to pick up his passport. She did not want to go, so she asked me if I would do it. He promised me some "goodies" as payment for my troubles. Well, why not? I had nothing planned for the day, and, hey, free coke was free coke.

He was like no one I had ever met before: secretive and sure of himself, good-looking, and lots of sex appeal. He had a mean streak he hid well, but I knew it was there. He had a loud laugh but not a happy one, more of an I-got-you-if-I-want-you type of laugh, kind of scary…and very attractive to me. This was one of the many times in my life I have asked myself, "What were you thinking?" Looking back, I wasn't thinking.

We arrived in Tijuana at some sleazy hotel. He got his paperwork; then we drove back. He asked me to come to his hotel in South Bay, and he would give me some coke, some good stuff. I wasn't going to pass it up. He had stashed more coke than I had ever seen before, a whole kilogram. I snorted some right away. "You want to help me package it up for sale?" he asked.

A dream job for me, you might say.

Funny that Dale did not touch the stuff, but I was free to do as much as I wanted. And I did. We ended up in bed, naturally, and then finished packaging the small little gram packs the next day. Dale fronted Dina and a few other friends some of the small packs to sell. The stuff was quality and not cut with baby laxative, so everyone snapped it up.

Dale and I became an item. I learned that he was planning to bring more coke back from Bolivia, lots more. He wanted me to work for him as his runner. By this time, I was really in love…sure that Dale was the man of my dreams. The thought that we were doing something illegal did not cross my mind.

It's important to note that in this early drug experimental time, the drug trade did not include guns, gangs, cartels, or violence. It was a different time, a mellow time of love, peace, and happiness. It may be hard to grasp this concept if you didn't grow up in this era, but no one wanted to hurt you or kill you over drugs or money. We all just wanted to party together. Date rape drugs or dousing another's drinks weren't part of the scene. It was a time of innocence. I know it sounds strange since I was on the brink of becoming a major drug trafficker, but it was not thought of in those terms.

I belonged to Dale, and he was smarter than anyone I had ever met. He assured me that I would be okay. Nothing would happen to me as long as I did what he told me to do. Yeah, I was foolish for believing him, but I bought it absolutely and whole heartedly. I was going to see the world with the love of my life. I had no fear and honestly did not think I was doing anything wrong. It was simply a matter of supply and demand. Dale told me I was perfect for it.

He had to go to Bolivia to get the cocaine ready for transportation. He wanted me to move to Northern California with Nellie, one of the girls I lived with. He gave me some money and told me to find a place near San Francisco. With the money he gave me, it was only enough to rent a small house in a horrible town called West Pittsburgh. Truly a hellhole. The local glue factory emitted a wretched odor.

Who did I have the gall to ask to help me move? You guessed it, good old Craig, who had a big van and a bigger heart. I have no idea what I told him, but he assumed Dale was out of the picture, for Craig did not know I was moving there on his instructions.

I still had my faithful JR, and Craig often visited. He was good at lots of things; I was cold-hearted and self-absorbed. When Craig visited, he brought his motorcycle. I had the small one he had given me, so we rode out in the country and around the small town.

I got a job working for a music producer. Around the first of March 1972, Dale returned and located us through Dina. Nellie and I applied for passports; mine was issued on April 20, 1972. Dale thought the hellhole where we lived was just that and moved us back to LA. Then he headed back to Bolivia. I took what little I owned, and we girls stayed at my mom's house. I stored my stuff along with JR there for a short time until Dale sent word for us to meet him.

We were given instructions on what to do. We had to buy tight, full-length girdles and ace bandages, lots of baby bottle liners, and duct tape, as well as short dresses. Nellie was to buy a girdle with a large breast size to take to Bolivia with us. We had no idea what we were going to do with these items, especially since Nellie had very small breasts, but both of us trusted Dale and asked no questions. We were to buy airline tickets to La Paz, Bolivia. On arrival, we went to the Sucre Palace (Sugar Palace) Hotel and got a room. Easy enough. Only one small problem: neither Nellie nor I realized La Paz is one of the highest places on the planet, and we immediately got altitude sickness.

We got to our hotel room where we collapsed on the beds, feeling sick. Two stupid girls pretending to be students holding up in the hotel, sick as dogs. The little Bolivian maid came in, took one look at us, and left. We had no idea what she was up to as she spoke no English and our Spanish was limited to *Dónde está el baño?* ("Where is the toilet?") She quickly returned with a pot of tea and two cups. I tried to tell her we were too sick for a spot of tea. But she insisted we drink, so we did. It had a funny taste, not like anything I'd ever had. Earl Grey it was not! But in no time we were feeling better than okay. We were great and ready to do some sightseeing around town. It wasn't until much later that we learned that the maid had given us coca tea! The stuff worked! We never felt so good.

Off we went. Before we got a block from the hotel, I was surrounded by a large group of Bolivian women shouting, "Henna! Henna! Henna!"

I had no idea what they were saying and did not want to stay around to find out. I slipped away from the group and found Nellie. She was dark haired and seemed of no interest to the women. Huffing and puffing our way back to the hotel while the mob of women pursued us, we managed to make it into the safety of the lobby, no easy task as the air up there is very thin. While the residents' lungs are adapted to that altitude, ours were not. Once inside I asked the manager what I had done wrong to attract so much attention. He took one look at my long very red hair and guffawed. Nellie and I exchanged puzzled looks. He warned me never to go out without wearing a hat or bandana, as the ladies wanted to know what brand of henna I used to get my hair that color! Why was I not warned of that little fact by someone? Anyone?

I took his advice and sent Nellie out to buy both a bandana and a big hat. With my red locks covered, we were free to wander un-accosted and take in the sights.

Dale joined us in La Paz and proceeded to show us how we were to transport the kilos of cocaine on our bodies. That's when we learned what the special clothing and items were to be used for. As I said, Dale was smart, and his plan worked for many years.

We filled the baby bottle liners with the powder cocaine, sealed them with the duct tape, put them into another liner, and duct-taped them again. Since Nellie did not have a big bosom, we molded her some great boobs made of the stuffed liners. Next we taped the cocaine-filled liners to our bodies. I have a swayback, so my back got a double packing. Once our bodies were packed with the cocaine-filled liners, we snuggly wrapped ace bandages around us. We put on the girdles last. I could carry quite a bit on my body. I was large breasted and wore a short dress with a low-cut neckline to attract attention to the "girls" rather than my drug-laden body. I was a tad uncomfortable! On that first trip, I think we managed to carry between the two of us around seven kilograms. We flew back on what was called the milk-run route, meaning we stopped at just about every country between Bolivia and Mexico. We appeared to be students traveling around South and Central America.

It was hot, and the coke started to smell even through all the stuff we were wearing. When that happened, we bought the cheapest perfume in the duty-free shops at the airports and doused ourselves with it. We smelled like a couple of French *demimondaines*. But it worked. We made it back to Mexico, where Nellie continued to Los Angeles alone, and I carried the whole load through the US border into San Ysidro, California.

Upon my return home, my mom told me that JR had gone missing. She had looked everywhere, including several dog pounds, and put up posters with a reward for her. I was beside myself and drove around my mom's neighborhood for days. I never found her. My heart broke. To this day I have no idea what happened to my beloved dog.

Nellie and I went to Bolivia again, did the same thing, same routine. Only this time as we were boarding one of the flights, disaster struck. As we got to the door of the plane, airport security officers were there, patting down every passenger. I went cold. We couldn't turn back. Dale was already on the aircraft, though he never carried any of the drugs and never traveled with us. I got to the security woman and glanced down the aisle at Dale, who had gone white as a ghost. Nellie was next to me, both of us minutes away from disaster. I did the only thing I could think of. As soon as the woman began patting me at my breasts, I started to laugh uncontrollably and acted like a little fool. Nellie followed my lead. We must've unnerved the security ladies because they gave us a quick going over and did not feel anything out of the ordinary. They waved us onto the plane. All that layering worked out just fine. Dale slumped in his seat, weak with relief, although he acted like he did not know us. It was close, but I trusted Dale's power over everything and felt no fear.

Since we were going back and forth so often, my distinctive hair made me stand out too much. So Dale got me a new passport in which I was blonde and had a different name. Eventually, I answered to many aliases over the years to come.

On another occasion on our way to the airplane to depart the small airport in Ecuador, a few National Guardsmen stood by their new fighter jet. Dale thought it was perfect for a photo op. How brazen could he be with Nellie and me packed to the hilt with cocaine and me in a blonde wig? Dale asked the guys if he could get a photo of us with them. They were all for it. We stood, arms linked, with these guys. One of them stared at Nellie's big cocaine boobs with his big gun drawn to add to the effect, smiling into the camera. Again, I felt no fear of discovery and smiled when told by my darling Dale. That photo is on my wall to remind me of what an idiot I was. But we pulled it off and boarded our aircraft with no further ado.

My fourth trip was the first one the authorities knew about. They have me crossing the border at San Ysidro in June 1972. Part of the indictment states that I possessed five kilograms and the other part says sixteen pounds. For the four trips across the San Ysidro border, which I walked over by myself, I think the figure was right around sixteen pounds.

The fifth trip included three other runners plus me, so we managed to bring about twenty-six pounds into Mexico; the others crossed the border holding nothing. Dale went back to LA, picked up our car, and rejoined me in Rosarito Beach, at that time a lovely little sleepy community with one small motel and open beach. We rented a small trailer home on the beach, and I waited there with the cocaine for Dale to return with the car.

The first night he showed up, he wanted me to cook dinner. I grew up in the restaurant business, but my knowledge of cooking was zip. My talent was in ordering off a menu. So Dale went to the sole tiny market and bought the makings for spaghetti Bolognese: mincemeat, fresh tomatoes, onions, etc. "I hope you know what to do with this stuff because I surely do not," I said.

He did—after a fashion. The small kitchen looked like a bomb had gone off after he was done, but the meal was edible. Since he cooked, I had to clean up his mess. The first gift my future husband ever gave me was *The Joy of Cooking*. I did learn to cook, if for no other reason than not to have to clean up his messes.

Smuggling drugs across the US-Mexico border increased, as did the means: false bottoms in car trunks and drugs inside spare tires. The authorities caught on fairly soon. So Dale devised another plan for my crossing. He put the twenty-six pounds of coke in the spare tire. We drove up to Tijuana and pulled into a dumpy garage. He replaced one of the car tires with one filled with cocaine. I slowly drove the two miles to the border crossing, coasting across with no problem. I picked up Dale on the other side. We drove a short way, pulled off the road, and changed the tire back. Then we went straight to the vacation home owned by his aunt who had raised him in Apple Valley to unload it; she was at her primary residence in Gardena. When we opened the tire, we discovered that the cocaine had melted into the rubber from the tire. I called it the BF Goodrich load. The only thing to do was to cook it down. We went to the hardware store, bought the acetone we needed, and got to work.

We proceeded to cook the rubber cocaine over a gas fire stove, not a smart thing since it is highly flammable. It was a long process. We cooked the cocaine down to liquid form again, strained the rubber out of it, and then spread the liquid onto large cookie trays to let the acetone evaporate. To hurry this step, we hooked up several heat lamps. Honestly, it looked like what it was: an early-day drug lab.

Three-quarters of the way through the process, Dale went blind from the fumes. I had told him to wear goggles, but he refused. I rushed him to the hospital. I have no idea what stupid story we gave them for his severe eye infection, but they bought it, put medicine in his eyes, and placed bandages over them. They told him to put the meds in every so many hours, re-bandage his eyes, and then come back the next day. I took him back to his aunt's. It was up to me to finish the cooking. Big trays of drying cocaine lay on every surface throughout the house. We managed to dry out most of it and package it, but quite a bit of the wet paste remained. Despite the problems, we managed to extract all of the tire rubber without blowing ourselves and the house to bits. We never went back to the hospital, but Dale's sight came back the next day.

While we were in South America, Dale's sister, Shannon, rented one of the first condos on the beach in Redondo Beach for Dale and me. She and I were the only ones who were to live there. No children and no pets were allowed…and no Dale, just Shannon and me. She had just moved us into this beautiful home, with a bedroom, bath, kitchen, and living area downstairs, and a loft and bathroom upstairs, when we got this load back. Dale decided we should get the stuff we had packaged to the sellers and dry the rest of it under the heat lamps in the loft.

After we'd set up the loft with the heat lamps drying the cocaine, we decided to fill up my waterbed in the downstairs bedroom then get some sleep while the stuff dried. Our condo was on the fifth floor, next door to the assistant manager. I got the hose hooked up to the kitchen tap, and just as the waterbed was almost filled, a seam burst. Water flowed straight down to the four condos below us and one to each side.

The poor folks were sleeping in their beds when the fire sprinklers came on, flooding their new condos.

The first knock on the door came from the assistant manager, wanting to know if we had been flooded. I humbly apologized and told them we were fine but one of the seams on our waterbed had split. He was not happy with us. The next knock came from the fire department chief, who wanted to inspect our condo for damage. This would not do at all. Even though Dale was racing around the loft, trying to get all the trays of cocaine paste into the small bathroom, the place reeked of acetone. I was a quick talker and flatly refused to allow them in, telling him that we were dry and had no damage.

The other people who lived in the six flooded condos all had to be taken to other units that had not yet been rented out. This was about two in the morning, and they were not happy with me once they learned who had caused the damage. Ballsy as we were, after the commotion had died down, we took the trays out of the bathroom and placed them around the loft under the heat lamps again. The drying process took the rest of the night. In the morning we packaged the stuff and took most of it to Auntie's house in the desert to store.

When we got back to the condo, I got a dressing down from both the manager and assistant manager. The new carpets in this brand-new project hung over the banisters. Clothing and other personal effects were hanging everywhere. I was not very popular. But the manager couldn't do anything to me. Nothing was in the lease prohibiting waterbeds. When questioned about Dale's presence, I explained that he was my boyfriend, there to help me move in as my roommate was out of town.

Neither Dale nor I were drug dealers; we only brought it in and fronted it to very good friends. When the quantities became larger, we sold the bulk to two partners, one located in Orange County and one in the San Francisco Bay Area. They bought everything we could get to them. We never kept the stuff with us for any length of time. They came, they sampled, they loved the product, as did everyone in South Bay, and we had no trouble getting rid of it. The demand was great because our coke was high quality—no additives, no crap in it, pure flake cocaine. The few pounds sold in South Bay became a legend. Very few informants were around in those days. If you got busted, you shut your mouth and did your time.

Between June and October of 1972, we must have brought in over a hundred pounds of cocaine. It got to be too much for me to cross over into the United States, even using the other border at Tecate. Dale found a pilot, Jerome, who was willing to fly the stuff from Rosarito Beach. So we rented a plane in Torrance. I stayed at the beach in Mexico. The guys flew low over the beach. I hid behind a bush on the beach. As the plane kissed down, I threw the stuff in. They took off, flying low to avoid the radar. It worked beautifully.

By September the authorities got wind of this superior product being sold in South Bay. They learned that Dina was one of the persons selling it. They also knew that she was not the one bringing it into the country, but they thought if they could bust her, she would talk. One of her connections, Bill, attempted to sell one pound of our cocaine to DEA agent Robert Lucido. Lucido busted him and tried to get him to talk, but he would not give up Dina. He was convicted and had to serve two years. He did his time, and we took care of his girlfriend (paid her quite a bit of money) while he was locked up. He never gave us or her up. As I said earlier, it was a different world then.

Unknown to me at the time, although I had my suspicions, Dale had a former girlfriend, Melinda, down in Santa Cruz, Bolivia, where the cocaine was processed. The coca plant is grown only in the very high areas of the Andes Mountains between Peru and Bolivia. It was legal for the locals to grow. Its use is part of the locals' lives. They use the plant for a number of medicinal purposes, including altitude sickness. They chew the unprocessed leaves, which turn their mouths red and ruin their teeth. The only place in Bolivia where it is hot enough to dry the paste is in a small town called Santa Cruz, which is where Melinda had been living in a house Dale had rented there.

Until this point, the runners and I waited in La Paz at different hotels. At first we always used the Sucre Palace. But on July 4, 1972, we decided to party in the hotel bar to celebrate Independence Day. Looking back, it was really stupid, but at the time it was a grand idea. The hotel was quite nice and had a fully stocked bar. We got into several bottles of Jack Daniels. The more we consumed, the louder we got. Wasted, we staggered up to the large room we all were sharing. We crashed and were sleeping peacefully until a loud knock at the door woke us up. I got up and made my way to the door. "Who is it?"

A gruff voice demanded, "Officers of Interpol. Open the door now!"

I did. When they shoved their way in, they found five very innocent-looking young ladies in their pajamas. They told us they'd had a complaint about us but said they must have been mistaken and left. The Interpol office was only two buildings away from the hotel. Had they been there an hour earlier, who knows what they would have found and subsequently done. So much for Bolivian Interpol efficiency.

After that we moved our digs and stayed at various hotels throughout La Paz, waiting until Dale came from Santa Cruz with the cocaine. Then we packed ourselves and began our journey back to the States.

In October 1972, Dale told Melinda that it was over between them and that he had a new girlfriend he was bringing down to Santa Cruz with him. She was nice enough to my face, but she had plans to get rid of me. A few days after my arrival, she took me to the town to help with the shopping. While we were walking through a crowded area, a man rushed past me with a blade and cut my Bolivian-made purse off my shoulder, slicing my upper arm in the process. My passport was in the purse. At the time I thought he was just a petty street criminal looking for cash. It wasn't until much later that I learned that Melinda had planned the whole thing.

I would have to return to La Paz and replace my passport at the US Embassy. Flights in those days in Bolivia were disorganized: you got a flight when you could and to where you could. There was usually a stopover somewhere, and this time was no exception. On the way to La Paz, I flew from Santa Cruz to the next town with an airport, Cochabamba. Since the airfield had no lights, I was forced to spend the night there.

Most of the hotels were built around an open courtyard, with the rooms on the upper floors. The doors were made of a wood bottom and a painted glass on the top part. When I was checking in, a local in the courtyard was well on his way to being quite drunk. Even with my limited Spanish, I knew he made a few vulgar remarks about me. I paid him no mind and went to my room. When I went out later to get something to eat, he was still there, still drinking out of his brown paper bag. When I returned, he was fully drunk and made a pass at me. I told him to go to hell, rushed up to my room, and locked the door. He followed me and banged on the door. No one was at the reception desk or heard the racket, even though I was screaming for help. He broke the glass of the door. I grabbed a chair and warned him that if he came in, I would hit him with it. Well, he came in and I hit him with it. Unfortunately, in his drunken state, he went over backward, falling over the banister and into the courtyard. That got people's attention. They appeared from seemingly nowhere.

The man was not dead; he was fine. I was detained until the National Police arrived about an hour later. They arrested me for attempted murder. I did not have any cocaine on me, nor was I using it at the time. (We may have been young and stupid, but I never used the stuff while on a trip.) The National Police did no paperwork on me. Instead of taking me to jail and charging me, they took me to the outskirts of town, to a rundown small hotel no tourists would ever use. Under the stairs was a convenient little room with bars on the windows, cleverly hidden if you did not know it was there. They detained me, setting a guard at the door.

For the next three days, the police chief brought several people, sometimes two or four at a time, all males, and all Arabs. They never said anything but just studied me. I tried talking to them. When they did not answer, I yelled. But they remained silent, watched me, then after a time left. Something was terribly wrong. That I had no ID, no passport, and bright red hair was a worrying factor, and no one telling me anything was frightening. I had no idea what was going on, but I knew I was in trouble.

The little guard who sat outside my door took me to eat three times a day. He spoke no English; I don't think anyone there did. On the afternoon of the third day of being held, and as I was being escorted back after lunch to my hidden room, a group of United States Air Force men came in. Their presence surprised me, and I wondered why they were here. While my Bolivian guard tried to hustle me back to the room, I pulled away from him and yelled to the Americans, "Guys, I have been held here three days, and they will not allow me to contact the US Embassy. I am being held prisoner. Please, before they take me someplace else, can you contact the US authorities and tell them where I am?" Good thing the guard did not understand a word I was saying or else he might have had me transferred where I could not have been found.

The very next day the cavalry arrived…well, one high ranking officer from the US Air Force rescued me. Then I started making a fuss about the $1000 I had when the police arrested me. I needed it to get to La Paz and back to Santa Cruz. The Air Force officer told me to shut up, not to make the situation worse. Of course, I didn't shut up. I wanted my money and accused the chief of police of robbing me. I hurled a few other insults his way while the Air Force officer kicked my leg under the table, signaling me to stop. Finally, I got the hint and went silent. After the two men exchanged a few words, the Air Force officer hustled me out of there.

When we were settled on the military plane that had brought him to get me, I learned the sordid story. Maybe part of what he told me was crap, but I believed him and still do today. He was not FBI, DEA, or CIA, only a military man. "Those airmen were at that hotel because a water main had broken in the center of town, and they had to find accommodations in a hurry."

"But why were the police holding me? What were they charging me for?" I asked.

His brows furrowed. "They were planning to sell you into white slavery. You were a perfect target: fair-skinned, red hair, as well as no ID, no passport, nothing to prove you had ever entered Bolivia. The only 'problem'"—he used air quotes—"with the sale was your age and your mouth. At twenty, you're a bit older than what they prefer. By the time you drew the attention of the airmen, your captors were haggling over the price." He went on to explain that I would've been kept drugged up in a harem until I accepted my fate. And then there was my big mouth that affected my desirability. The question was, how long would it take to tame this wild female?

Upon my arrival back in La Paz, several alphabet agencies interrogated me: DEA, FBI, CIA, and Interpol. They even gave me a lie detector test, which I passed. I made up a story about why I was there.

No matter how they tried to trick me into saying what they wanted to hear (I was a drug runner), I stuck to my story. Repeatedly I told them I was a student traveling through Central and South America. I was in Santa Cruz for one day when a thief cut my purse strap from my arm. I still had the wound on my arm that corroborated my story. "My boyfriend, Craig"—not Dale—"and I had a fight, so I was going back to La Paz by myself to get my passport. He was acting like a jerk, and I would not be surprised if he already left Bolivia and returned to Los Angeles." I never varied my story, never added to it.

They doubted my story but could not prove anything.

I was taken to stay with Mr. Mudd, the Assistant Counselor for the US Embassy, and his family for about two weeks. I had only the clothing I wore, no toiletries or money. His wife felt sorry for me and purchased a few pieces of clothing and necessities. During the two weeks, a handmade Bolivian card came to me through the US Embassy. It read, "I love you. Come home." I knew it was from Dale, and I thought by "home" he meant Santa Cruz, not Redondo Beach.

Finally, my passport was processed, and the embassy had no reason to hold me any longer. I learned that Mom had been on the phone with the State Department since she had found out from Dale what had happened. The things she did for me! She drove the State Department crazy. She paid for my ticket back to Los Angeles as well as sending me money through the embassy. I thought Dale was in Santa Cruz waiting for me. But in fact, he had been about two to three days behind me, trying to find out what had happened to me. Melinda finally confessed to him what she had done.

Right after he sent the card to me while I was at the embassy, he went back to the United States. I was deported from Bolivia for the first time and escorted to the airport. Being a small airport, only one international flight and one domestic flight were available at that time. Right after they dropped me off, I immediately bought a ticket to Santa Cruz with the money my mom had sent to me. The short flight arrived in Santa Cruz. Immediately upon disembarking from the plane, two men who spoke passable English approached me and said my name. I said, "No, not me." They didn't buy it and hauled me off to the Santa Cruz jail.

Whole families were in some of the cells, some held only women and children. I guess when mothers went to jail, the kids had nowhere to go but to stay with their moms. It was quite a sight, one I will never forget. Strange as it sounds, this jail had a funny homelike atmosphere. I was not put with the local population but held in the warden's office for my three-night stay. My only offense was not leaving Bolivia. I had been booted out of their country, but I had not left. They were understandably upset with me. When the US authorities discovered I was not on the flight back to the United States, and since the only other flight was to Santa Cruz, it wasn't hard to figure out where I had gone. They notified the Santa Cruz police to be on the lookout for me.

Aero Boliviano went on strike just as I was to be sent back to La Paz. The powers that be decided I would take the bus over the Andes Mountains to La Paz. The Andes is among the world's tallest mountain ranges. The roads were narrow, rutted, and generally in bad shape. I had some money, enough to purchase a warm coat for the trip. And what a trip it was. I have been on many buses and trains that would make most people white-knuckle their seats. But crossing the Andes on that bus was the worst. The bus can be generously described as rickety. Holes riddled the bus's body, including the big hole above my seat. The pass was frigid, and not only did cold air fill the bus but cold water dropped onto my head from the above hole. The bus made several stops along the way not only to take on passengers but also so we could buy hot tea or coffee at the roadside stalls and use the nonexistent bush for a toilet—that area is as barren as the moon. So I squatted away from everyone and hoped my wee did not freeze before it hit the ground—yes, it was that cold.

After almost two days and one night, I finally arrived in La Paz. I was again questioned why I had not left the country. This called for another story. I said that I thought my boyfriend was waiting for me in Santa Cruz—not untrue, just the name was changed. I stuck to Craig and never mentioned Dale. There was nothing they could do but get me out of the country as soon as possible.

I was held up a few days again at Mr. Mudd's house as the Bolivian farmers from the mountains were having a jolly, old-fashioned riot against the government. I don't remember what it was about, but I do remember the farmers brandishing pitchforks and shovels as they ran wild through the streets while the police tossed tear gas into the middle of them. I almost got hit by one of the canisters. I got my first and only experience with tear gas. That stuff hurts!

When things quieted down a few days later, I was escorted into the aircraft and buckled in. The flight attendants were told to watch me. One of the authorities stared me straight in the eye. "Go back to the United States. Never return to Bolivia. No ifs, ands, or buts!"

I had spoken to my mom and learned that Dale was in LA, so I was happy to go home.

Upon arrival in Los Angeles, not only did my mom meet me at the airport but also the DEA and FBI "welcomed" me home. I had only a small carry-on in which I had packed a change of clothes. The agents grabbed it and tore it apart. I had come directly from the jail in Santa Cruz, delivered again to Mr. Mudd's house, watched by everyone at all times, and then strapped into the aircraft that brought me back to the States. Did they really think I was going to score some cocaine and smuggle it in? Dale was at the airport, but he stood way off to the side. As soon as he saw me leave with my mom, he left the airport and joined me at her house.

Since I could not go back to Bolivia under my own name, I needed a new name and passport—fast. Actually, it was quite easy to obtain one. It required visiting a large cemetery and finding the marker of a child born about the same year I was but who had lived only a short time, less than a year. Taking the information on the marker to the library, I looked up the obituary in the old newspapers. From that I could access the death certificate, which stated the mother's maiden name. That's all I needed to get the certified birth certificate and thus a passport. It was ghoulish but easy.

We needed to go to Bolivia to get our cocaine before my new passport was ready, so we paid Nellie for the use of hers. She and I looked nothing alike, but I did what I could to create her looks, including wearing a dark-brown wig.

We stopped in Panama on the way to Bolivia. We went to the US base and found a friendly young serviceman who, for a small price, took us into the base stores. Prices were much lower on base, and we had no duty or tax to pay. Ghetto blasters were all the rage. Those big boxy boom boxes could hold a fair amount of cocaine once we gutted them. We used anything we could get away with to transport the cocaine.

During that first trip back after my being kicked out of Bolivia, we went to Lima, Peru, and crossed the border at Lake Titicaca. I, possessing Nellie's passports, along with four runners, hauled boom boxes, large radios, and even hairdryers and boarded a bus that took us to the border town on the Peruvian side of the lake. The road was a mere dirt track, and few tourists used this route. However, just our luck, some kind of riot had broken out in the town the day before we arrived. The way in was blocked by a bunch of rocks. Since the bus could not get through, the driver left us and all of our stuff a couple of kilometers outside the small town. We had no choice but to carry our belongings to the town, where we managed to find a place to stay. The accommodations were pretty bad, but it had beds.

The next morning the road was open. We went to the small immigration building on the Peruvian side to exit then took a boat over the lake to the small town of Copacabana, Bolivia. We picked the "finest" hotel. It was small and barely a one star. We visited the immigration office across the street. They stamped our passports. No one was the wiser that I had been extradited from their country not even two weeks prior.

We got back to La Paz using local transport. Leaving the girls in town, Dale and I flew to Santa Cruz to pick up the stuff. Our farmer took us and the cocaine back to La Paz. After gutting the electronic items, we packed cocaine in them, packed the girls with baby bottle liners filled with cocaine, and boarded the plane for our usual milk run back to Mexico. Jerome had hired a plane and picked up the stuff with Dale. The rest of us took the bus back through the border, and then we headed back to Los Angeles.

5

BUSTED

Things at the condo hadn't settled down after the waterbed fiasco. In fact, they were coming to a head. Clive, Dale's son, had been staying with Dale and me full time, but his sister was seldom there. Clive was a loud and spoiled child. Living next to the assistant manager, who kept an eye on who was coming and going at our condo, did not help. The manager issued our thirty-day notice. As it turned out, we did not have that much time to vacate.

Shannon and I were using cocaine. I never touched the product when we were on a trip, but when in the States was another story. One night while Dale and I were sleeping, Shannon got a bit too stoned and ran out of our condo with one of my dad's big butcher knives. Screaming and yelling, she ran into the assistant manager's husband. So much for our thirty days. We had to leave immediately. Dale and I were heading back to Bolivia soon, so we thought it best to purchase a house. We found one that was rundown in Redondo Beach and put it in his aunt's name because we could not risk spending money like that; it was a quick way to be discovered and busted. We had nothing in our name except a car that we had bought from my parents. We left Shannon to pack up the condo and hire a truck to move our belongings to the new-to-us Redondo Beach house.

About the time I had first connected with Dale, Mom and Dad remarried. They bought a plush restaurant. It came with a coffee shop attached to a bowling alley. My dad was doing okay. He and Dale developed a close relationship. Dale and I needed to launder money, as well as get our hands on large-denomination US bills. Dale and my dad became partners in the restaurant. Dale was a silent partner, and my dad got us the $1000 notes from the bank. It was much easier to smuggle this denomination than ten $100 notes.

On April 30, 1973, Mom, Dad, Dale, and I celebrated my twenty-first birthday at the restaurant. What we didn't know was that the DEA had their ears on us. The DEA knew what we were up to, but proving it was another matter. They had bugged our table, hoping my dad and Dale would discuss business. As it turned out, the big topic was the bartender who would not take my US passport as proof that I was of legal drinking age and refused to serve me a drink. My dad came unglued, threatening to fire the poor fellow.

Swiss Bank, Inc. had a branch in Panama. It was also my job to smuggle the money to Panama, where we deposited it into Dale's Swiss bank account on our way down to Bolivia.

We were making frequent trips to Bolivia. The two DEA agents, Lucido and Williams, were good at their jobs, but Dale was smarter. They just could not catch us. We never kept the stuff on us for longer than to get it to our guys or fronted out to good friends. Still we felt the heat. To throw the agents off, we took a legitimate trip around the middle of 1973.

It was great! We just traveled. No smuggling. We went to Ceylon, Pakistan, and India, where Dale bought me a custom-made coat made of cobra skins with the snake heads forming the hem. From there we went to Hong Kong, the Philippines, Turkey, Japan, and Thailand before returning to the States via Hawaii, where we rented a car and drove around the island. It was a fabulous trip. But it didn't make the DEA forget about us.

Dale would not stop drug trafficking. Even with the DEA watching us, we made several trips to Bolivia, bringing back a lot of cocaine. I used several passports. One time we crossed the US border in a Jeep with a camper on the back that was fully packed with product. We used a variety of runners, but the process was usually the same.

During these years we had a front man, our good friend Rick, who was also the father of my friend Anna's son. He owned a store in Redondo Beach that sold to the hip crowd. South American handicrafts were popular, and he sold some of our items we brought up with us. One time Dale purchased a lot of colorful skirts the Bolivian women wear. The problem was that Bolivian women's bodies are short and thick, especially their chests, mostly due to the thin air in the mountains. We transported the skirts into the States, but when Rick held one up and studied it, he burst into laughter. "What are we going to do with these?"

Dale was put out by Rick's reaction but quickly realized that he had made an error in sizing. When handed lemons, make lemonade, right? So he had the skirts made into floor cushions, which were popular at the time. They sold well!

After one of the trips back from Bolivia, we stopped by Rick's store. He signaled us to leave out the back and fast. It seems he recently had been busted for drugs and was out on bail. He was sure the store was being watched. We did not go home for a few days; instead, we laid low and waited to see what would happen. Through the grapevine we learned that he was in deep trouble, so we took the loss of our items in his store and let it be.

By late 1973, the DEA agents Lucido and Williams were working full time to bring Dale down. Things were heating up. We left the country again, bought a Mercedes van in Amsterdam, and drove across Europe into what was then Yugoslavia and Bulgaria. We went up to Denmark, loaded the vehicle onto a ferry, and went to Sweden, Norway, and then Finland. We planned to go into the Soviet Union. To do that we had to wait two weeks in Finland for the visas, and no way were we were going to do that. We were camping in the van, it was uncomfortable, and we were bored. We decided to head back to Amsterdam, sell the van, and return home.

I will never know the truth, but I have my suspicions about what happened next.

I had told Dale that this was it. We had enough money to last us for the rest of our lives, the cops were too close, and I wanted to quit. "By chance" we ran into a group of our old runners in Amsterdam. They were planning a trip to Morocco to make some hash oil and invited us to join them. Dale could take the lead—it wasn't that they were being generous; everyone knew he would have it no other way. There were three of us girls and four guys. The guys would fly to Portugal, and we girls would drive there, just in case anyone was watching us. Three girls driving to Portugal seemed very innocent. So we purchased another van and off we went.

We arrived in Portugal and met up with the guys in Lisbon. We rested a few days before heading to the coast and the ferry to Morocco. Our timing was awful. We arrived in a Muslim country during Ramadan. The locals were fasting till nightfall, making them a bit cranky as the day wore on. I'm not sure how it came about, but we rented a fairly large house in Tangiers for our base and spent several days there. Dale and the guys took off to the mountains to establish a base of operations and to find a Berber pot farmer who would let us make the hash oil on his property. The guys found a farmer who was more than happy to have us and our US dollars come to his farm. The setup was primitive. Dale and I slept in the van, Frank and Larry slept in a small room above the courtyard, and the others slept in tents. We lived with the sheep and other farm animals. It was freezing in the mountains, and we struggled to keep warm. We erected a large tent and put a big basin in it to heat our water to bathe in. We converted a shed into our bathroom and used another shed to cook the oil out of the hash, using a flammable liquid.

Every so often we traveled the long winding road down to Tangiers. It took hours. We purchased what we needed, spent the night in the rented house, then headed back up the mountain the following day.

The nearby village held market day twice a week. If you missed that, you were in trouble because not much was available elsewhere. The market was primitive but colorful. Cow heads sat on tables, their brains, a local delicacy, displayed for purchase. Some vegetables and meat were available, along with the numerous flies attached to them. We cooked everything well done. One day we missed the market and had no food. The family we stayed with was kind enough to give us a turkey—a live turkey. When it came time to kill the thing and prepare it, everyone in our group disappeared, leaving me to deal with this flapping, squawking turkey. What the heck should I do with this thing? One of the local guys who spoke no English put an ax in my hand and tried to instruct me in the art of turkey killing. I couldn't understand him, so I motioned for him to hold the bird still. I chopped off its head. Then I dipped the dead bird in a large pot of boiling water. Most of the feathers loosened and fell out. After taking the turkey out of the pot, I had to gut it and pluck the remaining feathers. Dogs have an amazing sense of smell, and from out of nowhere I found myself surrounded by a pack of them. After cutting open the turkey, I grabbed a squishy handful of guts and threw them to the dogs, which feasted on them while I cleaned the cavity then ran back to the relative safety of our little camp.

The family had an outdoor, baked-mud type of oven that stood almost as high as me. On one side of it goes the wood or fuel, and in the other, the food. The family was upset with me because I hadn't followed their killing customs, so they didn't help me with the fuel I needed to cook the turkey. I used the only thing I could think of: the fuel-soaked bricks of the hash from which the oil had been removed. We had a few poorly looking vegetables, so I stuffed them into the turkey and put the bird in the oven.

No sooner had I finished this task when everyone miraculously reappeared. No one could believe that I had killed and cleaned this turkey that was cooking in a primitive oven. It took ages for it to cook and had to be taken out and checked and fuel added every so often. Finally, it was done. It was the tastiest turkey I had ever eaten. Even Dale was impressed. Not so our hosts. They stayed mad at me for the entire week,

The small room over the sheep pen, where the two guys slept, was our communal living area. There we would sit, read, rest, or play cards. One memorable moment during our stay on the mountain came when one of the guys had an emergency while he was tending the oil. He had to go to the bathroom then and there. Just as he was finishing, the oil caught on fire. He stumbled out with his pants around his ankles, yelling for us all to come and put the fire out. We were laughing so hard it took a moment for us to realize that our oil was on fire! We formed a bucket brigade from the well to the shed. With the family helping us, we managed to put out the fire. We had to compensate the old man for the shed that was all but destroyed. Lucky for us, we were almost finished and cooked the rest of the hash outside.

All in all, I had a really good time up in those mountains with the family. Despite the cold and harsh living conditions, it was a great experience. We had become friends with the family and thanked them for everything. Naturally, we paid them more money than they had ever seen in their lives. They were happy, and we got what we came for.

We drove down to Tangiers to our house. Creating a false wall in the van, we packed the product behind it. With Dale supervising, it was well done and concealed. We shipped the van to Mexico. I flew back to the States from there.

Dale and I were arguing often. I wanted to stop immediately, but he insisted on doing one last trip for a small amount of cocaine. I stayed in the States and met up with Jerome, who also wanted out and was not going to do any more trips. He had a family and was scared the DEA was getting too close. They certainly were, as we were to find out soon enough.

Jerome met me at a hotel by LA International Airport. He had agreed to meet with Dale when he returned. The oil-filled van was already in Nogales, Mexico, along with the small amount of cocaine. To get Jerome to do this one last trip, Dale sweetened the deal: he bought an airplane that Jerome could keep, but we could use it when we wanted. The plane was in Jerome's name.

Dale and Jerome met two of the other guys in a remote part of Nogales, The cocaine and oil was concealed in scuba tanks.

The DEA had been watching us for some time and had approached my father and Nellie and persuaded them to cooperate to bust Dale, whom they really wanted. Willing and anxious to cooperate to get herself off, Nellie's testimony could have me facing twenty years in federal prison for using another person's passport. My dad had no choice. In exchange for his testimony, any money laundering charges were dismissed and I got off. Dale and I had no idea these deals were in the works right before Christmas 1973.

Jerome along with Dale flew the plane into Apple Valley, California. Having lived in this area on and off with his aunt for most of his life, Dale knew the place quite well. There was no safer place for the oil and cocaine but to bury it in the desert, which is where we hid our portion. Jerome flew the plane to his home in Kansas where he had moved his family. The guys who had been involved with this last operation got their share of the cocaine and the oil. A portion of their sales was to come back to us, as we had footed the bill for most if not all of the operation. We also gave them some of ours to sell as a favor to them for being a part of the operation.

The DEA showed up in Kansas not long after Jerome landed. Upon inspecting the aircraft, they found enough traces of the oil that had leaked to indict him. He was not the one they wanted and made a deal with him as well: his testimony for his freedom. I can't blame the guy. He had a wife and kids. With this latest development, our fate was more or less sealed. DEA could convict Dale under federal conspiracy laws.

We had no idea how close they were to us. We went about our business. January 11, 1974, we went to Shannon and her husband's house for the night. That day we had gone to a big RV show in Orange County. As we innocently viewed the boats and motor homes, DEA agents trailed us, hoping to catch us with the drugs.

Later that night while I watched the movie *Hawaii*, Dale drove out to Apple Valley with $26,000 in a Tupperware container to bury the money. He was not far from the house when at a stoplight he was suddenly surrounded by unmarked DEA cars. They arrested him. He was not allowed to phone anyone, and they held him until the following morning.

Meantime, the movie ended. I waited and waited for him to return. When the sky began to lighten in the early morning, I knew something had happened. But I could do nothing but wait. I was a nervous wreck, fearing I'd be picked up at any time. Finally, an attorney phoned and said that Dale was in federal custody and being transferred to San Diego to the federal jail.

6

Gone, Baby, Gone

My life as I knew it stopped. My situation shifted into a blur. I spoke to Emma, the attorney we had used for Dale's divorce. She was the only attorney we knew and who had helped us with small things in the past. She found good federal attorneys in San Diego who specialized in drug cases. I hired them for Dale and to help me and Dina. Dale told them where he had hidden the oil in the desert. But try as they might, they were unable to locate it. They had to take a shackled Dale out to Apple Valley in a helicopter. He immediately found it, and they dug it up. It was never mentioned in any of the indictments as to what happened to it.

Dale's bail was set at $500,000. Extremely high in 1974, equivalent to about $2.6 million today. We had the money to get him out, of course, but the Internal Revenue Service was waiting in the wings so they could seize the funds for back payment of taxes (we never filed a tax return for our drug money). The amount they said he owed was staggering. I have forgotten the exact amount, but it was more than his bail. Dale told me to do nothing but collect as much of the funds as I could from the people who still owed us, then get it and myself out of the country and to Switzerland.

The DEA had found the number to the Swiss bank account on the back of a photo of Clive. They did not know what bank in Switzerland, but Dale feared that given enough time, they'd figure it out. We had no idea what the bank would do since he was in jail for drug smuggling.

I did as I was told and collected thousands of dollars. Apparently, the DEA was watching me. Later, they told me that they had no idea how I had managed to shake them. They kept losing lost track of me, trying to catch me with anything—money or drugs. I watched my back but never noticed anyone following me. I will never know how I pulled it off. Not only did I collect almost all the money but I also slipped out of his aunt's house in Gardena with her help in the middle of the night with my niece's birth certificate. I caught a bus from LA to Bakersfield, then onto Las Vegas, where I got a flight to Miami, then to US Virgin Islands, where all I needed, at that time, was a birth certificate to enter. I had packed thousands of dollars on my body.

Getting out of the Virgin Islands was another matter. Since I wanted to catch a flight to Europe, I needed a passport. I don't know why, but the DEA never confiscated mine. I had to come up with some story as to how I had arrived and was leaving, not back to the continental USA but to Europe. I told immigration that I had come in by private boat with my boyfriend, and we'd had a fight. I left him and wanted to go to Europe. I produced my passport. They bought this ridiculous story, and I flew to Luxemburg, connecting to Switzerland.

In Zurich is a branch of Dale's bank where he had accounts and a safe deposit box filled with foreign currency and bonds. I first had to go to the bank and get all the forms that Dale had to sign and get notarized for everything to be changed over to my name. I got the forms and sent them by Federal Express to our loyal attorney, Emma, who was also a notary. As one of Dale's attorneys, she slipped them into Dale. He signed them, and then she notarized them and sent them back to me, a process that took about three weeks.

In the meantime, it dawned on me that I had missed my period by weeks. In all that had been happening, I had forgotten when it was due. I was almost positive I was with child.

I had developed a bad case of insomnia and had a horrible time getting to sleep each night. I would read in my hotel room until the early morning. One night, just as I was dropping off to sleep, I was awoken by the night manager, who had sneaked into my room at the small B&B I was staying at. He was trying to get into my pants. I was not in a deep sleep as he would have expected. I woke up and screamed. He rushed out, leaving me quite shaken. I packed my bag and got a taxi as soon as he went off shift. I could not make a fuss, having to keep a low profile. The last thing I wanted was to file charges against him and bring in the Swiss police to investigate.

I booked into a better hotel. It was February and bitterly cold. I stayed under the wonderful down comforter and read one book after the other, day after day, waiting for the notarized paperwork to come back from Emma.

The bank released all of Dale's accounts to me. They asked me where I wanted the funds transferred. I wanted all of the funds in the accounts in the form of gold, as Dale had instructed me. I followed his instructions to the letter, even if he was thousands of miles away in a jail cell. The bank officials were so shocked, I had to repeat myself. They looked at me quite unbelieving. I guess this was a first for them. Hey, it was a first for me as well.

They advised me that it would take several days to collect that much gold, thirty-six kilograms (about eighty pounds). The contents of the safety deposit box were all bonds and other currencies, so I took them to another bank nearby, where I rented a large box and deposited everything under my name. The gold was another issue. Eighty pounds is a lot to carry. It took me a few trips. I am sure the personnel at the bank I took it from were a bit miffed, but I hauled it all over to the new bank.

I returned to the United States. No one bothered me upon entry. I came back through New York and then went to Las Vegas. From there I took the bus to LA, where Emma met me.

I went to the doctor, who verified I was, indeed, pregnant and due in October. I immediately flew to San Diego to see Dale and tell him the news. I was so afraid he was going to blow, but he was very happy about the child, even if he was in jail.

Those were hard days. I had never had air sickness, but being pregnant, I got sick on my flights between Orange County, where I was living with Delores and Henry, Dale's mom and stepfather, and San Diego to visit Dale. The flight lasted only thirty minutes. I arrived in time to throw up, see Dale, go to the International House of Pancakes for my food fix—I was eating for two—then fly back and throw it all up.

I attended court for all of Dale's appearances. It was then we finally knew who said what—who had given evidence against Dale, including my dad. We were furious. I had no idea they had enough evidence to throw me into jail for a very long time.

This revelation triggered a three-year estrangement from my family. Looking back, I have never forgiven myself for what I put my mom through during all of this. But at the time, Dale was my entire life; everything was wrapped up in him. I did everything for him and whatever he asked of me. I asked no questions and had complete faith in him. You may be asking, "How stupid can you be, Paula?" But love is surely blind. I was deeply in love and totally blind!

It occurred to Dale that we should get married so that I could not testify against him. Since he was in jail and the authorities were not letting him do anything, he was not cooperating with them. They did not have to let us get married, for it was considered a privilege not a right, and he had been stripped of his rights. They were out to nail him and nail him good. Dale decided I was to go to Mexico and we would marry by proxy. Pete's brother, Harry, would stand in as Dale's proxy. We went to Mexico with the required paperwork supplied by Emma. Then it was discovered that we had done something incorrectly, so we had to do it all over again. The second proxy "wedding" was legal and binding.

The authorities advised Dale that they could certainly convict him and send him away for years, but they also wanted our two main buyers, James and Oliver. The authorities knew about them but could never bust them for anything. These guys were very, very careful and had great covers as legitimate businessmen. Unknown to the DEA, I had contacted them right after Dale's bust. They were lying lower than low, doing nothing but their legit business.

Auntie put her Gardena house up for Dale's bail and he was released on the condition he would set up our buyers. I picked him up from the jail shortly before Mother's Day. I have always wondered if DEA was watching when Dale and I drove off the road and made love on the way back to his aunt's house that wonderful day. It was great to have my man back in my arms after almost four months.

What came next was one of those "How did we do it?" moments. The day before Mother's Day 1974, I left out the back alley with Auntie driving her old pickup. I was scrunched onto the floor as she drove me to the bus station. I wore one of my many wigs and dressed to conceal my baby bump as well as thousands of dollars I "wore." I took a bus to Canada and made my way to Toronto, where the next day, right on schedule, Dale joined me. We met up at the city hall. We had successfully made it out of the United States.

Meanwhile, DEA agents were staked out in front of Dale's aunt's house. I have no idea why they had not covered the back alley access. Dale had said our plan would work, and it did. I had no fear but complete faith in Dale's plans. They had always worked in the past, and this time was no exception.

The day after Mother's Day, Dale was to contact agents Lucido and Williams. When they came to the door, Auntie said that she had no idea where we were then shut the door in their faces. They were furious, as you might expect, and quickly returned with a search warrant. To her credit, Dale's aunt remained cool and never gave us up—we never told her where we were going—despite the agent's threats against her for aiding and abetting. All they could do was take her house that she'd posted for Dale's bail. She, too, had complete faith in Dale.

When they didn't find us, they were so mad they brought a bulldozer in and tore up her backyard, looking for buried money or dope. She hated that house and had planned to sell it then move to her Apple Valley house. The agents could not prove she had anything to do with our escape, but they did take her house. (I had given her $500,000 to cover the bond and the house.) So she did not have to deal with selling the place and got all her money back. She was happy, and we were long gone.

Soon after, I was added to the indictment as a defendant and faced all the same charges: eight felonies. The date they filed against me was May 23, 1974. I was now in deep, deep trouble. No getting out of it no matter what my dad or anyone else did. I was wanted right alongside my husband on all counts.

In Canada Dale kept me out of sight. He found a guy who was willing, for a price, to sell him his identity. While he was looking for someone for me, I started bleeding in the middle of the night. Dale did not want to take me to the hospital, but I pitched a fit, so he had no choice.

I was admitted to the maternity ward and hooked up to all kinds of machines. Thankfully, the baby was fine. The placenta was low, causing the bleeding. I stayed in the hospital for observation for about a week. All the while I thought Dale was going to have a heart attack. We were on the run, and I was in the hospital. My red hair was like a neon sign that said, "Here I am!"

Dale found a girl who sold her identity to him. He had to get a passport for me using the girl's photo. It took some time, but both passports finally came through. We became completely different people and Canadian citizens.

I had traveled under many identities, with a variety of hair and eye colors. Most of the photos were not of me, but that had never been a problem, so I didn't worry that my Canadian passport photo was not of me. I simply bought a brown wig and used contact lenses to change the color of my eyes from brown to hazel. Voila!

Sometime after being released from the hospital, we left for Australia with a stopover in Singapore. Of course, I had packed my body with a lot of cash.

Being in Singapore after those months of being separated from Dale while he was in jail and then our time in Canada, all the while scared we were going to be caught, was such a release. Though we were still on the run, we were very far from the DEA agents. I learned much later that Lucido and Williams were looking for us and had a BOLO (be on the lookout) issued for both of us from the Mexican border and all borders south to Bolivia. Did they think we were stupid enough to go south, where they knew our routine?

We flew from Singapore to Sydney on Qantas airline. It was a great flight, and my morning sickness was long gone. We landed a few days before Australia changed its immigration laws. The day we arrived, being Canadian, we could apply for and get residence status for as long as we wanted. We could work and own property. Dale did all the paperwork and got us cleared. We were in.

We encountered one small problem. I did not have a smallpox vaccination, and because I was pregnant, I could not get one. If we had not stopped over in Singapore, it would have been a non-issue. Coming directly from Canada, I would not have needed one. But flying in from Singapore was another story. So Qantas had to pay for me to be quarantined for two weeks in a big house in Manly Bay, a beautiful setting right on the ocean. It was a sprawling place with lots of empty houses. It had in times past been used for the boatloads of people coming in who had to be put into quarantine. It was like a ghost town with just me and two registered nurses. A doctor from the government came to check me every three days to make sure I was not getting any spots. The house was old and cold, as it was winter in Australia. Dale could not come with me, so he got a room in Sydney and busied himself with making plans. As usual, I left all that in his hands.

I had problems of my own. How was I going to fool all three government workers for two weeks with my wig and contact lenses? I often locked myself in my room so I could take off my wig and remove my contacts. They knew me only by my passport name, which was new to me. Sometimes when they called out to me, it took a bit of time to remember that they were talking to me.

Both Dale and I struggled to get used to calling each other by our new names. Even after all the identities I'd had over the years, he had always called me by my real name, unless we were in the middle of a trip. But this was different. We were not on a quick trip. We were looking at the rest of our lives. We had to get used to it, so we never called each other by our real names, in private and certainly not in public. It took awhile, but we did get used to our new names. In time I rarely ever thought of my real name.

The nurses were very nice ladies who tried to teach me to knit. They had extra knitting needles, so I gave it a go. After I almost stabbed them, they thought better of it and tried me on crocheting—with the same effect. I was hopeless at both. They asked the doctor to bring me a needlepoint set. I could do that. I made a cute little sheet and pillowcase of Roadrunner for the baby.

They were curious that I never washed my hair and asked me about it one day. Again my imagination took over. "Oh, it's so cold, and I think

I'm coming down with a cold. So instead of getting my hair wet, I'm using a dry shampoo."

They bought the lie and never asked me again. Finally, after two weeks, Dale picked me up. Free at last!

He decided to go up north out of Sydney. He had been checking on properties to purchase and wanted to buy a little motel on the beach. But our gold and most of the money were in Switzerland. We needed to access it and change the accounts to his new name. Since the US government had never taken my passport, I still had it and had smuggled it out. With no vaccinations needed to go to and from Switzerland, we went. Things went smoothly. I transferred *everything* to his new name.

While he was in jail in San Diego, I could have taken everything and just run. I was not wanted at the time and would have never been indicted had I not run with him. But I loved Dale, and the thought never crossed my mind to leave him. I gave all of the money and gold back to him; never mind it was I who had done most of the hard work in earning it, and I had taken all the chances, not to mention I had put my life and liberty on the line so many times. Nope, not good old loyal me; he was my man, and I trusted him like a fool in love.

Upon our return to Australia, we bought a vehicle and drove north to the New South Wales–Queensland border, where we looked at several properties and finally purchased a nice twelve-unit motel on a beautiful beachfront called Cabarita Beach. The motel, the Cabarita Beach Motel, had a beautiful view of the sea with a swimming pool overlooking it. We bought it from a family with nine kids who lived next door, which would be a blessing when it came time for me to be a mom. I knew very little about newborn babies.

This area was pristine, with only a few houses and the Cabarita Beach Hotel. The hotels had a women's bar, a men's bar, and a bottle shop. The nearest hospital was in a town called Murwillumbah. I found a good doctor. During my first visit, he discovered I was anemic. He told me to drink sherry to help my blood. I hated sherry but it was doctor's orders, so I went to the hotel to get some. I was new and had no idea about the separate bars for men and women. I marched in, very pregnant, to the men's bar to get a bottle. Gasps from the male clientele greeted me. I gazed across the horrified faces, not understanding what

I was doing wrong. The minute I opened my mouth and spoke in my American accent, they realized I was not from there and kindly asked me what I wanted. I told them I needed a bottle of sherry, on doctor's orders I quickly added. They directed me to the bottle shop and advised me of the way things worked there. What a fuss! But I never made that mistake again.

In August we decided we should get married—this time not by proxy. We went to Tweed Heads to the City Hall to do the deed for the third time, if you count the two Mexico proxy proceedings. We were told we needed two witnesses. We knew no one. So we got a police officer and a very drunk stranger off the street. We paid them to witness our holy union.

Early October came, but the baby did not. The doctor considered inducing labor but then decided to wait another week or so, as first births can be late. I was sick to death of being pregnant. It had been months since I'd seen my feet. I had gained over sixty pounds. When I was in Canada, I ate and ate, and in quarantine, I did the same. I was a blimp. For the first time in my life, I was fat all over, not just the baby, but all of me.

The second week in October I took matters into my own hands and decided to try drinking castor oil. I had heard that was what they used to induce labor. The taste of this stuff was worse than horrible. I chased it with pineapple juice. (To this day I cannot drink pineapple juice.) Stuff came out all right. I had a trash can in front of me while I sat on the toilet. But still no baby.

With the baby two weeks overdue on October 18, the doctor decided to either induce labor or perform a C-section. I was admitted to the maternity ward, where they promptly handed me some castor oil to drink. I tried to tell them that I had already done that, but they made me drink it anyway. Although it was not as much as I had taken on my own, the results were the same: I got sick. The next step was to give me injections, which worked. I finally went into labor on October 20, and then was I sorry! This kid did not want to be born. Period. I had a horrible time: over twenty hours of labor, hard labor. It started in my back then wrapped around me. I thought I would die. I cried and cried. I told them I had changed my mind; I did not want to have a baby.

To make matters worse, the maternity ward was in the midst of a renovation. The delivery beds had no stirrups, so I had to hold up my legs with my hands. By the time the baby came, my inner thighs looked like mincemeat.

At some point they took me to X-ray, thinking they would have to do a C-section after all. I was so small-boned, they weren't sure I could have a vaginal delivery. I begged them for anything to help the pain, but they did not believe in using pain medication until after the birth. At some point Dale told me to shut up because I was embarrassing him. The midwife, an angel of a woman, rubbed my back for hours. I was grateful when she threw Dale out of the delivery room.

The doctor came in to check me from time to time. He told the midwife he was going to dinner and to call him when the time came. I am in serious pain and he is going to dinner? After twenty hours of the most horrible pain I had ever experienced, my baby girl finally entered the world, weighing seven and a half pounds and measuring twenty-one inches long. She was a big baby for a small girl like me. When I first heard her cry and they laid her on my chest, it was like a miracle. She was so lovely and healthy; all the pain was worth it. However, I finally got the pain medication and slept for hours.

Dale had decided I would not breast feed as I had a motel to run and could not have a baby sucking on my breasts while checking in our guests. At the hospital I received injections to dry up my milk before releasing me two days later.

The family from whom we bought the motel lived next door, thank God, as I had no idea what to do. The woman was a wealth of information. I ran to her for every little thing.

We named our daughter Irene Salsman. We had to use our alias last name on her birth certificate; however, she would have several names in her lifetime. She was a good baby, never sick, and slept through the night at only one month old.

I got serious about losing the weight I had gained. The two-story motel also provided breakfast to our guests. Doing the cooking and running up and down the stairs with breakfast helped me to lose weight and get back in shape. I went on a strict diet and lost it all in about two months. It felt good to be down to my normal size, about a hundred pounds, and in my bikini again.

Business was good. The motel was located off the highway on the way to the Gold Coast, a nice stopover en route.

When the baby was only three months old, we had to go to Switzerland to get some funds. Irene needed a passport, so we applied for and received an Australian one. We could not risk taking her to the Canadian Embassy to register her there—who knew what trouble the two people we had bought our identities from might have gotten into. Dale decided that after leaving Switzerland we should go on to Hong Kong. At that time, Australia was just introducing color television to the country. So we purchased ten color TVs and thousands of pirate tapes, which were, of course, highly illegal. We removed the covers, making them appear as blank tapes; the covers as well as the tapes had a barely noticeable code on them and were packed and shipped separately. We then had an agent ship everything to Australia a few weeks apart so nothing would arrive at the same time. The TVs arrived first, and I had no problem collecting them from customs. I said they were all gifts and didn't have to pay any duty. We sold them and made quite a bit of money.

A month later the supposedly blank tapes arrived. There was nothing illegal about the "blank" tapes, but because there were so many, I had to pay a small import duty on them. Sometime later all the original covers for the tapes arrived. The customs agent raised an eyebrow at them and asked what I was going to do with all the covers. Off the top of my head I came up with a clever deception: "I'm going to use them for wallpaper."

I know that sounds stupid, but the agent bought it and let me in with thousands of tape covers. We spent hour upon hour matching the covers with the tapes, then sold them at flea markets, making a lot of money from them as well.

It was about then that Dale decided we would renovate the motel and build kitchenettes in the downstairs units. We built another unit at the end of the motel that was smaller than the owner's unit we lived in. We could rent that one out for more money to families. Our little unit was big enough for us, and it was easy to keep clean. We hired only one lady, who lived close by. She helped me clean the rooms, which was also my job. Dale's job was the renovations. When that was done, his only job was to keep the pool clean.

I am sure he had a local girlfriend on the side that kept him occupied. I was so busy doing all of my jobs and taking care of the baby, I didn't have time to give much thought about what he was doing or with whom.

Once the renovations were complete, he quickly became bored. I was tired of him and his cheating. To try to save the marriage, we decided to hire a manager to run the motel while we went on an extended trip. Irene was then six months old and could have her immunizations. The managers moved into the original owner's unit. We stored our things in the small unit.

We left Sydney, with me in my disguise. Most of our luggage contained Irene's baby food. Unfortunately for me, she could not wear disposable diapers because they gave her a rash. I had to hand wash diapers for the over six months we were on the road.

We went to Indonesia, first Bali, where we stayed on the beach in a thatched cottage. It was a lovely spot. Dale decided we should try Irene on some local food. Much of it contained peanut butter, and he thought she could eat it. It didn't take long to learn that it wasn't such a great idea. It gave her diarrhea. And I got to hand wash all the dirty diapers. I put my foot down; she would eat only baby food from a jar while we were traveling. We would stock up on more when we got to Europe.

It was not Dale's nature to travel any other way but by local transport or hitchhiking, so that's what we did. I am grateful that I got to see the world at ground level. This was 1975, and not many backpackers took to the road—none with a baby.

We hired a motorbike to explore the area. Irene rode between the two of us. I put her in a sling that went over my shoulder and held her close to me. The local women used this with their babies. I had tried to use the Western baby carrier that had a metal frame and you wore it on your back. But it was cumbersome and got in the way. The local "carrier" was much better.

We were on our way to see a famous temple when Dale stopped the bike. Forgetting to put his foot down, he jumped off, leaving me on the bike with Irene. It turned over with my leg pressed against the exposed hot pipe. I held Irene above my head to protect her, but by the time Dale picked up the bike, my leg had been severely burned. The locals applied some kind of medicine on it. It blistered something awful, and, oh, did it hurt!

By the time we got back to town and our cottage, I was writhing in pain and barely able to walk. The blister was bigger than the size of my hand. Dale said we should pop it, another of his many health suggestions I listened to. After he did the deed, I washed my leg and the wound. The water was not fit to drink, so why I thought it was okay to wash an open wound in it I have no idea. But I did. Sure enough, it got infected. I had to go to the doctor and get proper ointment and antibiotics to cure the infection.

From Bali we went on to Jakarta on the main island. We walked about seeing the sights. The next day someone from the hostel where we stayed ran up to us, waving the newspaper. My mouth dropped open when I saw the picture on the front page. Irene was hanging off my back. The caption read, "Baby Sight Sees as Well." We were celebrities, or at least the baby was.

In Jakarta, Irene came down with a cold. Dale's medical advice was to bundle her up to keep her warm. It was very hot, so she naturally started running a temperature. The higher it got, the more clothes he thought we should put on her. She didn't improve. Panicking, we flew to Singapore, where we thought the doctors would be better. We took her to the hospital. The nurses looked at us like we were really stupid. They stripped off Irene's clothing and put her in a bath of cool water. Her temperature lowered. They gave us medicine for the cold. She was fine. I felt like a complete idiot.

From there we went to Malaysia. The city bustled with people and activity. Cassius Clay (later known as Muhammad Ali) was fighting. The only accommodation available was very basic. We didn't stay long because of the crowds.

We went to Thailand, and then Dale said we should go to Laos. The Vietnam War was still raging, but our troops were pulling out. The day we arrived, Laos fell, and thousands of people came over the border. One was a former runner of ours, Katie. We could not believe we ran into her after all this time and in of all the places in the world. We were already in a hotel, so we got to keep our room. I was sure Dale had cheated on me with Katie during the drug-running days. I was not so pleased to see her as Dale was. Somehow she got a room in the same hotel; I had my suspicions about what Dale did to make that happen but could not prove it.

We saw the sights then moved up the peninsula. We flew from Thailand to Nepal, arriving during the monsoon season, so everything and everywhere was wet. Just try drying diapers in that weather! I had to hang them out of bus windows when traveling through the country. The locals were kind to let me use their windows. We stayed in a lodge in the middle of a lake in the small sweet village of Pokhara. The rains were heavy, so I had all the diapers draped over the fireplace in the main lodge to dry. The locals likely thought we were a bit mad traveling to these out-of-the-way places with a very young baby, especially during the rainy season, but they were very kind and helpful.

Dale got sick and had trouble deciding what end to put on the toilet. He suffered from diarrhea and throwing up. I found this funny and laughed myself silly, much to his displeasure. But what could he do? He was too sick but to put one end down on the toilet just to have to turn around to throw up in it.

India was next on our itinerary. We flew there around July, traveling all over by local transport, mostly buses. When we could, we hitchhiked; it was easy getting rides with a nine-month-old in tow. We arrived in Delhi around August, and I don't think I have ever been hotter in my life than there. We put Irene in and out of the shower to keep her as cool as possible. India was great and a friendly place with courteous people. Though curious about this white baby being hauled around, they never tried to touch her or hassle us in any way.

We took a small boat down the Ganges River, a sacred place, and watched as dead bodies were transported on the back of bicycles to where they were cremated. The stench is not so easily forgotten. The Taj Mahal in Agra was amazing. I have a photo of baby Irene sitting in front of it.

We made it up to Kashmir, where it was peaceful and, thankfully, cool. There were lots of hippy types using pot and hashish in the open. Instead of coffee houses, the city had pot-smoking cafés—good quality pot. We stayed on a houseboat. Decades before Uber Eats came into fashion, little powerboats would deliver food, drinks, and pot right to your houseboat door. If you wanted to go to the mainland, you just hopped aboard and they'd take you there. I loved it there; it was a paradise at that time.

Pakistan was another story. We went overland to Karachi. Everything was fine until we crossed the border. Troubles with Irene began with everyone wanting to touch her. Dale or I carried her on our backs or slung over our shoulders at all times. Whoever wasn't carrying her walked close to her to swat away everyone's hands, or else I think the poor child would have lost a foot along the way. It was a constant battle to keep her safe from grabbing hands.

We traveled to Peshawar and crossed over into Afghanistan, a county rich in history and tradition. In 1975, the Russians had not yet invaded. Irene cut her first tooth while we were there. I loved it there; it was peaceful, and everyone was friendly.

We went over the high pass between Afghanistan and Iran. The road was primitive, but the scenery was incredible. Iran was a bustling busy modern country in those days. The shah was still in power, and everyone had new cars and TVs. We spent the first night just over the border and arrived in Tehran the following late afternoon. Finding a place to stay was a big problem: no vacancies anywhere in the town. We finally found a small hotel that made room for us. I think because of Irene they felt sorry for us. .. . or thought us complete idiots to be hauling a baby all over the globe.

By this time we were a bit travel worn, so we flew to Istanbul. We loved the bazaar and mosques, the history and traditions.

Heading to Europe, we flew to Greece, where we restocked our almost empty duffel bag of baby food. After the peanut butter sauce experiment in Indonesia, I had decided to wait until we were back in Australia to start feeding Irene "people" food.

We visited all the normal tourist sites in Athens then went to some of the islands. In Santorini, one of my favorite places, we rode donkeys up a steep rock face to get to the small town. In those days there were not so many tourists. Irene rode in front of me on the donkey without any issues. That child took everything in stride, no matter where we traveled. I guess riding a donkey was just another means of transportation to her.

The Greeks eat dinner late and take their afternoon naps seriously, so we did the same. Wonderful! The islands were beautiful, and we could take Irene into all the bars with us. Greeks love babies. Some nights I would lose her for hours as she was passed around to all the people in the bar, who would dance her around Greek style. She loved it. I was taken with Greece; it was fun and safe, and the people were warm and welcoming.

From there we flew to Cairo, Egypt. We hired one of the many horse-drawn carriages to take us to the pyramids. You can't do this now, but we walked right up to the pyramids and the Sphinx. No one hassled us or charged us a fortune to see them. We were free to explore as we wanted.

Each time we crossed over a border to enter another country; I had to wear my wig and contact lenses. We were breaking every law in the book, but it was our way of life, and I didn't think anything about it. Never once did Dale or I call each other by our real names. We became and remained our aliases until the bitter end.

We flew from Cairo to Khartoum, Sudan. If I thought it was hot in India, I was in for an unpleasant surprise in Khartoum. We landed at about five in the morning. It was still dark, but the temperature was around 35° C or 95° F. The sweat dripped off of us. Right then I said, "What have we done now?" Why we bothered going there, I don't know, but we thought it was a good idea at the time.

Irene was a big crowd draw, and once again we were protecting her little limbs from grabbing hands. We found what we thought was a decent hotel, although it lacked air conditioning—but it did have big powerful fans.

As the sun came up and the temperature rose, we stayed indoors and kept Irene as cool as we could. She fell asleep; poor little thing was pooped and as hot as we were. We wanted to leave the next day but had to wait three days to get a flight to Nairobi, Kenya.

Nairobi was a hectic capital city. We stayed only a few days to catch our breath before hitchhiking to the Maasai Mara Game Park. First, *no one* hitches a ride into a game park; everyone uses either a tour company or personal vehicles. We were stuck at the entrance to the park for hours. All the vehicles going in were tour companies, and they did not give us a ride. While there, we got friendly with the Maasai tribe that lived near the entrance. All the women were eager to see the little white baby and wanted to hold her. As I lifted Irene into the waiting arms of one of the women, Irene took one look at the big ear lobes and took in their colorful traditional dress then opened her mouth and let out a god-awful yell, scaring both the woman and me. Eventually, she quieted. We visited awhile, giving Irene time to get used to the Maasai people. She finally allowed them to hold her.

We waited for hours, trying to get into the park. Just when we thought we should find a place to stay the night, a couple in a vehicle stopped. Surprised to see us out in the middle of nowhere with a baby and trying to hitch a ride into the park, they gave us a ride. We went to the lodge our hosts were going to. Our accommodation was in a great safari tent, complete with an en suite bath. It was amazing and simply wonderful. The tent came with beds, electricity, and a bath. I loved it. We stayed a couple of days, went on game drives, and had a ball! We hitched a ride back out with some folks leaving the lodge who also found it quite strange that we were there with no vehicle or a tour group. To us, it was not unusual, but looking back, I see what idiots we were.

We got back to Nairobi and flew to Mahé, Seychelles. Though it was a beautiful place to end the long trip, I hated the huge spider webs that stretched from tree to tree. I never saw any of the builders of these webs, but I was quite certain creepy giant spiders had made them. Other than that, it was paradise. I was able to put Irene down on the floor where she finally started to crawl. Poor kid hadn't been able to be put down on a floor long enough to even try until then, and she was over a year old.

Near the end of 1975, Dale left us to return to Australia while he went to Switzerland to visit the bank. He did not come back for a couple of weeks. I did not doubt that he was meeting a woman there. I was weary of his unfaithfulness. But what could I do? Like it or not, we were fugitives together.

About two days after my arrival in Australia, I experienced a migraine. It came on like a flash. The only thing I remember is screaming, holding my head, and bouncing around the bed from one side to the other. The manager heard the ruckus and called an ambulance. While I went to the hospital, our next-door neighbors took Irene. They picked me up from the hospital after I had been given an injection of powerful pain medication. When I woke up in my bed, I learned that I had slept for twenty hours.

Since Irene was over a year old, it was time for her to start eating solid food. I started with a scrambled egg, thinking it was something mild and easy to digest. Shortly after eating it, she broke out in a rash all over and her little body swelled. Panicked, I ran to my neighbors, who loaded us up and took us to the hospital. I learned that lots of babies are allergic to eggs. Okay, well that's good to know, but it would have been better had I known it a few hours earlier. Poor kid had a mom who knew nothing about babies. With the help of my neighbor, we transitioned Irene to solid food. What I would have done without this woman is beyond me.

By the time Dale got back from his little adventure in Switzerland, I was done. I'd had enough of his crap and was moving to Sydney. He promised to be a good husband, to be faithful and honest, and to be a good dad. I believed him again, and we decided we would all move to Sydney. We left the manager in charge, packed a bit of our stuff, but left the big things in our small unit, and moved down. We rented a room in a big house in a nice area called Belleview Hill. The house was in probate, where five or six other people were living.

We developed friendships with those already living in the house, and, true to form, Dale started cheating on me again. This time no amount of begging and promises could make me believe him. I told him to move out; I was staying, and he was going. After a lot of fighting, he moved out but only on the condition that I research and find him another identity. I agreed. I could do it just as easily as we did in the States... well, kind of. I went to the public library day after day, searching the obituaries in the newspapers for births and subsequent deaths. After many long days, I found a match in the age of a child who had died in infancy: John Cross, a name I would soon forget and remember only years later.

I found a babysitter for Irene and got a job as a waitress in a coffee shop on the ground floor of a big complex called Australia Square. The upper floors had many offices and a nice dinner house at the top. The waiters and waitresses worked a split shift in this restaurant. They served lunch then closed for a few hours before opening up for dinner. While they were on their long break, they hung out in the coffee shop because it was too far to go home just to turn around and come back. One of the guys from, of all places, Canada took a liking to me. Just dandy. He thinks I am Canadian, but I know nothing about Canada.

Every time they came in, they sat in my station, making it impossible not to have contact with the guy. I tried to stay busy, but the middle of the day was slow. Changing stations with another waitress did not work either; the group simply shifted to my new station. He continued to flirt while I tried to find something other than Canada to talk to him about. He finally asked me out. I must've had that deer in the headlights look because he took me to the side and said, "Hey, I know you are not from Canada. I don't know where you are from—probably the US. I don't care why you have a Canadian passport. I like you and want to go out with you and I won't tell anyone anything."

His friends were mostly from the UK, so no problem. I started dating him. Eric ended up being one of the nicest guys I have ever met. After a few months I told him a bit about my history, and true to his word, he never told anyone else. My secret was safe. Dale was gone. I had no idea where, just that he was not around. For that I was grateful.

My photos for *Playboy* all those years ago never appeared in the USA as promised, but they did appear in Australia. Eric saw the ad for the booklet, recognized my picture, and ordered a copy. I was so embarrassed, but he loved them.

I got another job at a fine dinner house in Rose Bay, a floating restaurant that paid much better than the coffee shop. Miriam, one of the girls who was living in the big house I was renting a room from, and I had become especially close. Since she worked days in an office and I worked nights, she watched Irene for me, who was about two years old.

We had big dinner parties at the house on the nights I was off. Miriam and I cooked gourmet meals, like duck àl'orange. My cooking had come a long way from the early days. Funny as it sounds, one of the few things I took with me when I fled the States was a gourmet cookbook my dad had given to me years ago. It had my name inscribed on the cover. Dale had insisted that I cut it out, but I still had the book.

My housemates and I spent good times together. We smoked a bit of pot, nothing serious—no hard drugs—had BBQs at friends' houses. I had a nice group of friends, and we all got along well. It was the best of times I had in Australia.

Eric and I had a falling out when I found out he had slept with one of my friends. He apologized and said he loved me, but after all of Dale's cheating, I had no tolerance for cheating. We remained friends.

Around the middle of 1976, I entertained the idea of going back to the United States. I was in such turmoil. With Dale not in the picture, if anything happened to me, Irene would be an orphan. Even though Eric and Miriam knew something about my past and that I was from the USA, I never told them the whole story. It was a very hard decision to make, one I worried about all the time. Going back held the very real possibility of a long prison sentence. Although I was certain my mom would take custody of Irene, who would have her family around her, losing my daughter for all that time seemed unbearable.

7

LIFE ANEW

After months of stressing about returning to the United States, I finally called my brother. I was so happy to hear his voice. He had been worried about me and was relieved to finally hear from me. Oh, how I missed him and my mom and dad!

I had to go back, no matter what was in store for me, for my daughter's sake. Many people have asked me, "Were you scared to go back?" Honestly, I have no idea if I was or not. Rather than being scared, I felt numb.

I called my mom right after talking to my brother. She cried with happiness. I had hurt her so badly; I felt so guilty. I had no money to purchase tickets, so she bought them under the names I gave her. I learned that she was still in contact with DEA agents Lucido and Williams. They had become quite friendly over the years. She assured me that they were after Dale. Even though I had been indicted after leaving with him, they said they would help me. My mom notified them that I would be coming back but through Canada. I could not take the chance of coming directly from Australia into the United States with a false passport. I was in enough trouble as it was.

Once I had decided to go back, I told Miriam and Eric a bit more about my situation. They had thought it was something like it was but had never questioned me or made me feel uncomfortable about not telling them.

Me with my wig and contacts and carrying my Canadian passport, and Irene with her Australian passport, it came time to leave. It was hard to say goodbye to all the friends I had made—harder to think about what was waiting for me when I got back. A few months before Rod Stewart had released the album *Atlantic Crossing*, which became my story. I was crossing stormy waters just as the song "Sailing" on that album said. My legs felt like lead as I boarded the plane. I almost turned back. If my friends had not been there to support me, I might have. But the die had been cast, and people were waiting for me—some I longed to see. And then there were the authorities, whom I was dreading to face. I was clueless as to what they were going to do to me, regardless of what they had told my mom. I was in deep trouble.

I faced at least a twenty-year federal jail term on the one count of using another's passport, not to mention the eight felony counts I was up against. I prayed Mom could gain custody of Irene. None of this was my daughter's fault, and she did not deserve to be put into a foster home. I felt certain that Mom, being the fighter she was, would never stand for that. No matter what, she would get custody of her granddaughter. At least I could find solace in that. But the flight back to Canada was hard, and I was scared to death. I had to face the music for what I had done for and with Dale. I took with me only what I could carry since I had absolutely no funds from the drug money; in fact, I had no funds at all. I was returning penniless with an almost-three-year-old child who would tip the scales in my favor.

After the long flight back, I arrived in Canada. Upon showing my Canadian passport and Irene's Australian one at immigration, they took our passports and escorted me and Irene to a waiting room. *I am going to be busted in Canada now as well for using this girl's ID.* I had no way of knowing if the girl whose name I had used for almost three years was wanted for murder or anything else. As I waited for the immigration officer, I broke out in a cold sweat. I knew I was going to land in jail here.

Fear does not touch what I felt. I can find no words that adequately describe my feelings. After what seemed to me hours but was only five minutes, the immigration officer walked in holding our passports. He stared at me before quietly asking, "Why didn't you register your daughter as a Canadian citizen while in Australia? It is her birthright. You should take care of this at once."

My heart stopped. I was not going to jail here and now? I assured him I would take care of it at once. He handed me our passports, and with great relief, I left his office, fighting the blackness that threatened. When I got to the first bathroom I could find, I threw up.

My next task was to purchase our tickets to LA. No problem, I had the money. But as I was buying them, the ticket agents asked me for the $300 I needed for the Americans to let me in. I didn't know about this new rule. I had the money for the tickets, but that left me with only $30. In hindsight, my situation was ironic. I was a US citizen with several felonies against me, but I couldn't get back in to turn myself in to the authorities who were waiting for me. What a mess. Of course, it wasn't funny at the time. My only choice was to call my mom and tell her the problem. Bless her, she said, "Use the money you have to get a room at the airport now. When you're settled, call me back and tell me where you are. I am getting the first flight out to you." After all, I had put her through, not one "I told you so" crossed her lips. Just love and help.

As it happened, that airport had small rooms to rent. It had only a small bed, toilet, and shower, designed for long layovers. I got one and called my mom, who had already booked her flight and would be there in about twelve hours.

Although Irene was great on the plane, the last few hours of her sensing my extreme stress took its toll on her. We got some food then went into our little cubicle. We slept for about eight hours straight. Mom arrived on schedule. Oh, what a reunion we had! Neither of us could stop crying. She held her second grandchild like she was made of gold; there was no separating them. She stuck like glue to Irene, who sensed this woman loved her very much. She fell in love with her grandmother from the first moment. I will never forget it. After all the pain and shame I had put my mom through, all she had for me was pure love.

We went to the ticket counter to book the flight back home. Now that my mom was with me, I felt at peace. I was heading for big trouble, but it was okay. My daughter would be safe with my mom.

We arrived in Los Angeles without any problems. The DEA had paved the way for me. I was aware there was a BOLO—be on the lookout order—issued against me. While at the airport, I stepped into the bathroom and destroyed the false Canadian passport, flushing the pieces down the toilet. I had to keep Irene's passport because it was the only ID the child had, but the photo on it was taken when she was three months old. Despite all the assurances from my mom that the DEA was not going to arrest me on the spot, I was still looking over my shoulder the whole while, expecting someone to yell "Stop!" at any moment. It was one of the longest walks of my life out of the airport to the car with my dad waiting for us. He was happy to see me. The past was behind us and that was that. One look at his granddaughter, his only grandchild, and his heart melted. Love at first sight.

At the time, my parents owned the rights to all the food and beverage facilities in a big hotel, the Ramada Inn, across the street from Santa Monica High School. It included a coffee shop on the ground floor and a nice dinner house restaurant with a great bar, which had a large window that looked out to the pool. The top floor was enormous and had a big apartment, where my parents lived. It also had a very long bar and a huge banquet room. I started working for them right away, in part to show the authorities that I was working and to keep busy. But I was a nervous wreck. It did not help matters that I would not answer to my real name for about a month. It drove my dad crazy, as he would call me by *Paula* to pick up an order, but it had been so long since I'd used my name that it didn't register with me. It's like I didn't hear it. My dad was never a patient man, so this was a constant irritant to him.

The reunion with my brother was a very happy one. We had been close, but behind all the happy reunions was that nagging in the back of my mind: "They will be coming for me soon; then what?"

To the credit of DEA agents Lucido and Williams, they gave me about a week to spend with my family. Then the time came. They set up an appointment to meet with me at the restaurant. None of us knew what was going to happen. Were they coming to arrest me? My mom and I had it all arranged: if the worst happened, Mom would get custody of Irene.

The day and time arrived, along with the agents. They conducted the interview mid-morning, after the rush of high school kids had come and gone, when it was slow in the coffee shop. No handcuffs came out as we—Mom, Dad, me, Irene, and the agents—settled into a booth. They advised me to contact my attorneys. I would have to turn myself in the following week in San Diego to the federal court. They gave me the day I was to do this. I had already contacted our old attorneys in San Diego, the same guys who had represented Dale all those years ago. They were happy to take my case and knew the story already. My dad was paying their fee. They were good to us and charged a small percentage of their normal fee. I had no money at all except what I earned in tips waitressing for my parents, and that just barely paid for my cigarettes.

On the appointed day, my mom drove me to the San Diego court. We knew I would not be going back with her and Irene, who was too young to realize what was going on, thank God for that. She never knew the terror I was feeling, but my mom did and tried her best to assure me that she and Dad would do everything they could to keep me out of jail. That did not do much to help my fears, for I knew the DEA was not going to let me go with all they had against me.

This time the handcuffs did come out and were placed on my wrists. I went with the DEA agents to court for my arraignment. My attorney was present so I felt a bit better. The assistant district attorney who was going to prosecute me was my old "friend," the one who prosecuted Dale, the one I had chased down the courtroom hall, spitting at him. The judge who would hear my case was the same one who had sat on Dale's case. It just couldn't get any worse. Shouldn't these guys have retired by now or moved on? No, they were still there and very happy to see me.

I was handcuffed to an African American woman who had been caught crossing over the Mexican border with a gram of heroin taped to her tummy, a federal crime. Her bail was set at $5000.

Then the judge called me by name, said how happy he was to see me again, then set my bail at $100,000. The poor girl linked to me turned a much lighter shade, tried to scoot as far away from me as the handcuffs would allow, and said loudly, "What the hell did *you* do? Who are you?"

Shocked, I could only whimper, "Nothing, really."

My attorney tried to argue for lower bail but to no avail. They placed me in a holding room, not a cell, and gave me a minute with my attorney. I advised him to tell my mom not to post bail, just to take care of Irene.

I was taken to MCC (Metropolitan Correctional Center), the federal jail used for federal offenders waiting for trial and sentencing. I processed in right in time for dinner and was last in line. As far as jails go, a federal one isn't as bad as county jails. The accommodation and food aren't so bad. Being the last served, all the tables were full except where one girl wearing a red cape sat alone. I found the cape a bit odd as the rest of us were in prison garb, no capes for us. Thinking nothing of it, I asked if I could sit with her. She nodded. I ate what I could, which wasn't much because my guts were in knots, and I was just plain scared. After dinner we were ushered into the common areas where each set of four cells surrounded a central sitting area. The layout was not horrible, with only two girls in each cell. The cells had solid doors with a sliding window so the jailers could check on us. The toilet was just there, no privacy. Everything was bolted to the floor, but it was not as oppressive as I had imagined.

A girl came up to me in the common room and said, "Hey, do you know who you ate dinner with?"

"Well. No. She was not exactly a chatty Cathy now, was she?"

The girl told me that my red-caped dinner mate turned out to be Lynette Fromme, also known as Squeaky Fromme, one of the Manson girls. She had never been indicted in the 1969 Tate–La Bianca murders, but she, along with several others, had carved crosses in their foreheads during Manson's trial in the early '70s and had taken up wearing the red cape as a sign of solidarity for him and the others who were convicted of the murders. So that was what was on her forehead and why she was allowed to wear her red cape. She was in prison for the attempted assassination of President Ford. I was told to stay away from her because she was dangerous. Oh joy, and I just had my first prison meal with her. Lynette had her own cell as the authorities had the good sense to keep her by herself.

Another celebrity was also in jail with me: Patty Hearst, although she was isolated from the general population, and we never saw her. I was lucky and got a cellmate who was also a drug offender. So my first, and I was sure not my last, night in federal jail began.

The next day I was taken out of my cell and put in a room where my attorneys and several officials sat. On the table was a polygraph machine. They hooked me up and the questions began, all of them related to where Dale was and what name he was using. As funny as it sounds, after all the time I spent researching the new name for him, I had forgotten it. It was not until years later that I remembered it. I did not know where he was or what he was doing. I had no idea where the money was, and I certainly had none of it. The only thing I could answer was the name I had been using and about Irene. I was questioned for three days, and my story was always the same: the truth. Because I did not lie, I passed the test.

The jail was not uncomfortable as jails go. During the day, they let you watch TV or read, but the nights were horrible. Sleep was impossible, with swirling thoughts that I would not see my child until she was almost grown. They were surely going to throw the book at me…and they had every right to do so.

My attorneys visited me, as did my mom, all assuring me that things would be fine, or at least not as bad as they could be. All I kept thinking was that the DA and judge hated me. What chance did I have with them controlling my fate? No matter what anyone said, I was sure I was going away for a very long time.

On the fourth day, I was called back to court for a bail hearing. I had no hope of getting out. To my complete surprise, the judge dropped my bail and let me out on my own recognizance. I couldn't figure what was happening. It was like a fog lifted, and I could see daylight once more, but I was sure it would not be for long. I was released into my parents' custody, which was fine with me. There was no other place I wanted to go to. I was out, and my baby girl was with my mom to pick me up. I was free. But for how long?

I was assigned a court date and had to talk to the probation department several times during the three-month ordeal. They were still stuck on getting me to tell them where Dale was, but I didn't know and couldn't tell them anything. He could have been anywhere in the world.

The three months went by way too quickly. My attorneys could do little to defend me because I was guilty and everyone knew it. But the authorities did not want me; they wanted Dale. They were quite sure I would never have gotten messed up with any of the illegal activities had it not been for him, and they were probably right. My juvenile record, which my dad had paid a lot of money to have sealed, came out during this period. Don't kid yourself; it's never sealed and follows you your entire life. The courts have access to it and can use it, as they did with me.

For the next three months, I worked for and lived with my parents. I went back and forth between Los Angeles and San Diego. It was a very long three months waiting to see what would happen to me.

A sealed probation report is not opened until the day of sentencing. No one sees it until then, not the judge or the DA. The DEA agents were the first to tear open theirs, followed quickly by my attorneys. After glancing through the report, my attorneys called a recess and asked to see the judge in his quarters before he handed down his sentence. I sat, handcuffed, knowing the recommendation was a minimum of one to five years in federal prison. I didn't know what the final decision would be, but I would forever have a federal felony against me. It could be worse. I could get twenty years.

I tried to prepare myself to be led back to MCC, where I would have to wait to learn where I would do my time. It could be anywhere in the United States. I prayed whatever facility would not be too far for my mom, dad, and brother to visit. I was not going to allow Irene to visit. I did not want her to have memories of me being in jail, bad enough she would have to know I did time. All this ran through my mind for what seemed hours and hours as my attorneys and others met with the judge. It was only about an hour.

Finally, all parties emerged from the judge's chamber. The DEA agents and my attorneys wore smiles, the probation officer scowled, and the judge...well; he was a judge and looked like judges are supposed to look. I couldn't read the DA's face since he would not look at me.

The judge cleared his throat and went over all kinds of things. I didn't hear it all; my mind had shut down. Then certain words seeped through: *reduce, probation, terms.* The DEA had convinced the judge to let me go with just probation!

The DEA desperately wanted Dale, so they convinced the judge, who held my life in his hands that sooner or later he would try to contact me and see his child. This could be instrumental in leading them to him, so the best thing was to let me go. They pointed out that I was Dale's captive, under his spell, which was pretty much true. That I had already served almost three years living in fear as a fugitive, and as soon as he was out of my life I came back and did the right thing demonstrated this very fact. Plus, and this was a big thing, I had no funds from the drug trafficking and was penniless with a three-year-old child. It would serve no purpose to further ruin my life. I had shown remorse and sorrow for what I had done. Yes, I was truly and thoroughly sorry.

Although I had been convicted of trafficking over thirty-two kilograms of cocaine, I was sentenced to five years under federal probation with no prison time. What the heck? An hour ago I had been trying to come to terms with where they were going to send me and how long until I would be able to see my baby, but now I was relatively free to go. My family surrounded me, all of us in tears and hugging one another.

At the time I thought how very lucky I was, but it was not until much later, over thirty years later that I knew it was not luck at all. God had a plan for me. It didn't play out for many years, but it was His plan nonetheless.

I was immediately faced with another problem: the convoluted mess with Irene's birth certificate. The mother's name on it was not my legal name. How would I put her into school and prove I am her mother? I'm not sure how it happened, but with the help of my attorneys and the stroke of a judge's pen, my daughter had a new name: Amelia Petty. I was given the task of naming her. I gave her my maiden name since that was what I was going by. All of her documents were changed at the federal level. She received a Social Security card with that name, and the record of her childhood shots she received in Australia were changed as well. She had a new legal name. Though her birth certificate retained the Salsman name, we never had to use that document. Her Social Security card was sufficient.

The nightmare was finally over.

True, the feds are watching me closely, but it was not to catch me but to nab Dale when he got the urge to see his daughter. They did not know Amelia's dear old dad very well. He never came to see us or even tried to contact us. Dale did not love anyone. He only understood possessing people and things. Once I had no value to him, he moved on.

I felt freer than I had in a long time. I got my driver's license back, and my old name was restored. I was getting used to being me again. It seemed like a long bad dream had finally ended.

8

Party and Crash

A new year: 1977. I continued working for my parents. I wanted to be out on my own. Probation terms stated that I had to have permission for any change of address. My probation officer had to know where I was at all times. I received permission from the court to move into my own place, a small apartment in Hawthorne.

For part of the year, I did nothing but keep my nose clean and have only an occasional drink.

I was my dad's best bartender at his restaurant. When I was not doing that, I waitressed. I worked the big banquets. Because I had started so young waitressing, I was exceptional at it. I ran circles around the other girls.

Some of my old friends learned I was back. I located Anna, who was still living at her parents' house and still in contact with Rick, the father of her son. I found out through her where everyone was hanging out. The old nightclub we used to visit, the Flying Jib, had burned down. Some of my old friends got together and built a new one in Redondo Beach, which is where they could be found any given night. I had no restrictions as to who I could see or where I could go other than I was to have no contact with any felons. Maybe some of the old gang were convicted felons, but it was a public place. I walked into Sweetwater, as the nightclub was called, and there they all were, the old gang. A lot of my friends were surprised but happy to see me. They peppered me with questions, mostly about where I had been for the last few years. They were taken aback to learn that I'd had a baby while I was a fugitive.

It was good to be back with so many of my old friends, many of them from when I was in high school. We recalled good memories of the parties and the fun we'd had. It seemed light-years away, but it had been only a bit under six years. I felt alive again. The past was done; I could go on with my life. I was still young, "hot," and ready. I did not dare go anywhere near drugs, but I did drink. Although every time I got drunk, I also got sick and suffered from horrible hangovers.

Little by little I started to smoke pot again—just pot. I had been smoking pot since I was fourteen, so it was a natural part of my life, and I did not see anything wrong with it. I could drive and I was always in control (not so when I drank too much).My probation officer did not test me for drug use.

I had stayed in touch with Eric and my Australian housemates. In the middle of 1977, Eric and one of the other guys got a job as waiters on a fancy cruise line that would be docking at the Los Angeles harbor. It was amazing to see them again. Eric said he was still in love with me. But I was not the same person I had been in Australia. I liked him and would always fondly remember the times we had together.

Eric and a couple of the other Australian guys came over to the States and stayed awhile. Anna and Eric hooked up, and her sister, Heather, fell for one of the other guys. Everything was fine as far as I was concerned.

I met a long-haired hip guy named Mike at Sweetwater. Never good at picking the right guy since I'd tossed aside Craig, I fell for him. It would always be downhill for me in the romance department.

Since it was not hip to live in Hawthorne, Mike and I moved into a very small place in Redondo Beach. Smoking pot gave way to the occasional snort of coke at a party, and I took acid or mushrooms if I could find them.

Anna and I started going to Hollywood. I loved LSD. I dropped it right before we arrived in Hollywood. I could go all night, come down, and drive home early in the morning. Amelia stayed with my parents.

While I had been out of the country, Anna had become good friends with a major music producer. We got backstage passes whenever we wanted, no strings attached. It was great being back in that concert scene and the parties after. I was on unsupervised probation and doing everything normal twenty-five-year-old girls did: party, drink, drugs, and sex.

Mike and I didn't last long; I wanted to party, and he did not want to work.

Patty, a dear friend of my mom's, worked for my parents at the restaurant. She talked me into going back to school to take a course to be a loan processor. If I did well, I could have a career in a mortgage company or bank. I completed the course and also took an accounting course.

I partied hard, but I also worked very hard. I worked all the big banquets, weddings, and important events, either tending bar or waitressing. I was the head bartender as well as the head waitress. Sometimes I worked a big banquet, got home at 3 a.m., snatched a couple of hours of sleep, and went back to work a breakfast banquet at 8 a.m. Amelia stayed with my mom, living in the apartment on the top floor of the hotel.

At the time Anna and I were drinking White Russians. After one hard and heavy Mexican wedding reception, I asked Mom for a bottle of Kahlua. As I was leaving the storeroom, my dad saw me with the bottle, had a fit, and came after me. I took off to one of the elevators to go to the top floor where my mom was. He took the other. We came together about the middle of the big banquet room. Both of us were tired and not thinking well. Before I knew it, we came to blows, shouting and yelling. My mom and brother ran out of the apartment to find me and my dad going at it. He was a lot stronger than I was and had me in a headlock. I did the only thing I could: I bit him…hard. It got him off of me, but to my horror, I had drawn blood, and it dripped down his arm. My mom and brother pulled us apart. Both dad and I were spitting mad. Mom told me to leave. I took my bottle and left. The three of us decided that since Dad and I couldn't get along—things had been building for quite some time—I shouldn't work there anymore.

I got a bartending job in Inglewood, on the corner of Imperial and Crenshaw, in the middle of LA's African American neighborhood. Mine was the only white face for miles. When I applied for the job, they were a bit surprised, but with my previous experience behind a bar and my mom's outstanding recommendation, they hired me. It ended up being one of the best jobs. I worked for some of the nicest people I have ever worked for or have even known. The locals loved me, and I loved them. They were always very sweet and gave great tips. I worked only four nights a week, but I earned enough to pay my living expenses and hire sitters for Amelia. I never needed money to party because everywhere I went, somebody else picked up the booze and drug tabs.

One night Anna and I were at a concert at the Shrine, nothing big, so we were not backstage but just hanging out. We were a bit bored since the band wasn't good. Two good-looking guys starting chatting us up. They said they lived close and asked us to their house to party. Like so many things in my life, it didn't go well. Anna and I ended up being some of the first girls to be given the date rape drug, which was almost unheard of in 1977. We did a few lines of coke, and then the guys got us some drinks. The next thing I knew, I was waking up with my pants down with a passed-out man beside me. I got up very carefully and found Anna in the living room in about the same condition. I got her up, and we hurried out of there.

Once we were a safe distance away, we took stock. Neither of us had drunk enough to pass out. Especially since we were so full of coke. No way did I pass out on my own. The guys had slipped us something that knocked us out.

We were okay and only about a mile or so from the Shrine. We found the car fast enough, but what a sight we were: unkempt, makeup smeared, wearing skimpy party clothes, and walking down the street at 6 a.m. We were mad at the guys. We would have most likely slept with them; they didn't have to dope us up.

Wizard, one of my oldest friends from the beach, had had a crush on me for years. We decided to rent a big house in Redondo Beach, in a nice area. There was never any sexual thing between us, not for his lack of trying; I was not into him that way. For the most part, he accepted that and was one of my best friends. Quite the character, he set me up with some of his cool friends. I usually ended up in bed with them.

He introduced me to a lot of his friends, including Sean, who lived about six hours from LA. He was quite rich. His family owned a large successful ranch up there. He liked to party, so he frequently came down and stayed with one of the gang. He was hip and hot and welcomed anywhere. He always brought "goodies" with him. I slept with him once, but it was much better to be his friend rather than lover.

Life and parties went on. Sean and two of his friends shared birthdays at about the same time. In the summer of 1978, they planned an enormous party at the ranch—a three-day, invitation-only bash. Being the biggest ranch and richest family in the area, they hired security guards to keep out uninvited guests. The party was anything goes, do as you want, and no worries about cops busting in. In fact, some of the local cops partied with the best of us. It was a ball! The theme was "Great in '78." There were wet T-shirt contests, which I won my fair share. Rooms were available for sexual activity as were a few hot tubs. You name it, they had it.

They'd hired a full catering staff. Large BBQ grills were set up, with a variety of beef cooking, salads, and all kinds of food were for the taking. There were about two hundred of us happy, dopey people. In a big vat we brewed pomegranates and made wine from them, added booze, and cooked the stuff. It was potent, but after the first cup, you were hooked.

One of the birthday guys took a liking to me, a big guy, Jacob, a good friend of Sean's. They had grown up together and were the best of buds. The second night, or should I say early morning, we were partying and getting cozy when he asked me to come back to his house—he lived close by. That sounded good. I was tired and in the mood for a hot bath and a comfortable bed as we had been hosing each other down. That started my brief but happy affair with Jacob. This guy was big, well over six feet tall and broad. You just did not mess with him as evidenced by his actions the next day back at the party when one of the guys tried to hit on me. Jacob put him in his place with just a well-placed word.

About this same time, my parents retired to Grover City up by San Luis Obispo, an area with lovely sand dunes. Many people went up there to play in the dunes with three-wheelers or their 4X4s. I had a 4X4 CJ-5 Jeep. Wizard and I went there often. He had friends in the area, and we'd go there to party and play around with my Jeep in the dunes. Wizard and my mom got along very well. I think it was because my mom knew he cared for me.

After the big party, Jacob and I kept our affair going. I drove up to see him on my days off. He was a wonderful big bear of a guy. One weekend Wizard and I went to the dunes in separate vehicles. We were going to drive my Jeep into the dunes and have some fun for a day, and then I was going to go see Jacob. One of the dunes proved to be too much for the Jeep. One of the motor mounts broke and the frame got a bit bent.

Since my uncle had one of the only frame-straightening machines around, I took my parents' Lincoln Continental to see Jacob until my Jeep was repaired. The road over to Jacob's house was through an area called Kern County, with Bakersfield as the county seat. It was at the time a redneck place, with cowboys and the like, as well as big farms that employed many undocumented Hispanic laborers to work these citrus and other fruit farms in the area.

The two-lane road was a typical country road, with only farmland on each side. My daughter was in the car with me, so I was sober as a judge. I was driving behind a large truck and could not see around it so to pass. I had to go into the oncoming lane a bit to see if it was safe to pass. It was at the exact moment another vehicle, also behind a large vehicle, did the same thing. We side-swiped each other. My vehicle went to the oncoming side, as did the other vehicle. My car ended up in a ditch.

No one was hurt; my daughter was fine with only a scratch on her hand. I took four-year-old Amelia out of the car and set her in the orange grove way off the road. I told her to stay there until I got back. As I was walked over to the other car, two cars passed us and did not stop. I was off the road and approaching the other car. I could see that the girls in the car were unhurt, and the car had little damage. Just then a third car came along and ran me over, dragging me about ten feet before hitting the other car.

We were in the middle of nowhere. I was going into shock. I don't know when or how, but my daughter was suddenly beside me. I asked her to get my purse and the blanket out of the trunk of the car. Upon impact with the ditch, the trunk had popped open, making it easy for her to retrieve it.

I was a mess. My left leg lay at an impossible angle. I felt blood running down my chin—a lot of it. I did not want Amelia to see me like this. She got the blanket and I worked it over myself. I have no idea how long it took for the ambulance to come, but I was in shock and pumped with adrenaline, so the pain had not set in. I was transported to the hospital in Bakersfield.

The cops took my ID and looked up my record, finding my federal probation status, and the reason I was on it. They seemed eager to put me behind bars, where they figured I belonged. When I got to the hospital, they said they would not treat my daughter until I gave them a blood test—they were sure I was high on something, a big drug smuggler like myself.

I had no idea if my daughter was hurt. I had only seen her right after being hit and was not sure if she was okay. Things were a bit fuzzy, and the pain came on with a fury. They took my blood before they would give me any pain medication. Then they let me see my daughter, who had a cute little pink adhesive bandage on her hand. Thank God she was okay. I had them call my parents.

I was put into traction; my left femur was broken right above the knee. My chin had a large gash. Had I not put my hands up when the car hit me, my whole face would have been a mess. My hands and knees were full of asphalt and grit.

The cops were not happy that my blood test came back clean. They wanted to charge me with drunk driving and threatened to do so but couldn't because I was not drunk. They placed me under arrest for reckless driving, the only thing they could do.

My emotional state was off the charts because contact with any law enforcement meant the feds could put me away for five years. I was waiting for them to come along at any time. Every time the door opened, I feared it was them coming to get me. I was so afraid, as I had been arrested and this was more than contact.

My parents arrived with my brother. They contacted the bar I worked at and told them where I was and what had happened. About two days later, twenty African Americans, coworkers, and customers drove the distance up to see me; a three- to four-hour drive. It was wonderful to see everyone as they all walked in. The nurses and hospital staff watched, their mouths hanging open. It was the only bright light since the accident, and I loved them for coming. One of the gals who worked the day shift told me she would swap shifts with me when I was able to get out and be on crutches, and my bosses assured me that my job was still there.

Traction was hard on me. I was so light; the heavy weights pulled me to the foot of the bed. Every hour I had to hoist myself back to the head of the bed, but the weights pulled me back down. I continued to worry about the feds coming to get me. I couldn't sleep with all of this going on. Everything combined to make me an emotional wreck.

After a few days, the doctors presented me with my options regarding my leg. I could stay in traction for six to nine months. Seriously? No way. My second option was to be in an almost full body cast for about nine. Again, no way. That left me with the final option: insert a rod into my leg from my knee to my hip. I would have only a small scar at the top of my hip. I would be on crutches for a year or so, and then the rod could be removed. Okay, now we were talking. I would at least be mobile. I could handle the crutches and only a small scar.

They took me into surgery. Once I woke up from the surgery, I saw that my leg was wrapped up and hurt like it was on fire. But the pain meds were great. I was in and out of consciousness for a day or so. Then they started slowly backing down the pain meds, and I started coming around.

The scar was not a small one on my hip; rather, it ran down the outside of my left leg from hip to knee. It was brutal looking and hurt something awful. My chin had stitches; my right leg was full of asphalt as well as my elbows and part of my arms and hands. The doctors said that I would be able to walk at some point, although I would limp for the rest of my life. The asphalt would fade in time, the stitches would dissolve. After thinking long and hard and considering I could have died, the prospect of a few scars did not seem that bad.

As soon as the hospital released me, the Bakersfield police brought a wheelchair and took me to the local jail. My parents were waiting to bail me out. Still, I was sure the feds would be arriving soon because being arrested meant I had violated the terms of my probation.

We found out later that the other two drivers involved had no driver's licenses or insurance and were in the country illegally. Yet the police laid the fault entirely on me even though I was a citizen with a driver's license and insurance. In the cops' eyes, I was the drug smuggler from Los Angeles and therefore the guilty one. My parents and I worked out a plan for the five years I would be in federal prison; we were so sure they would pick me up for violating my probation. I had resigned myself to this fate, sick at heart that I would not see my daughter until she was almost ten years old.

But they never came for me. Eventually, I stopped worrying about it, although it did take quite some time for me to stop shaking when someone knocked at my door.

In the end, after all my court appearances, which my parents had to drive me to, I received a fine and had to complete a hundred hours of community service, which had to be completed within six months. That wasn't too bad, but being on crutches complicated where I could do this. Community service usually involved picking up trash along the freeway or some other physical activity. But one thing I could do was fold lap sponges and sterilize hospital equipment at Harbor General Hospital.

Wizard was upset with me for not calling him first after the accident instead of my parents. But I reasoned that they were closer and they were my parents. At any rate, it was time for me to move. I rented a small apartment in a dingy little area that I could afford. I had to sell my Jeep because I could no longer drive a manual transmission vehicle. My father traded it in for a small automatic so I could get to work, Harbor General, and El Camino College, where I was taking classes for accounting—all in upstairs classrooms. I got pretty good at walking with my crutches in a very short period.

During this time, I indirectly heard from Dale for the first time since I had left Australia. My attorneys in San Diego had gotten word to him that I was seeking a divorce. Through the attorneys I learned he was still on the run. When the divorce came through, he paid me $10,000 in lieu of monthly child support payments. Essentially, he didn't want to hear from me or Amelia regarding any financial needs. The divorce covered all of the bases, including both of our aliases as well as our real names. I got full custody of Irene-Amelia. And that was that.

Anna and I still partied. I hobbled around on my crutches backstage. The stagehands would set me up to the side of the stage with a chair and a little table for my drinks. Crutches worked out quite well for getting parking spaces at clubs. If we saw a good space, I hobbled over and stood in the space until Anna, or whoever I was with, could get to it. Who was going to run down a woman waving her crutch in the air, yelling, "Oh no you don't. This space is mine." Drivers must have thought I had lost my mind, but it worked and no one ran me over. I had to watch how much I drank when out. I was wobbly to begin with. I could not go to the bar to get my drinks; the waitresses took pity on me and made sure my glass was full. I still partied with my old friends from the beach area. Life went on, crutches and all.

By the beginning of 1979, it was time for me to start thinking about a real job—a career—and getting a life. I had attended Mortgage Broker School and Jr. College. Although it was hard to say goodbye to all the really good friends I had made at the bar, it was time to move on. I got a job at a mortgage broker company as a junior loan processor. I learned fast and was soon processing the loan application from start to final approval and handling my loan representatives. These were the men and women who went out and got the loans from Realtors and did all the leg work. After the head processor got another job, I was promoted and got a big raise.

Anna's older sister, Heather, was reliable and had a steady professional job. She needed a roommate. We had known each other for ages, our families were very close, our dads were selling cars and making deals, and we all got together for Christmas and major holidays. It was a no-brainer that we rent a nice three-bedroom in Torrance, which was a step up for me. I had all the furniture Dale and I had brought over from Taiwan, hand carved and beautiful. I also had some antiques. Heather had practical things like a couch and a better refrigerator. We both had our own bedroom furniture. So we set up housekeeping, and it worked out well. We got on easily, and she and Amelia loved each other. When Anna would get on one of her self-destructive binges, we refused to let her come over. But she spent many days and nights with us. She was still my best friend, even with her issues and problems.

At the very end of 1979, Heather and I bought a home together in Wilmington. The area was not the best. The house was a little thing and even had a small backyard, but it was all ours. We got an adjustable-rate mortgage. I processed it, got it approved and funded quickly since we were both employed in good jobs and our credit was the best you could have. I was twenty-seven, and Heather, twenty-nine. We were hard-working girls.

Anna had a son, Darrell, whom she had given birth to at sixteen. He and Amelia were fast friends, a kind of big brother to her. He lived with his grandmother as did Anna when she was not with us.

Anna and I still partied, and if Heather did not want to go with us, she babysat Amelia. You would think that my party days would have been over. But this was the lifestyle I had always known, and I saw nothing wrong in it. It was still drugs, sex, and lots of rock 'n' roll.

At the beginning of 1980, I was doing very well in my job. I was good at getting difficult loans through. It took a lot of imagination and a fair amount of baloney to accomplish. I was a natural. I got better and better at it.

It was time for the rod to finally come out of my leg, and it was not soon enough for me. My leg ached a certain way if rain was on the way. I grew weary of forecasting the rains. My mom took me in to have it removed. It was a simple day surgery. All went well until they tried waking me up. I just wouldn't come out of the anesthesia. I flat lined for a short period, and they had to inject adrenaline into my IV to get me to come to. I have no memory of it. I only remember coming to with a lot of faces peering down at me, calling my name. Later my mom told me what had happened and how frightened she and the hospital staff were. They handed me the rod. I could not believe that enormous, god-awful piece of heavy metal had been in my leg for so long. No wonder I could predict the weather.

The doctors in Bakersfield had been right about one thing: I would be on crutches even after the rod was removed. It took another three or four months before I could walk without them, but then I had to use a cane. I determined that I would not limp for the rest of my life. I worked that leg, painful and hard as it was. But after another two months, I could walk without the cane. I still limped a bit, and that just was not going to do it for me. So I walked and walked and worked that leg until after about six months, I walked without a limp. Sometimes it would bother me and I had to steady myself, especially going up stairs, but the limp was a thing of the past.

In late 1980, I started looking for a new job. My current employer, a small independent broker, was having problems and couldn't pay me an income that was in line with my experience. This period was bad for the mortgage industry. Interest rates were 13 percent and even higher. I answered an ad in the paper for a managerial position at the biggest mortgage lenders in the country: Country Wide Funding. The business structure was different from other mortgage lenders. They didn't use loan representatives, so no commissions to pay. This meant that their fees were usually lower than the independent lenders. They had offices everywhere, all run by a manager and an assistant. Those two handled all the work of that one office except for the funding, which the head office in Los Angeles did. I did not think I had a chance of getting the job of manager of my own office, but I did! Thus began my long and successful career. I would make lots of money, and there was only one place for me to go: up.

I was very good at what I did. I knew how to work the system. I could get a loan through when no one else could. Bad credit? No problem. I took the basic facts of a client's problem that landed them in a mess, and by the time I got done with it, it was a work of art, a story to weep over. Those people deserved another chance and should be able to own a home. Yes, I made it happen for them.

I started my new manager's job at the Hawthorne branch, a somewhat shabby little town in South Los Angeles County. The office was established since it had been there for some time. The cliental was already in place. I walked into a solidly functioning office that bore the name of a well-known and respected large company. My assistant manager, Gertrude, was an older woman. She knew her job inside and out, but she did not want the responsibility of managing the office. I was eager to prove myself in the big boy's world. My salary was over twice what I previously had been making. The first thing I bought was a brand-new double-door refrigerator, top-of-the-line with water and ice dispensers in the door. It seems funny now but that is what I wanted. No more defrosting the old one and plenty of room. It took up a lot of space in our little house. But Heather was delighted with it as well.

Our families were growing closer together. Anna, Heather, their brother, Chad, both sets of our parents, usually my brother, Pat, and his current girlfriend, as well as Darrell, Anna's firstborn son, and Amelia were a happy lot. When we got together, we had fun times. Darrell and Amelia were like brother and sister; my dad and Don, Anna's dad, typically sat with a bottle of whiskey between them and discussed the decline of Western civilization. Francis, Anna's mom, and Irene, my mom, did the cooking with Heather and me. Anna was the baker of the family and always took charge of the pies for whatever holiday we were celebrating. Thanksgiving, Christmas, Easter, Mother's Day, we spent together. It was so normal, and it felt good to be normal with a normal life, and to work in a profession that held great promise for advancement—and it was legal!

The authorities caught Dale around 1980, but that is his story to tell. He appealed to me to write a letter for him, asking that he be incarcerated near Los Angeles so he could see his daughter. I did so, but that was the last I heard from him.

Anna and I decided we should go out to the Colorado River over one of the three-day holidays and see what was up. At that time, it was cool to go out to Parker, Arizona, make friends, and party. We did not take the kids the first time we ventured out. We didn't know what to expect except that we would be camping. We packed our sleeping bags, skimpy bikinis and other clothing, and an ice chest filled with wine coolers, Kahlua, vodka, and milk, and drove the seven-plus hours. I drove. Anna was our bartender along the way.

On the first trip out, we didn't know anyone and had no place to stay, so we camped in a designated area. Early the next morning, we sat in our bikinis by one of the boat launches and waited for a ride in someone's boat. It was not long before we were offered a ride in a ski boat with a nice guy, Jerry, who lived in Parker. He worked at the high school as a maintenance guy and had off every weekend. His first love was the river. We became friendly as the day wore on. He gave me a full day of skiing lessons. Jerry was patient with me because my leg was not that strong yet. He managed to get me up on two skies the first day. I was never the sporty type, but skiing was different; it was the in thing to do. When we told him we were camping, he insisted we stay at his place.

We gathered our things at the campsite and moved into his trailer. A lot of people in Parker lived in trailers. Jerry had no air conditioner but instead had a swamp cooler, which kept the trailer cool but also humid.

Jerry fancied me, and I thought he was very nice. He had a ski boat and a place to stay, so he became my new Parker boyfriend. The cycle began almost every Friday night after work. Most times Heather would also go, and Anna and I would load up the kids, Amelia and Darrell. We arrived in the early hours of the morning, when Jerry was expecting us. He had the spare room ready for Anna and Heather, as well as the couch made up for the kids. I hopped into bed with him. After a few hours of sleep, we got up and headed out to ski all day. Jerry taught us all how to ski.

The river had several places where we could pull our boat in, have a few drinks, eat some food, and rest a bit before continuing to ski the river. It was so much fun, and everyone was happy. We had all of Saturday and more than half of Sunday to ski and party. We left Parker late Sunday afternoon and arrived back to Los Angeles early Monday morning with just enough time to get a couple of hours of sleep, leave the kids with Anna, who did not have a job, and go to work. The kids slept in the car all the way back, and Heather and I were still young enough to be able to work on a few hours of sleep.

We went to Parker every weekend that summer. Moving into fall, we cut back to going once every two weeks. Then as winter came on, we went only once a month. It wasn't long after that our fascination with the river faded. Jerry and I remained friends, but our relationship ended.

Anna and I were making new friends while going to concerts again. When we were not attending a concert, the three of us went clubbing. Anna and I met a new group of people in Santa Monica. I immediately fell for one of the guys, Howard. He worked for his dad, who owned an exclusive shoe store in Santa Monica. Howard knew all the right people and had all the right drugs. I was in love with him, but he was not with me. He continued to see other women. When I found out I was pregnant with his baby, I did not bother telling him. I didn't tell anyone. I had another abortion. I felt nothing. I now know that I was committing murder, but at the time I was just ending an unwanted pregnancy. I was going up in the world and the last thing I needed was a baby to care for by myself. Howard and I were through anyway.

We did a lot of family activities with the kids. Heather, Anna, and I took Amelia and Darrell to all kinds of places: Sea World in San Diego, San Diego Zoo, and Santa's Village, Universal Studios, the Renaissance Fair, Disneyland, and Knott's Berry Farm. We had a relatively normal life. It was fun, and we had money to spend on the kids. We always threw nice birthday parties for both kids and usually took them to some restaurants that were for kids like Chuck E. Cheese, or we would take them and their friends to an amusement park or just have a big party at the house.

In my job I also met some nice escrow officers as well as Realtors who became friends. One of the Realtors was a guy named Roger, a sweet guy. We became good friends. Through Roger I met an escrow officer from a well-known and wealthy Los Angeles family: the Carrians. I started using her company as much as I could for my clients who needed an escrow company. I eventually became friends with their friends, who were all professionals and liked to party.

Heather and I started going to the upscale Marina Del Ray to party. The men we were meeting had money and were business professionals like we were. We frequented the ritzy Jockey Club, which was all about horse racing. It was part of a big club with its headquarters in New Jersey. I met one of the owners of the Los Angeles–based club, Bob. Handsome, charming, and quite a bit older than I was, he treated me like a queen. We started going to the club all the time. It was fabulous to be around all these people with so much money. I never had to pay for a drink. After the first time Bob and I slept together in his high-priced condo in Marina Del Ray, he sent me two dozen long-stemmed roses. No one had ever sent me roses, let alone twenty-four red gorgeous ones. For awhile, my one-night stands came to an end as our relationship continued.

Bob had to travel to New Jersey for a meeting with the head office. He flew ahead for the meeting, and he flew me out there a few days later to be with him. The company had a fully furnished apartment for all the hotshots who came in. We stayed there. We went to the horse races, a first for me, and sat in the best box seats that the Jockey Club always had reserved. I was in heaven. This was serious money, and these people had the class to equal it. The first few days were just grand. We ate at the best restaurants, went to the best clubs. Bob treated me well. That is until one morning he asked if we could stay in and if I would fix breakfast for all of us staying there: two guys, Bob, and me. I did, and when I asked the guys to help clean the kitchen since I'd made the food, Bob stepped in, and in front of the guys told me in no uncertain terms, "You made the mess, so you clean it up." No way was I going to let him treat me like this, especially in front of the guys, who thought the situation immensely funny.

I saw Bob's true colors: he only wanted me on his arm like a trophy. I was young and hot, and he was aging. He didn't care for me. I stormed out of the kitchen, packed my stuff, and told him to get me to the airport. I was leaving. He did not expect that. None of his young girls had walked out on him until he was ready for them to go. Well, money or not, I was done with the charade. He tried to talk me into staying, but I had seen through him. I went back home and never heard from him or saw him again, which was fine with me. I felt used, and I was not accustomed to that. I was usually the one doing the using, not the other way around.

From then on I picked up any guy who struck my fancy. I did not want any relationships. All I wanted was to know I could get any guy I wanted for the night, and after that night, it was over.

I was making a reputation for myself in my business, even among the regular Realtors who had used Country Wide funding exclusively for years. They told their friends who told their friends, and suddenly business picked up.

At the beginning of 1982, one of the new Realtors in the area who had been referred to me for some difficult home loans approached me. He wanted to introduce me to an escrow officer who owned a very busy office in South Gate. Ellen was a hard worker and had more business than she could handle. She had a large staff, but she wanted to spread her wings and open a mortgage company. She needed someone to run it for her and to train her son, Eddie, as a loan representative. I was highly recommended. Ellen and I met and came to an agreement. I would open the company in the building she owned next to her escrow office. She would pay me a good basic salary as well as pay a commission on all the business I brought in. I gave Country Wide my two-week notice, and I moved on and up. The training I received from Country Wide had been extensive and would help me greatly in the years to come. But I wanted more: I wanted to be my own boss. I wanted the power

Ellen was doing some kind of business with a guy named Pete, who was selling jewelry to her and her large staff. Eddie was in awe of Pete. Pete had a thing about him: he could talk the talk and walk the walk, and he wanted to be in on the loan representative training with Eddie. Ellen agreed. Pete was a smooth talker. Even if he did not have a clue what you were talking about, he could convince you he did. He could and did learn quickly and did very well.

I had a large following. A lot of the Realtors who'd used Country Wide followed me to South Mortgage. Within a short time, I was making money hand over fist.

It was time I had a better car. My dad got me a deal on a flashy car with a sunroof. However, when it rained, the sunroof leaked. We had it sealed time and time again, but it was an ongoing problem with that car. It leaked only a bit on the passenger side, and it did not rain much in sunny California, so it was not a big problem.

Anna had met a handsome guy by the name of Hess, and none of us thought it would last because Anna could be difficult at times. But Hess appeared to be a gentle soul. He was an engineer who was book smart but street stupid. Anna and Hess were complete opposites, but he was in love with this crazy unpredictable woman. To our surprise, he proposed and they married in July 1982. It was an uphill battle from then on. They would fight, and Anna would come and stay with Heather and me. If anyone could get her to calm down it was me. I did love that woman, but she was self-destructive. She had gotten into heroin years before. Getting off of it and staying off was an ongoing battle. She always ended up going back on it.

Heather met John, a nice guy, and spent a lot of her time with him. She eventually moved in with him and left me with the house. I bought her out. But since we had gotten a loan that required very little down payment and had an adjustable-rate mortgage, the house had little equity. We parted very good friends and have remained so to this day.

In January 1983 I took up snow skiing. Amelia and I went to Wrightwood, the closest ski area to Los Angeles and only about a two-hour drive. Then we went to Big Bear, a bigger and better ski area. Amelia took ski instructions from the professionals, but I just muddled about until I got the hang of it. At best I am an adequate skier. One of my Realtors had a condo in Mammoth Mountain, the best ski resort in California, but about an eight-hour drive. Amelia and I went up there from time to time.

Life was good. I was making so much money I did not know what to do with it, so I spent it on skiing and trips to Mexico for Amelia and me. Sometimes I took friends to Ensenada for the weekend. I rented houses on the beach. We'd party at Hussong's, the best and oldest cantina in Ensenada, and then move the party to the house. On one occasion, we were drinking lots of tequila, and I was very much into mine. It did not matter if it was shooters or margaritas or tequila sunrises, I loved the stuff.

We got a sitter, a local woman, for the kids when we went into town. When we came back, she went home. She was very good with the kids and I paid her well.

That night we had Mescal, a potent spirit with a worm added to the bottle. I was drunk and determined to get to the worm. Everyone was betting I would not swallow the thing. Of course, I had to be the best of the best and take them up on the bet. Yep, I did swallow the thing. Not long after I was sicker than I have ever been on alcohol. I threw up until there was nothing left in me, and then just kept dry heaving. I was sick for two days, delaying our return to Los Angeles. That was the last time I have ever touched tequila.

Things were starting to unravel at South Mortgage. My income was over $9000 a month. Pete was getting fed up with being Eddie's keeper. Eddie wanted to go everywhere with Pete. Pete was tired of Eddie hanging on to him. Pete convinced me we should start our own mortgage company. By February 1983 we had an attorney draw up the corporation papers, register it with the state, and do all the paperwork necessary to start a mortgage company. We decided to open our office in Redondo Beach. Many of my clients were located around the South Bay, so Catalina Capital, Inc. came into being. We were located on the ground floor of a three-story office building right on Pacific Coast Highway in Redondo Beach. It had two private offices, one for me and one for Pete. I hired an experienced loan processor, and we hired Sherry, Pete's girlfriend, as a junior loan processor. In those days there was no internet, even fax machines were not part of the office equipment. All of our documents had to be delivered by a messenger. I had my own since we were always busy.

The loans were funded by a savings and loan, a bank, or private investors. I had great connections from my time at South Mortgage. When we opened Catalina Capital, I had meetings with many of them and got approved by all of them. Soon I got my FHA (Federal Housing Administration) and VA (Veteran's Administration) approval to underwrite the loans that fell under either government guidelines and would be insured by the government. Many of the loans we did were government-insured loans.

You had to qualify for a loan, everything had to be in writing, and the rules and regulations were tough. The escrow companies gave us their escrow instructions that had to include monies already paid to the escrow company for the deposit. Many requirements had to be met to get a loan to final funding. I knew all of the rules and almost always got the loans approved and funded by the lenders on the first try.

Not long after we opened, I successfully processed and funded a loan for one of my Realtors, the listing Realtor, Catherine Whiting, whom I had never met, was skeptical. The loan was difficult because the buyers had bad credit. They had tried the mortgage company Catherine usually used but were unable to get it approved. My friend told Catherine, "We have nothing to lose. Let's see if Paula can get it approved."

Catherine was reluctant, but she had nothing to lose but the commission on the sale if the loan did not go through. It took a while and some fine-tuning, but I got it approved and funded. This became the start of a very lucrative relationship as well as a wonderful friendship between Catherine and me. We became good friends, one of the best Realtors I have ever met. I have met and done business with hundreds, but no one came close to Catherine. This woman could sell sand to a Bedouin in the middle of a desert, she was that good. I became her personal mortgage broker.

I always had a fondness for shopping at the nicer secondhand stores. Even though I was making more money than I needed, I still shopped at them. In California, and especially where I lived, the secondhand stores stocked great clothing, including Jimmy Cho shoes, Channel, Neiman-Marcus suits and dresses—designer clothing for a fraction of the cost. So I dressed like a million bucks for pennies and no one was the wiser. I had a fondness for shoes, which I am very hard on, and wore only the best brands; the higher the heels the better. I would not be caught dead in anything less than three inches. I am short, so high heels worked out very well for me. The same with boots, which I had dozens of. I had a shoe for every occasion. I was always dressed to the teeth, very business-like.

My voice is low and hoarse. Most people who had only spoken to me on the phone pictured me as a large African American woman. They were shocked when they met me, a five-foot-two-inch, 105-pound redhead. Inevitably they'd say, "Your Paula?!"

I was aggressive and demanding of both my staff and anyone I did business with. However, almost every Friday, I closed the office an hour early and took my staff to happy hour. I was tough on them but rewarded them well and paid them very well. If any of them had a birthday, I took them all for drinks and usually dinner or lunch.

I worked late every day, not leaving the office until well after seven or eight, and always Saturday. Catherine and I did some of our best work during those quiet hours.

By the middle of 1983, Pete decided we both needed not only new cars but Cadillac's. He had a friend who was a dealer. My credit history was the best you could get, and I had every credit card imaginable with high credit limits. My employment history had been steady and constantly moving upward. I got immediate approval for two brand-new Cadillac's. Mine was burgundy, and Pete's was dark blue. Both had the aluminum grill on the front as well as the roof. They were stunning. I loved that car and leased both of them.

Anna and Hess were settling down. Anna was pregnant and became Amelia's babysitter. My long working hours did not matter as Anna loved Amelia as her own. Amelia had grown up knowing not only Anna but also the entire family, so Anna was like a part of our own family.

Anna would feed Amelia, take care of any problems, and make sure Amelia did her homework. If any problems popped up that she couldn't handle, Anna called me.

Catherine had an escrow company she always worked with, so it was natural that two of the escrow officers, Susan and Cynthia, and I also became good friends. Between the four of us, we made some serious money and put numerous people into their own homes. I had other Realtors and escrow companies I worked with, but the bulk of my business came from Catherine. We also dealt with title companies. All of these people were professionals and had money and condos in the best ski areas in California—mostly in Mammoth Mountain.

We took many vacations with Catherine and her family. Sometimes others would join us. If I was seeing anyone I thought worthwhile, I allowed him to come up with us. Catherine had two children, one girl several years older than Amelia, whom Amelia looked up to, and a much younger son. We always took the kids with us and had some great times on that mountain. After the kids went to bed, we usually partied with a bit of cocaine and drinks in the hot tub.

Skiing is an expensive sport, but we had the money to enjoy the slopes. Ski resorts are amazing places. The kids usually skied the smaller slopes while we met them at one of the resort's many eating and drinking places at the end of the day. Amelia was getting quite good as I continued her skiing lessons at Mammoth. They were costly, but they made my only child a better skier and gave her skills that would keep her safe from injuries. So it was money well spent.

Mid-1983 I wanted to move out of Wilmington and into the best part of San Pedro, up on the hill. Catherine found me a great home in the right area with good schools and clean streets. The house had a three-car garage as well as a one-bedroom unit on top that had an ocean view. I rented out the house in Wilmington, which covered its mortgage payment. The new home was very expensive at the time: $250,000. I processed the loan, got it funded, and we moved in. It was a lovely big house with a large front yard, nice grass, and a brick wall around the back. The garage opened up to an alley, had electric garage door openers for my precious Cadillac, and a door that opened to my backyard.

The stairs leading up to the rental unit above the garage were off the alley, so the renter never had access to my yard or home. It was perfect. It also had a funny little room with a bath in the backyard that remained empty. Anna and Hess lived only about a five-minute drive away, making it very convenient for Anna to take care of Amelia. I had everything going for me.

Catherine's house was in Palos Verdes, a wealthy area located farther up the hill from San Pedro. We held many parties there. Susan and Cynthia came to most of them, bringing their families too. In the early '80s, cocaine was still the rich man's drug. At these parties, we all would bring a bit, pool it together, and share it. The kids were forbidden to go into Catherine's master bathroom, where we kept the cocaine and paraphernalia. If you wanted a little, you helped yourself. We were not addicts, and no one got out of hand. We were all professionals. It was just clean good fun. We were all rolling in money and were classy folks respected by our peers and admired by many of our colleagues.

I was working some unbelievable hours because business was brisk. My business was my life, and it enabled me to provide a wonderful home for Amelia as well as buy her about anything she wanted. The only thing she did not have was a mom she saw often. For that I have always been sorry. At the time I thought I was doing the right thing for my child.

We went places. My friend Roger kept his powerboat in my garage, and we had many wonderful weekends going to lakes. Many times my parents would meet us. He and my dad got along very well. My parents had a fabulous thirty-five-foot motor home that slept us all. Roger and I had always been dear friends, nothing more. He loved Amelia, and she loved having him around. He was a great guy with a terrific sense of humor.

At times I would go to the clubs with my friends and pick up a guy if I felt like it; use him, abuse him, then send him on his way in the middle of the night. I was getting a bit tired of it all and started spending more time with my brother, Pat, and his girlfriend, Evelyn. Pat could still party me under the table though he was almost eighteen years my senior. His roommate, Carl, was about ten years older than I was. One night after we had all been out, we went to Evelyn's house. Before I knew it, Carl and I were going at it hot and heavy. He was a dear guy, really sweet, and well over six feet tall. He had a presence about him that demanded respect.

We were polar opposites but became a couple. He liked country and western music; I liked rock 'n' roll. He loved baseball; I had never watched a game in my life. Regardless, we had a great relationship. I went to their house in the San Fernando Valley, or he would drive down to see me. I liked being with Carl. He never tried to tell me what to do. He had a quiet way about him and let me be myself. I never cheated on him, and we were not only lovers but also good friends. I settled down and did not pick up any more guys. I had a steady boyfriend.

We still smoked pot and did the occasional snort of cocaine. I had a big circle of friends who often came by the house. Carl called them my entourage. Many times Pat and Evelyn came to my house for the night and brought Carl. I had the extra bedroom, and it was so nice to spend time with my beloved brother. Had I known that I would not have him for many more years, I would have spent even more time than I did with him.

My dad never smoked, but he had a lung disease and was sick for ten years. His health had been getting worse. Mom took care of him. As they traveled the country in their thirty-five-foot motor home, he was connected to his oxygen mask. They came to my house many times to visit. They had moved to the desert town of Banning, where the warm dry air was much better for his lung condition than the ocean air in Grover City.

At times Anna and I would "slut out" and go to Hollywood to the Roxy or Rainbow night clubs. When you go to Hollywood, you wear the least amount of clothing possible without getting arrested. We wore our "slut out" clothes and went to have fun not pick up guys. Most times we drove the short distance to the Valley (San Fernando Valley), woke up Carl in the middle of the night, and spent the night there. He was very understanding about my need to let loose every so often and never had a problem with it.

Business was great, and I had a steady boyfriend everyone liked. He fit right in with my circle of friends. Since he was my brother's roommate, they had all the same friends who accepted me as well.

I was at the top of my game. I needed no one. I had always believed in God, although I never thought much about Him. I did not worship Him, but I did have some scruples: I tried not to use His name as a swear word even though I cussed like a drunken sailor, especially when I was mad. But I tried not to ever misuse His name, and if it did slip out, I always said, "Sorry, God." That was about the extent of my religion. Since my days at the Catholic schools, I did not trust any religion. I did not think I needed God. I was doing fine all by myself. It would be much later when I realized that although I had turned my back on Him, He never turned His on me.

Our house was in a family neighborhood. Halloween is a very big thing in the USA. That year, 1985, my accountant, Nancy, made Amelia a cute princess costume, complete with a crown. I put a bit of eye makeup on her. She looked so cute. She had just turned eleven and was such a great kid. It's too bad I missed so much of her growing up because I was working all the time.

About a month prior, Anna had been staying at my house with Carol and Dan, her second son and third child, taking care of Amelia. She received a few phone calls from a guy named John Cross. He told her that I would know who he was.

I had no idea. He never left a number and always said he would call back. She'd tell him she did not know when I would be back as I worked last many nights. During this time, I felt that someone was always watching me. It was creepy and made me uneasy. I told Anna about it and warned her to be on the lookout for any suspicious characters lurking around. I was afraid someone was watching my daughter. This went on for the whole month. I was sure I was being followed to work, at home, everywhere I went. It was not my imagination. I have never had a flashback from any of the LSD I took, so it was real. I just had no idea what was going on. But then the feeling ended and the presence was gone, so I just let it go.

9
SUCKED BACK IN

On Halloween day I left work early. It was a big day for Amelia. I had to stop at the store and buy tons of candy for the many trick-or-treaters who came to our door. As soon as I walked into the house, with my arms full of candy for the kids, the phone rang. Before Anna could pick it up, I grabbed it. Nothing could have prepared me for who was on the other end of the line. Before Carl and had I started our relationship, I had been seeing a man by the name of Dale but had not heard from him in ages. So when the voice on the other end said, "This is Dale," for one moment I thought it was him. Then I realized it was my long-lost ex-husband.

I fell to the floor, dropping the bags of candy, scattering them across the floor. Anna rushed to me, mouthing, "Who is it?"

I was slow to recover and told Anna that I was okay, to leave me alone and take Amelia to help her put on her costume.

Dale said that he wanted to see me. He was out of jail and staying at a halfway house in Long Beach. I asked him if he had a weapon and why he wanted to see me. It had been years, but I had never stopped loving him in my heart. I remembered the good times, but in my wildest dreams, I never thought I would hear from him again. He wanted to see me and Amelia.

"Why after all this time do want to see us?" I asked.

"Can I just come over and talk to you and see her for a little while?"

My heart melted along with my legs. I was barely able to get up and onto a chair. "As long as you don't do anything horrible to me, you can come over."

"Honest. I have only good intentions."

I believed him and was about to tell him where I lived.

"I know where you live. I'll be there in a while."

I thought it odd that he knew where I lived. But as confused as I was, I let it pass.

I did not tell Amelia about the call from her dad, and she went out with her friends to trick-or-treat in the neighborhood. At dusk she returned. She was busy handing out candy to the few kids still out when the knock came on the door. She answered it to find a familiar-looking man. I had shown her photos of her dad and never said a bad thing about him. When she became quiet, I turned around and saw Dale flashing his award-winning smile.

Awkward does not come close to describing this situation. I managed to eke out a greeting, ask him in, and introduce him to his eleven-year-old daughter. Amelia had not a clue what to do, but when Dale opened his arms to her, she naturally fell into them. Dale could be a real charmer when it suited him, and right then he was at his very best.

My heart was doing summersaults all over the place. After he hugged Amelia, he asked if he could speak to me in private. Anna was still there, so she and the kids stayed in the living room while I took him to my room. I hadn't a clue what he wanted to talk about.

Dale always had some kind of hold over me. How he did it, I can't say, but he could control me, and I seemed unable to stop myself from doing exactly what he wanted me to do. At this point I was so taken aback at his sudden arrival, I could barely think straight. All I knew was that the love of my life was back.

Dale was at the top of his game and wanted another chance. He said he was sorry for everything he had done to me in the past, with his cheating ways, and that he had always loved me.

Funny thing was that I had never stopped loving him after all those years. I guess all I had achieved without him or his help was to prove that I could.

I learned that he had been sentenced to the maximum prison term, which was five years, for bail jumping all those years ago. He had served his time someplace back East and had been transferred to Terminal Island, the federal jail near Long Beach, very close to San Pedro, about six months prior to his release date. At that time he had hired a private detective to find me. There had been someone following me all that time; it was not my imagination. No wonder he knew my phone number and where I lived and worked. Now that Dale had recently been released from federal prison, he lived in a halfway house in Long Beach.

Dale still had all the money in Swiss bank accounts that I had left him. He never gave it up; he did his time and waited it out. He had bought a motorcycle after getting his license back. He seemed so sincere in wanting Amelia and me back and being a family again. We talked for quite a while, hugged and kissed and made up, so to speak.

I was still seeing Carl. I had to make the horrible phone call to tell him that Dale had come back and I was going to give him another chance. I also told my brother and mom and dad. They were all very surprised and not at all sure about it. But there was nothing anyone could do. I was still in love with Dale.

The halfway house and his parole officer allowed him to move in with me, almost at once. I was a proper businesswoman and also the mother of his daughter. We decided that his son, my stepson, Clive, should move in with us. His mom agreed since Clive was too much for her to handle. Now we were a "happy" family. Truly, I thought this was wonderful for Amelia to have her father and brother back in her life. My life was complete, and it felt great.

Dale was always making money; he was very good at it. But now that he was on parole, he had to make sure his income was from legal means. Most major cities in the world have mobile food carts, and Long Beach was no exception. Dale talked a teacher from a vocational school into having his students make him a food cart—a school project he called it and paid next to nothing for it. He had to have a license to operate one in the city, so he talked me into getting it. Dale hired some Vietnamese guys to do the daily selling. He supervised, bought the stock, and counted the money. This initiative pleased his probation officer. In time he'd had enough of that and sold the cart to the guys who were working it.

Dale had been in the halfway house with a funny character that had been in and out of federal prison for most of his life. An older man with a huge belly that made funny noises, he was a professional con man. For some reason Dale thought we needed a butler and that this man, Andrew, would be perfect. I had that little self-contained room in the backyard that was perfect for him. I told his parole officer and the prison board that I would hire him to watch the kids when they got out of school and take care of the house while Dale and I were at work. They released him into my care.

He told the kids all kinds of funny stories. He seemed harmless; even my mom thought he was a good guy. He was a good cook and cared for the kids and was loyal to Dale. I had a butler, even if I did not need one. I thought I was doing a good deed by helping him to adjust to life on the outside. He became depressed at times, and then he'd get some cheap wine, get bombed, and hide in his room for a few days. We left him alone until he eventually came out of it and resumed his duties.

One day about a year later, I was at the office. I phoned home to see how things were. A strange man's voice answered. I demanded to know who he was and why he was in my house. He demanded to know who I was. I was upset that a stranger had intruded into my home and was making demands of me.

When the man finally identified himself as an agent for the Secret Service, all I could think of was what the heck were they doing in my house? I learned that Andrew had made a call to them threatening the president of the United States, and they were there to pick him up and take him back to prison since he had violated his parole. I was beside myself and told them I would be right there. They said that there was no need because this had nothing to do with me or my family. They were just there to pick up Andrew.

As it turned out, Andrew wasn't able to function outside of prison. He'd spent so many years there that it had become his home. He didn't feel safe unless he was behind bars. Sad, but true. Andrew left a note to thank us but said that he wanted to go back. He was sorry for causing the problem with the Secret Service. That was that; the last we ever saw or heard of him.

My father was getting sicker. We took the kids more often to see him. Mom, Dad, and Dale reconciled with one another. My family accepted Dale back, thinking he was a changed man. For the moment, we were a happy lot, except for my dad's health. Though Dad and I had had our differences over the years, we had mended our relationship long before. He was my dad, and I loved him.

On November 22, 1985, my mom phoned and told me that Dad had been admitted to the hospital. He was very sick and I needed to come now. He was indeed very bad off, and the doctors did not expect him to live much longer. This took my breath away. I felt empty knowing I would soon lose my father.

The next day Mom, Pat, and I were at the hospital, gathered in my father's room. My dad was on life support, and my heart was breaking. He had signed a DNR (do not resituate) order. It was my mom's responsibility to determine when to take him off life support. The time had come. As the three of us stood around his bed, to my shock and surprise Dad opened his still very blue eyes, looked right at me, just me, and blinked. I knew that he was aware of what was going on. He indicated that he was tired, done with living, and was ready to go. His look told me, "Do it. I love you."

Mom saw the look on my face and had watched the unspoken exchange between Dad and me. She, too, understood. She gave the order to turn off the machines and let him die in peace.

Devastated, I cried and cried. My mom had taken care of him for so long. Toward the end of his life, she had finally told him that she loved him, making his dream come true. He died knowing that the only woman he had ever loved finally loved him.

My mom and dad had already chosen his burial plot on a hill in the San Gorgonio Memorial Park. Mom, the strongest woman I have ever known, took this situation in stride and kept on living life.

Dale was hanging around the office more and more, doing some running around for me. Since he was there and could make deliveries, I let the messenger go. Catherine and my circle of friends loved Dale and were happy for me that I finally had the love of my life back with me.

We went to one of the many ski shows that are common around Southern California. We purchased skis so we did not have to rent them anymore. We went to the local ski areas around Los Angles, the same ones Amelia and I had been going to. We went to Mammoth Mountain a few times for some serious skiing.

Dale always had an angle. He discovered that if he acted like we were interested in purchasing one of the many time-shares at the best ski resorts, we could get free two-night accommodations at them. Time-shares were just starting to be offered at the time, and Dale was one of the first to take full advantage of them.

He convinced many of the salespeople that we were interested, and since I was a mortgage broker, they were willing to let us stay free for two or three nights, hoping we would purchase one. The residences were very nice, fully furnished, typically with Jacuzzis, and overlooking the ski slopes. Of course, we never intended to purchase a time-share; it was just another one of Dale's scams. At the time I did not see anything wrong with going along with Dale, but it was dishonest; however, we did have some very nice free accommodations for our ski vacations. I should have realized right then that he was back to his old ways. But I did not want to see it, so I didn't.

Being the scam artist he was, Dale immediately recognized my business partner, Pete, for what he was: a con that had been using me for years. It was time for him and Sherry to go. Pete had seen it coming the minute he met Dale, so it came as no shock to him. He had already made other arrangements to work for someone else, so the parting was painless. I do think it saddened Pete to part with the Cadillac, but he did since they were both in my name and I had always paid not only the hefty lease but also the insurance. Dale took Pete's Cadillac as his to drive.

Not even six months had passed since Dale had reentered my life when he started making big changes in it.

I had been the vice president of the Women's Professional Mortgage Brokers Association of South Bay, and through this, I knew many of my counterparts throughout the area. Although we were competitors, we were also friends. As such we exchanged information and contacts that could help us all. One of these contacts was a company in Florida to whom I sold many of my loans. That put me in another league. I now processed the loans, copied the loan packages, and shipped them to the Florida company. The FHA- or VA-approved loans were no-brainers. I was an approved underwriter for both. Once I approved the loans and the company received the paperwork, the funds were immediately transferred into my account, thus making me a mortgage broker/banker.

I handled the disbursement of funds to everyone, sent the packages on to FHA or VA for them to insure. I had no corporate surety and they never asked me for one. At times my account held between half and three-quarters of a million dollars in it prior to disbursement. If I were unscrupulous, I could have taken the money. But the thought never crossed my mind. I was a legitimate businesswoman and loving it.

Life with Dale was wonderful…or so I thought. He was loving and generous. We were the perfect happy family now that we were back together. We were going to grow old together and enjoy our grandkids with each other. Oh, how wrong I was! But at the time I saw what I wanted to see.

We decided to move the company to San Pedro. We found a nice office building right off the freeway. It was convenient, and my clients moved with me. I had a few staff changes as well. Dale found Penny, a bright hard worker who quickly learned the business. Dale also convinced me to hire a Cambodian guy, Chue. Both Penny and Chue were willing to work for less money than I had been paying.

Business went on as usual, though my working days were a bit shorter. I still worked on most Saturdays.

In the middle of 1986, Dale found a property in San Pedro. Two houses sat on a big lot on a hill. The top house had been destroyed by a fire and was condemned, but it had a marvelous view of the ocean. It was about sixty steps straight up from the lower house, with lots of space between them. The bottom house was livable to some extent. It had been divided into two living areas. It was a mess and needed to be refurbished from top to bottom. The owners were anxious to move to the suburbs. Overall, it was a great investment as the asking price was almost a steal.

I let Dale talk me into selling my lovely home in the best area of San Pedro and purchasing the property. Amelia was horrified. The sale of my home was quick, as was the purchase of the Channel Street house. I processed the loan and got a special FHA loan on it. The loan was for the value of the houses once they were refurbished. We started work on the top house first as it was the one we intended to live in. We gave the tenant notice and moved into the bottom house. The rental unit was in horrible condition, so we all lived in the very small unit on the bottom. It was a far cry from the luxury Amelia and I had been living in, but we made it work.

Dale and I started having issues…and it did not take long before he started seeing other women. We had some vicious fights. He would get me into the vehicle and take me out to a place above Long Beach called Signal Hill, a horrible desolate place where the oil rigs stood. He called me every name he could think of, then he would insult my mom, whom I loved so dearly, as well as my brother. I tried everything to get away from him, even jumping from a moving car. But he sensed I was about to do this, grabbed a fistful of my hair, and yanked it to the steering wheel, trapping me. He droned on and on until he had his say. Then he would just stop and then drive back home. I told him he had to stop or we were finished for good. I was not going to put up with it. He was always very sorry, saying that it was because of all the pent-up hate for the time he was in prison. Of course, I forgave him again and again.

10

Spit Out

My brother was not well; he had cancer and was in and out of the hospital. It devastated me because I loved him so very much. We went up to visit him in the Valley as much as possible. One horrible day, I was at the office when Mom called and told me to get to the hospital. Pat had been readmitted and was very sick. Amelia was in school, so I told Dale to pick her up and tell her I had to go to the Valley.

I arrived moments after my brother had passed away, December 19, 1986. I went into shock. My only brother was gone. It was too much to bear. The doctors had to give me a sedative to calm me. Mom was the voice of reason, as always. My loss is still with me, as is the pain.

I phoned Dale and told him not to say anything to Amelia. I wanted to be with her when she learned of her uncle's passing. But he did not wait and dropped the bomb: "Your uncle is dead."

She was very upset that I wasn't with her. By then her relationship with her dad had cooled.

I got back the following day and consoled Amelia. She loved her uncle Pat, her only uncle. My mom insisted on burying him in Texas next to his father. Mom and I drove there, leaving Dale and Amelia in California. I did not think it was good for Amelia to see how upset I was. Once we returned from Texas, we had a memorial service for Pat with all of his friends. Although I mourned for months, I had a life and had to go on.

There were big warehouse stores in California. Some of them required memberships, and some allowed only business owners to join.

Dale had me join all of them because the prices were cheap and the products were of good quality. We also had all the big hardware stores that sold everything for home improvement, from floor tiles to nails.

Dale started checking them out while I was at work. I did not know what he was up to. I don't know how it all began, but Dale devised a scam. I have no idea how I let him talk me into it, but going along with him was easier than fighting him. I knew it was horribly wrong, but to save my family, I gave in. Dale went into the stores and changed the price of things. For example, he took the sticker from typewriters and put them on fax machines, which had just come out and were very expensive. He put several fax machines into his cart. While he was doing this, I was browsing the store. Then I would take the cart with the fax machines, go to the checkout, and pay for them. I walked out with several fax machines for the price of typewriters.

Then we went to another store of the same chain, sometimes a couple of hours away, to exchange them—one at a time. We had no receipts to get our money back, so we exchanged the fax machines we bought at the typewriter price, getting credit for the expensive fax machine price. I came up with stories, which the clerks believed. I was good and I got away with it every time. If a manager gave me a hard time, I got loud. I dressed in very expensive clothes, portraying a successful businesswoman going off at the manager. They always capitulated. With the credit we received, we purchased food, clothes, or whatever they carried.

It was quite a feat to come up with something like this, but this was Dale. If he'd had a proper upbringing and schooling, there is no telling what good he could have accomplished with his intelligence. He could have been anything. But that was not the case, and he turned to crime, something he was very good at. His plans were unbelievable and they worked, though they were wrong.

The stores that did not carry building materials Dale scammed for everything they had: a leather couch, clothing, food, even a satellite TV—just by returning expensive goods we had paid almost nothing for and receiving credit. I have no idea how we got away with this, but I guess the same way we got away with smuggling. Dale was just too good at this type of thing. Even though I hated doing it, I knew I would be okay. I still believed in him and that he could pull it off.

Using the gains from this scam on the Channel Street renovations meant that we were refurbishing it with top-of-the-line materials for very little money.

Dale found a condemned property on Orange Street, at the time one of the worst crime areas in all of Long Beach—probably all of South Bay. The property was held up in probate. Two of the ten heirs were young kids living in foster care, and the other eight were adults, heavy drug users with no place to go but the house. They entered through a crawl hole. Dale spoke to one of the heir-druggies, who said they'd be happy to sell the property.

Dale hired an attorney to handle the probate and the purchase of the property. As it stood, the property was worth nothing. The attorney drew up a contract that gave each of the heirs $1000. The court approved everything, designating that the funds for the minors would be put into a trust for them until they reached eighteen years of age. Probate was closed and I became the owner of this awful property.

When we finally got into the house, it was so much worse than I imagined. There had been no running water or electricity in the place for over a year. The first time I walked in, the most horrible stench assaulted me.

Human excrement in the bathroom was everywhere, not only all over the floor but also up some of the walls. I swallowed hard and fast to keep from throwing up. The rest of the place was just as bad with spoiled and rotting food, used needles, and drug paraphernalia. Add to that torn moldy clothing and trash of every description littering every room. The agreement stated that we would not pay anything until the house was refurbished. Dale was so happy showing me what we had purchased for only $10,000. All I saw was a disaster.

Dale started work on it using the local Cambodian and Vietnamese laborers who lived in the area and needed the work. Every room had to be taken down to the studs, and even some of them had to be replaced. Dale "purchased" all of the building materials by scamming them: cupboards, sinks, toilets, floor tiles, roof…everything. In the end, we renovated the crap property in the middle of the worst neighborhood in Long Beach with top-of-the-line everything. What a waste. The property was not worth the effort. But Dale was so proud of himself.

The eight heirs–drug addicts did not want to wait for their money and were constantly asking Dale for an advance for their part. Dale had the attorney write out a form that Dale would fill out and have them sign each time he paid them an advance, which was almost every day. Before the renovation was even complete, we had paid them everything we owed.

Work on our house was still going on when the Orange Street property renovation was done. Much to Amelia's and my horror, we moved out of the Channel Street house, which was still a big mess, and into this house. The Orange Street house was nice on the inside, but the neighborhood was the problem. Almost every night we heard gunshots. Fighting in the streets from drug wars was common. In short, we were miserable.

James, a handsome guy and one of Dale's former inmates, was released from prison. Full of charm, just like Dale, the two got along well. Dina, Dale's ex-wife, and he started seeing each other. James alternated staying with us and Dina.

The fights between Dale and me worsened. Catherine had told me time and time again that she had seen Dale driving around in the Cadillac with another woman. I did not want to believe her; I tried my best not to. One day when we were still in the Orange Street house, I was just about to leave for work and take Amelia to school when the phone rang. The woman on the line asked for Dale.

"Who is this?" I said.

"I'm Dale's girlfriend. Who are *you*?"

"Who am I? I'll tell you who I am. I am Dale's *wife*."

"No way. Dale said you and he were history. We've been together for months."

I figured out that this is probably the woman Catherine had seen with Dale.

I hit the roof. I told Amelia to get her stuff because we were leaving her dad. She was so happy! She had lost all respect for him by this time and had been hinting that I should leave him once and for all.

The Channel Street house was in disorder with all the building still going on. It was livable to a degree, but I did not want to be where Dale could easily find us; not knowing how he was going to take me leaving him. I phoned a good friend of mine and told him what had happened. Jim insisted that Amelia and I come to his house for the time being. He had a large beautiful house near Marina del Rey. I left Dale a note telling him to phone his girlfriend. It was over between us.

Amelia and I packed all of our clothes. Everything else was in storage. As fast as we could, we drove to Jim's house.

I phoned the office and learned that a very angry Dale had been there looking for me. I was to call him at home. How dare he? What right did he have to be mad at me? He was the one caught red-handed cheating on me! I did phone him. He demanded that I come back and bring his daughter with me.

I was steaming. I was done.

Then he made some very nasty threats. "If I can't have you, I'll kill you."

Jim insisted I hire a bodyguard before I went back to the office.

Later that day I again phoned the office and was told that Dale had been back several times, demanding to know where I was. Nobody knew where I was, so they could not tell him; however, he made threats to them as well.

An armed bodyguard was a good idea, so I hired one. Jim traded vehicles with me to make me less noticeable. The following morning my bodyguard followed me as I drove Amelia to school and then went on to work. Sure enough, Dale was parked around the corner. The minute I got out of the car, he ran toward me. He stopped in his tracks when my bodyguard stepped in front of me and ordered Dale to hold it right there. Even Dale was not stupid enough to try to get to me with a 250-pound armed bodyguard protecting me. He huffed away, yelling over his shoulder, "This is not over!"

He started sending me flowers and singing telegrams. He even sent Amelia all kinds of gifts to try to win us over. I stood my ground. No way was I going to be treated the way he treated me and thought he had the right to.

After a couple of weeks, Dale slowed down on his quest to win me back. So I thought it would be safe to have the bodyguard only when I arrived at or left the office. Amelia and I were still staying at Jim's house when one night when I was working late. Amelia wanted to go to the Channel Street house to spend the night. I did not think it was a good idea but gave into her. I did not think Dale was around.

The minute I got out of the car, Dale appeared out of nowhere. He attacked me from behind, knocking me to the ground. I landed on my purse. He sat on my back, hitting me.

Amelia yelled, "Leave her alone!"

"Get into the house and call the police!" I told her between Dale's pounding blows.

She hurried up the steps and into the house.

Of course, Dale knew the police station was just a five-minute drive from the house. He hit me a few more times in the head and he jumped back into his car and drove away, as fast as he had come.

The cops showed up, but he was already gone. I refused to press charges. I knew that if I had him arrested, he would make sure I ended up dead. He always said he would never go back to jail and would kill anyone who tried to put him there. I knew him well enough to know this was no idle threat. Amelia and I stayed at the house that night with no further appearances from Dale.

The next few days my office filled with flowers, cards, and presents—from candy to expensive perfume. He sent more gifts to Amelia. He begged me to forgive him, saying he just flipped out that he could not live without me. On and on it went until I finally gave in and told him I would meet him in a public place to discuss this.

He cried and begged me to come back to him. He wanted us to go to Club Med, an all-inclusive resort, for a week to work it out. He wanted us marry again, said he loved me, that he always had. Stupid and blinded and in love, once more I agreed.

We went to Club Med in Ixtapa, Mexico. It was a glorious time with just the two of us. Amelia stayed with a friend for the week. He was loving, generous, and attentive...again. I thought he had changed.

How could I have been so wrong so many times? I wanted to believe him. I wanted to see what I wanted to see. We decided to get remarried in Las Vegas; on May 31, 1987, I became his wife…again.

The top house at Channel Street was finally completed, and we moved from the Orange Street house. Though the renovations were done, it was an odd house. Dale had scammed the doors but got the outside doors wrong. Rather than opening inward, they opened outward. This was also true of our bedroom door. The bathroom and laundry room were downstairs. We had gotten a nice Jacuzzi bathtub that Dale installed incorrectly, so it leaked. There were so many problems with his construction. Unless you lived there, or you knew about construction, you would not have been able to tell anything was amiss. We moved, and Clive came to live with us again.

11

On the Road Again

Dale wanted to travel again. I did too. When we traveled, we got on well and were happy. I wanted us to be happy together, for I still loved him. He decided, and I agreed, that it was time for me to close the office

We wanted to go to China, but Amelia had only her Australian passport. I had renewed it, so it was current. She would need not only a visa to go to China but also a reentry permit for the United States. Brazen as we were, we went to the Federal Building in Los Angeles and told them our daughter needed a reentry permit to come back into the United States. The officials asked to see her passport as well as ours. They took one look at our last names—Dale's and mine were the same—and checked Amelia's. Confusion clouded their faces. They asked us why our child did not have the same name as we did. And why did she have an Australian passport rather than one issued by the United States? The story came out, the whole mess about our past. I swear that poor guy just looked at us like we were insane. You could not make a story up like ours. He had no idea what to do with her or us. He phoned Washington to ask how to proceed. I was told to bring all the papers from the court proceedings regarding her name change.

That left them even more confused. On discovering that Irene Salsman had become Amelia Petty with just the stroke of the pen of a hotshot from the State Department, there was nothing they could do because the State Department trumps the US Citizenship and Immigration Services. After many phone calls to his superiors in Washington, he told me to get several affidavits from my mom and dad,

Dale's mom and stepdad, and Amelia's dentist—I have no idea what the dentist had to do with anything; he had only known her as Amelia Petty. Dale and I had to write affidavits explaining everything: the details regarding the birth of our child in Australia, our fugitive status, and why her birth certificate stated her parents were Lea Ann and Michael Salsman. I felt sorry for this guy. I don't think he had ever encountered a muddled mess like this one. He could do nothing to Amelia because she was an innocent child whose parents were both American.

We had so many documents; the file was an inch thick. Finally, after several days of grappling with this, he threw up his arms and asked, "Okay, what name do you want this child's passport issued in?"

That struck me as a bit funny. I could have changed her name—again—to whatever I wanted it to be. But we stuck with Amelia and gave her a new last name: ours. For the first time, we all had the same last name. Of course, we notified her school and had her last name changed there as well. Her name would not change again until she married.

My daughter has in her possession all of the documents regarding her many names. She dare not lose any of them, for it would be a mess to prove her identity. I had no idea when I became a fugitive and used an alias that would affect my daughter to the degree it did. You never know how your wrong actions can touch your loved ones.

Our visas for China were no longer an issue.

I officially closed Catalina Capital in June 1987. The office had been winding down slowly for months, and the staff saw the end coming. We closed very quietly—no party, no nothing. I just moved all of the office furniture to the garage at Channel Street or sold what I could.

Dale wanted to take ten-speed racing bicycles to China, even though such bicycles were inappropriate there. The kids and I tried to talk him out of taking them and gave our best arguments. Dale had his mind set and refused to listen to any of us; so against all of our wills, he won. It was easier to go along with him than to fight him. It was a battle I knew would not end well. Naturally, we scammed the bicycles, which took a few days; how we got them out of the stores without being caught is beyond me.

At the beginning of July, Dan, me, Amelia and Clive and our bicycles flew to Hong Kong. We rode them around for a bit, but the narrow roads with too many vehicles created a hazardous situation. Dale found a guy who would store them for us for a few days, guaranteeing they would be safe.

For a few short days we were in heaven. We shopped, took the ferry to Hong Kong Island, rode the cable car to the top, did all the typical tourist things, tried different foods, and had a really good time. We were the typical, happy, well-to-do all-American family.

We entered China through Canton (Guangzhou). We rode the bikes everywhere and soon found out that we were up against very experienced bike riders. At that time there were very few vehicles and almost everyone rode bikes. However, their bikes were sturdy and had big tires, all with loud bells. We had these stupid racing bikes that were not made for the roads in China, the gears were a hindrance, not only to us but to those we shared the road with. Other riders gawked at us Western people riding strange bikes. They got too close to us and either ran into us or ran us off the road. We needed bells for our bikes, and we got them.

Some of the people spoke English; especially those who lived in the big towns. The Chinese were courteous, friendly, and kind…except when you got onto any public transport. The kindness ended and bedlam ruled.

The distances in China are vast. We could not ride from town to town, only when we arrived in a town. We got to be more aggressive riders; it was that or be run over.

On July 12, 1987, we boarded a train for Guilin, where we discovered that it was every man for himself. We arrived early so we could secure the bikes in the baggage car. We found where we had to board the train, and though we had first-class tickets, so many people were shoving and pushing to get on the train, it was an uphill battle to get through the throng of people.

We traveled through China, taking buses and trains. It was always the same: too many people shoving and yelling. The countryside was lovely. But as we had tried to tell Dale before we ever left the US, the bikes were a constant problem. Every time we went to collect them from the train's baggage cars, we found the locals riding them around the baggage collection area. The gears would be off, and we had to wrestle our bikes back from them. Clive and Dale would have to put the chains back on and reset the gears.

We stopped at many little villages and some larger towns on our train journey toward Shanghai. Some we stayed at a night or two, and some we just passed through. By this time, we had learned how to board the overcrowded train: Dale and Clive pushed Amelia and me through the windows to secure our seats.

Along the way to Shanghai, we stopped at towns that were listed in the guidebook as interesting sights. But it soon got to be just one more temple or monument with steps—China has steps going up everyplace.

In one small town where no one spoke a word of English, we passed by a typical restaurant. Outside were a few monkeys in a cage. Dale and I knew they were for someone's dinner. Amelia thought they were cute and wanted to pet them. It broke my heart to have to tell her the awful truth.

The hotels we stayed in were very basic. Actually, we had no other choice. It was basic or nothing.

In another larger village, we went out to dinner, finding the best-looking place we could. No one spoke English, and the menus were in Chinese. We looked at what everyone else was eating. I spotted a platter that held what looked like a nice vegetable, maybe eggplant. To order, we pointed to it and the bowl of rice and indicated bottled beer for us and cold drinks for the kids. The woman smiled and took our order.

In no time she brought us our platter of *eel*. It did not look like it had been cooked. I am sure all of our eyes bugged out as we stared at this horrible shimmering platter of the snakelike fish. We did not want to offend anyone by refusing it; after all, we did order it. But none of us wanted to touch it.

Some guests had just arrived and sat beside us. They had not ordered yet so we pointed to our eel and in sign language offered it to them. Dale took it to their table. They were most grateful and could not thank us enough.

We ate our rice, drank a couple of beers, and hurried out. From then on, I always made sure I got a close look at a plate of food before ordering it.

We finally arrived in Shanghai the last week in July. The kids were weary of traveling and begged Dale to let them go back to the States. They could stay with Dina and James at our house. I was dead set against it. I was not going to let Amelia go back to stay with Dina. Dina and Dale were Clive's parents, so his going back was their decision. But Amelia was not. We phoned Dina, who assured us that everything was great and the kids could come back. She and James would watch them. It was three against me. Dale, Clive, and Amelia begged and begged me to let her go back and stay with Dina. In the end I gave in.

We did a lot of shopping in Shanghai. We purchased a twelve-piece setting of china in an amazing pattern, including the little cups for sauces. We also bought two lovely Chinese side tables. We packed the dishes into the side tables, padded everything with the kids' clothes, wrapped it in bubble wrap, and taped it well. That was to be the kids' baggage for their trip home, one for each. When we took the kids to the airport and checked them in, we got a bit of hassle from the airlines, but each table was within the weight limit, although they barely fit on the luggage carrier.

In Shanghai we picked up some great bargains on jade necklaces, earrings, and bracelets as well as other typical Chinese handicrafts such as the carved figures of the Chinese years—twelve of them.

Dale decided to sell the bikes and found a buyer in no time. Shanghai is the financial center for China, so many businessmen were eager to have them. We sold them for less than what they were worth but a lot more than what we had paid for them.

We stayed a week and then booked our cabin for the cruise down the Yangtze River, one of the most famous Chinese rivers and a must-see for any tourist. We left the Shanghai skyline behind us, a beautiful sight and much smaller than it is now.

Our cruise took us first to Nanjing, which had an amazing bridge over the Yangtze River. It also took us through the gorges between Wanxian and Chongqing, an awe-inspiring sight.

On the first day of our four-night cruise, a Chinese child about five years old decided to be my friend. She was obsessed with my hair and tried to get it out of the braid I wore. Had the ship not had a fully stocked bar with lots of beer, that child would have driven me crazy. The only way to lose her was to escape to our hot, steamy cabin that had only a tiny fan that moved around the hot air. When I thought she had gone back to her parents, I would venture out, but in no time that child would find me. She spoke no English, and I never did see her parents.

Wuhan was a delightful surprise. It was a bustling city with one of China's most famous temples. Yellow Crane Temple was so large it could be seen for miles. It was a favorite of Chinese and foreign tourists. Wuhan also had several Buddhist temples and Mao's Monument. We visited them all. By the end of the day, we were well and truly worn out.

We purchased several Chinese souvenirs: masks, traditional hats, as well as some very nice trinkets. Dale and I were together and not fighting. It was like we were starting over. When we traveled, he was sweet and kind, nothing like he was when we were home. I prayed it would last.

Our next stop was Xi, famous for the Terra Cotta Warriors. It is a large site. Years ago this complete army of Terra Cotta Warriors with chariots, horses, shields, and everything an army in those days would need was discovered. In all my years of traveling, it was one of the most incredible sites. Although only about half of the site had been excavated when we were there, what we saw was massive. It took my breath away. The scope of it was beyond understanding. Each warrior looked different from the others; each horse and chariot was unique.

We went from there to Ming's Tomb and the Great Wall. Both were amazing.

We flew into Lhasa, Tibet, the first week of September and stayed at the only nice place. We didn't have much choice. The options were really bad or really good. An American celebrity was staying at the only good one: Dan Rather, the newscaster, was filming a documentary on the area.

Tibet in the '80s was still very much Tibetan. It was its own country and very different from China. The people had their distinct customs and traditions. They did not look Chinese and were warm, kind people. Lhasa means "Land of the Gods" and sits at an altitude of 3,650 meters (almost 12,000 feet) above sea level. It has been the center of politics, culture, and religion in Tibet for more than 1,300 years. It is also home to the center of Tibetan Buddhism, the Portola Palace.

To see the Portola Palace was worth the trip. It was impressive! It took all day to see only a fraction of it.

I don't think anyone had updated the toilet facilities since 1645. I have relived myself in many places under all kinds of circumstances. That it stands out in my mind says something about my bathroom experience at the Portal Palace. The palace itself is breathtaking. When you get to the top of it you are in the clouds and out of breath because precious little air is up there. It's weird because the air is brisk and cold but because you're up so high and closer to the sun, you are cold and hot all at the same time. What a rush! There are numerous palaces and temples as well as monasteries. Three of them are extraordinary: Sera Monastery, Drepung Monastery, and Ganden Monastery.

It snows in Lhasa only about once or twice a year because of the perpetual bright sunshine. Daytime temperatures in September are usually a high of 50°F. You wear layers of clothing. It's cold in the morning, and when the sun is high, it's warm, so you shed the outer layers during the day and then add them back as evening draws close.

We ate only breakfast at the hotel and visited many restaurants that served local food. Most of it was very good. On our fifth and last day before we were to take a bus over the mountains and back into China, we ate at a small place called Top of the World Restaurant. Spaghetti with meat sauce as well as beer was on the menu, which sounded wonderful—something different from the yak burgers we'd been eating.

When we got back to the hotel, everything broke loose. I was violently throwing up, and my period came early. At this high altitude, it was not good.

I was sick all night. Because of limited transportation, we had to leave early in the morning, taking the bus that ran between Yecheng in Xinjiang, China, and Lhasa, Tibet, once a week. If we missed the bus, we'd miss our flight out of Beijing to Burma.

The highway winds its way among five mountains soaring more than 5,000 meters (16,400 feet) and runs 1,455 kilometers (902 miles). I was so sick; I had to be hooked up to oxygen. Breathing through the mask made me feel a bit better. The journey should have gotten us to civilization and a hotel room in a day. We were scheduled to arrive late that afternoon. But about every four to five miles, a pile of large rocks blocked the road. Everyone had to get out of the bus and walk around them. The driver let me stay on the bus. I think he was afraid I would never make it, and I do believe he was right. Once everyone had disembarked, the driver drove the bus off the road a bit and around the rocks. Then everyone got back onto the bus. It was the craziest thing.

No one could tell us why the rocks were there. I didn't care why as long as we got down the mountain. I was so sick and in pain and suffering, I started to worry that I would not survive the trip.

The bus started to emit some strange and worrisome noises that got increasingly louder until the bus shuddered to a stop. I hoped and prayed I was hallucinating this and we were still on our way. But no. We were stranded in the middle of the road at the top of a mountain—beautiful but desolate.

There were no cell phones and nothing on the road but some wild horses and us. Dale and the driver ran off to get help. I slept. When I woke up, the sun was on its way down, so it about two or three in the afternoon. No one knew what to do. I was very weak since I had not eaten anything since the spaghetti the night before, and I had thrown up that. Between the food poisoning, high altitude sickness, and one heck of a monthly cycle, I was sure I was going to die on that mountain. And I was getting very cold. I bundled up and sucked my oxygen.

About an hour before dark, two big army trucks arrived. Dale and the driver were with them. What a welcome sight! I perked up a bit and thought that maybe I would survive.

Just as I thought it could not get any worse, I was told the diesel-powered truck would tow our bus to the army barracks about fifteen miles away. They hooked up the bus, and as the truck was pulling us, its diesel fumes were blowing right back to us. I was sure it was the end. I had no choice but to endure the journey in agony. It was freezing, and I was hungry and thirsty.

On arrival at the army base, the commander had his six highest-ranking guys surrender their beds to us. Dale and I had one room. He pushed the beds together to conserve our body heat. We put on every piece of clothing we had with us, but even with the blanket, we were very cold. And to top it off, the toilet was a bit of a walk. I had to make my way there a couple of times that night in the dark. Alone. The one good thing was we were so high that the stars were incredibly bright, so I could see quite well.

When morning came, we were given some tea and bread. A guy in a pickup offered to take us the last few hours down the mountain to civilization; everyone but me piled into the bed. I was still unsteady, and although I felt a bit better, I was not at all back to normal. The road was not bad and the rock piles were no longer an issue, so we managed to get through.

We stopped at the top of the mountain, where we had a fabulous view of Mt. Kailash. The rest of the trip down the mountain and back to Beijing was uneventful, and we made our flight to Burma.

Arriving in Rangoon, Burma, was an experience. Burma had been cut off from the rest of the world for a very long time. It had been only recently that foreigners were let into the country. I am almost positive that I was the first red-haired person they had ever seen. Upon arrival we had to take off all of our jewelry, which they put into a big envelope and secured with a wax seal. We could keep our watches and wedding rings. We had to surrender our cameras to the authorities. Everything would be returned to us on leaving the country. We were told where we could stay. It was comfortable and had just been renovated to accommodate the foreigners starting to trickle in. We spent a couple of days looking around, but our activities were limited to what they wanted us to see. Many places were off bounds, and we knew that we, along with everyone else, were being watched. My hair made me a bit of an anomaly with the locals, who stared at me wherever we went.

We left Burma and headed home, arriving in Los Angeles in mid-September. We took a taxi home to San Pedro. The kids were there, but they were alone.

— 12 —

WILD LIFE AND HEAVEN

We settled back in and started thinking about going on an extended trip to Africa. Dale wanted to look into some kind of pot deal, but I just wanted to see Africa—I had wanted to go back since our first visit there in 1975. I thought that if he were to get a pot smuggling operation going, he would have to do it without me. I did not say this to him, but I just went along. We wouldn't take the kids because it would mean pulling them out of school. My mom was happy to stay at our house with both the kids for the six months we would be gone.

Dale had to take bikes and camping gear with us because we were going to bicycle through Africa. I don't think he gave that enough thought as Africa is a very big place. But there was no arguing with him. We scammed the bikes and gear again. We got new backpacks, bikes, and bike saddles. We were going to South Africa first. It was still during Apartheid, so we went to the High Commission of South Africa in Los Angles to get our visas. At that time they did not put a South African entry stamp in your passport because many countries in and out of Africa would not let you enter their countries with a stamp from South Africa in your passport. Instead, we carried an official paper, thus allowing us to visit other African countries. No flights were available from the US to South Africa, so we flew to London and from there to Johannesburg. After two long flights, we arrived in South Africa on March 3, 1988.

After all that flying I was tired and wanted to rest, but we had to ride our bikes from the airport to Soweto, another long trip that took us over five hours. By the time we arrived, my back had two bruises, one down each side where the backpack's metal frame rubbed. We found a dumpy place to stay in. I fell into bed and slept for twelve hours. The first thing I did when I got up was to take the metal bars out of the backpack.

We were in the heart of Black South Africa in 1988, Apartheid South Africa, and an amazing place. We met some cool local guys who loved us because we were Americans. We had a good time and stayed for a few days, sampling some nice smoke, as well. After all, that was Dale's reason for being in Africa. When it was time to move on, I was in no hurry to get back on the bike for another long-distance haul, but Dale was.

We were only going to Sun City in North West, a province of South Africa. The resort was located near the city of Rastenburg and had several nice campsites near the luxury resort. We peddled a bit of the way but hitched some rides, with people in trucks or pickups to accommodate out bikes, managing to get there in one day. The following morning, we were ready to rub shoulders with the rich folks at the resort and got a ride in.

The key to getting into these places and using their facilities for free was easy. We simply acted as if we belonged there. We walked in wearing shorts and went directly to the toilets, where we stripped down to our bathing suits. Then we picked up our towels for the swimming pool and grabbed a lounge chair. We were in business. I lay by the pool with my book, chilling while Dale wandered around checking out the place until lunchtime. We put our shorts back on and ate lunch in one of the restaurants. We looked like any of the other tourists. Dale had made friends with some of the staff who lived close by. They all lived together in flats and had lots of room, so after lounging around by the pool for the rest of the afternoon, we were invited to stay with them for a few days. They had a bed, and I was a bit tired of sleeping on the ground in a sleeping bag. They were lovely people, very hospitable, and liked to party.

We visited a few game reserves in the area. One of the biggest was the Pilanesberg Game Reserve, which was close to the resort. We took the tours offered through the resort and paid cash as opposed to having them put the charge on our room that we did not have. It was not allowed to go to these places on a bike. It would have been a perfect place if not for Apartheid always in the background rearing its ugly head.

We wanted to go to Lesotho, but it was too far to bike there. We hitched rides and biked some of the way. In all, it was a grueling four-day journey. Several times when hitchhiking on the motorway, the cops chased us off. But as soon as they left, we got back on and resumed our hitchhiking.

We finally arrived in Maseru, the capital of Lesotho, a very small country surrounded by South Africa, an independent country but with most of the stores and infrastructure as South Africa's. There was nothing to see, but we rode around the county on the only road that dead ended at the top of a mountain. It was getting late and too far to ride back down. We were cold and it started to rain. We found a small guest house and restaurant. We ordered some food, and just after it arrived, a guy drove up and came into the restaurant. He was about the only person we had seen for most of the day in this isolated place. We got to talking. He insisted we go back to Maseru with him and stay at his house. He and his wife had lived in Maseru for twelve years. He worked with the government through a UK organization. They welcomed us into their very nice house. They showed us all the sights and gave us a history lesson. They would not let us pay them for anything. Honestly, it was great to have someone else to talk to besides Dale.

After four wonderful restful nights with our friends, we crossed back into South Africa and proceeded to Durban. It was a long stretch, and even getting rides for long stretches, it still took us days to arrive. We camped along the way, and while in Durban, we ate at some very good seafood restaurants. We arrived at Hluhluwe Game Park via Richards Bay and St. Lucia, which took days to get there, even with hitch hiking a lot of the way. At this rate I was sure we would never get to Kenya before our six months were up! Outside of Hluhluwe, in sight of the entrance to the game park, Dale was in front of me when a lizard flew into my face. I screamed and fell off my bike, badly scraping my knees, legs, and arms. I was hurting. Dale had no sympathy at all. He started yelling at me, concerned because the camera was in my saddlebags. Riding all the way to Kenya was not looking good.

We stayed at a nice campsite for two nights for a much-needed rest. We went on a couple of game drives, saw some great animals. I was in heaven.

Dale grew restless and said it was time to move on. We were riding and hitching when possible. It was raining a lot more, making biking uncomfortable. We finally made it to the small Kingdom of Swaziland, a mountainous country. At this point I was ready to pay someone to steal the stupid bikes and put me out of my misery! I was desperate when Dale decided that this was not working and we were two idiots on bikes. We sold them for a good price.

Without the bikes, hitching rides was a lot easier and the going faster. We met many interesting people, and some invited us to stay the night at their homes, many of them on farms. It was a great experience to stay with both black and white families, enabling us to get a better idea of what was going on in the country. We listened to and saw both points of view on Apartheid.

We crossed from South Africa into Zimbabwe at the main busy border post at Beit Bridge. Trucks, cars, and people lined up to cross the border. The last ride from Messina, the last town on the South African side of the border, was with two Zimbabwean businessmen going all the way to Bulawayo, exactly where we wanted to go. While we were waiting, I looked around the ground and saw that it was covered with the most hideous large hard-shelled bugs that looked like mini-tanks. They were everywhere. I was told they were harmless, but I did not take any chances, jumped back into the car, and would not get out. The immigration officer thought it was so funny, he did not make me get out of the vehicle to take my paper visa and stamp me out of South Africa; he let Dale do it for me.

The Zimbabwean officers stamped us into Zimbabwe. This seemed perfectly normal, but farther north we would find out what that little stamp would cost us.

Bulawayo is the second-largest city in Zimbabwe after the capital, Harare. The country was pumping. The white-owned farms stretched for mile after mile. The surrounding villages were prosperous and the cities bustling. The campsites were clean and well managed, the grocery stores were full, and the prices were reasonable, including beer.

We took a bus to Masvingo, the nearest town to the Zimbabwe Ruins, the largest collection of ruins in Africa south of the Sahara. We stayed at a lodge in Masvingo and hooked up with some other travelers who were going to the ruins the following morning. We tagged along with them. It was a lovely day.

We went through the capital, Harare, stayed one night, and then took the morning bus to the town of Victoria Falls. Zambia and Zimbabwe share the world-famous Victoria Falls, which forms a partial boundary between the two countries. Victoria Falls was jumping in those days; the bars were lively with locals as well as backpackers from all over the world. We met many people and had a great time. We viewed the falls and saw the David Livingstone statue. We camped at a clean and secure municipal campground that was only a two-minute walk from the center of town and a ten-minute walk to the falls.

Victoria Falls is not the highest or the widest waterfall in the world, but it is considered the largest based on its width and height. The spray from the falls soaks the visitors; it was lovely, and the weather was quite warm, so our clothes and hair dried quickly.

The locals call the falls *Mosi-au-tunya*, meaning "the smoke that thunders." When David Livingstone first saw them, he was so impressed he named them Victoria Falls in honor of Queen Victoria and wrote, "No one can imagine the beauty of the view from anything witnessed in England. It has never been seen before by European eyes; but scenes so lovely must have been gazed upon by angels in their flight." And I agree with him.

After a few days, we walked over Victoria Falls Bridge to the border of Zambia. It had been independent for only twenty-four years, and the economy wasn't stable. Most backpackers avoided Zambia because the accommodations and availability of goods and services were limited. Soft drinks in bottles were rare, but beer was plentiful. It was sealed and cheap, so it was much safer to drink than water. We got a room since there were not many safe places to camp. We stayed only two nights to see the falls on that side.

We took the bus to Lusaka, the capital. It took all day. The bus was not that bad, and the fare was cheap. We were only passing through but spent an afternoon at the Inter-Continental Hotel pool and had a great lunch…acting as if we belonged. The following morning, we arrived at the congested bus station and hopped on an early bus to Chipata on the border of Malawi.

Chipata is a busy border town. We arrived late in the afternoon and found a place to stay the night. We were just passing through on our way to Malawi. The ride we got to the border the following morning was going all the way to the capital city of Lilongwe. We did not spend too much time there because we were anxious to get up to Lake Malawi and the beaches.

After a few false starts, the rides taking us only a few miles at a time, we finally hitched one to Nkhata Beach. The couple who had picked us up were about our age and going to the same budget accommodation we were—a nice enough place right on the beach, with a restaurant, fully stocked bar, and a nice campground. There we took a boat trip out on Lake Malawi, the ninth largest lake in the world, the third largest and the second deepest in Africa, and a haven for backpackers.

Traveling with Dale was traveling with the perfect man I had fallen in love with so many years before. He was kind, generous, and great fun to be with.

We stayed a couple of days, but it was almost the middle of April, and we had a long way to go and a lot to see. We hitched a ride to the Tanzanian border. The officials scrutinized our passports when they noted we had entered Zimbabwe at Beit Bridge. They knew we had been in South Africa. We tried to talk our way around it, telling them we did not have a South African stamp in our passports, but if we had crossed at Beit Bridge, we could have only come from South Africa. And if you had been in South Africa, you were not allowed into Tanzania.

They demanded we go back. This was a problem. It was late in the afternoon, and Karongo was the nearest town, about twenty-five miles away, and no buses or other transportation were available. Going back was not an option. We bartered back and forth. They pulled everything out of our backpacks and gave us a hard time. We were in the middle of nowhere. I was carrying thousands of dollars, well-hidden on my person. We were in a sticky situation, and they were not being kind or welcoming but hostile, insisting we go back. It was getting later and later, and we were getting worried. Dale continued to barter with them.

They wanted our watches, T-shirts, shoes…anything. Finally, Dale offered them $100 to let us go on. Ah, they only wanted a bribe, and that was their price.

It was getting dark, and it was about 100 kilometers, or two hours, to the nearest town in Tanzania, Mbeya. We needed to get a ride soon or we would be stuck at the border with nothing around it. One of the maintenance workers at the border was driving to Mbeya, so we paid him to drive us to a reasonable hotel. We arrived after dark, relieved but hungry and tired

Mbeya is hilly and the temperatures mild, accommodation and food reasonable; it is a very nice town. We stayed for a day and had a much-deserved rest. Early the following morning we took the bus to Dar es Salaam, the capital. It was a long, bumpy, crowded, hot ride with frequent stops. It seemed to take forever. Once again we arrived late. Hot and tired, we wanted nothing but a cold beer and a comfortable bed. We got both.

Dar is a nice enough town for an African capital, so we wandered around. Dale thought I should get my hair done, African style, in tiny braids. I let him talk me into it, knowing nothing good could come from it but worse hair. I sat for hours on the floor between two local girls in a hair salon as they worked nonstop until my whole head was braided. My hair is so thick; they did not need to use any extensions as they usually do. It turned out quite amazing, but it was heavy and itched like mad.

We took the ferry over to Zanzibar, a city steeped in history as a hub for the slave trade. We stayed in the old Stone Town and enjoyed the beach and the bars. While in one of the bars four days later, my head became especially hot, heavy, and itchy. I decided the braids should come out. We had made friends, and a couple of them wanted to help me take out the braids. It took some time, but when they finished, I was very sorry I had done it there. My hair stuck out all over. I could not go through a doorway without my hair brushing both sides. Everyone thought it was great. No one had ever seen a white person with a red giant Afro! It was a long time and many hair washings later before I finally tamed my hair.

We got back to Dar and left the following morning to Arusha, the tourist hub, the dropping-off point for all excursions to Ngorongoro Crater and Serengeti National Park. We took the local bus all day with the Massai people dressed in their colorful robes, jewelry, and beads. We planned to stay at a campground that had a lovely lodge overlooking the crater. The bus was old and the roads rutted, and we bumped along for hours. We finally arrived hot, tired, and sore. We found our site, put up our tent, and then went to the lodge. It was my thirty-sixth birthday, so we had a party at the lodge. Many of the guests, as well as most of the staff, drank with us until the early morning.

When the sun rose over the crater the next morning, it burned off a layer of clouds, revealing a spectacular view of the crater before us. The party left me with a whopping hangover, so I slept most of the afternoon. But it was a birthday I will always remember. Africa moved into my heart and made itself at home.

The following morning we went on our safari down into the crater. The lodge had packed us a lunch, and we left right before sunrise. We traveled down through the clouds along a winding road. It was as if we'd gone back thousands of years to another world. It's simply one of the most stunning places on the planet. Had it not become the world's sixth-largest unbroken caldera, what is now known as the Ngorongoro Crater, it could have been a towering volcanic mountain as high as Mount Kilimanjaro.

The area contains over 25,000 large animals, including black rhinoceros, wildebeests, zebras, and much more. The game viewing is amazing. I had never seen so many different animals in one place. It is still one of my favorite places. We stayed an additional day and moved on to Serengeti on May third, about two months into our journey.

The Serengeti National Park is 5,700 square miles and is Tanzania's oldest and most popular national park. It is one of the Seven New Wonders of the Word. The animal population is spread out all over the park rather than concentrated as they are at the Ngorongoro Crater. But seeing the game there was every bit as spectacular as at the crater.

We got there by hitching a ride with some people leaving the crater. They were staying in a luxury-tent camp, so we decided to stay there as well. We booked it for two nights. The luxury tents were amazing, just as

I'd remembered from Kenya in the '70s, complete with toilets, showers, and lovely comfortable beds. The lodge had a lighted water hole, and at night it was incredible to sit out there with our gin and tonics after an amazing dinner, watching the many animals coming down. I was in heaven and could have easily stayed there for the rest of my life.

It was again time to move on. We got a lift to Musoma, where we stayed at a real fleabag place. From there we took the ferry across Lake Victoria to Bukoba, where we again stayed at a horrible place, full of big black bugs and no hot water. It took some days of hitchhiking and hopping what buses we could to finally get to the border of Rwanda.

This was before the war. The country was hilly, green, clean, and beautiful. Goods and food were inexpensive and plentiful. The people were friendly, and accommodations came with running hot and cold water. After the last few days of roughing it, we were ready for a nice place to stay a few days while we explored the city.

We took a bus to Gisenyi on the border of the then Republic of Zaire (now DRC) where the accommodation was horrible, but we were there to go to the mountains to see the mountain gorillas. We paid a hefty price of $40. The gorillas were beyond anything I had ever seen. It was worth the money to see them up close.

Then we hitched a ride and returned to Kigali and stayed a few days. We took an early morning bus to Entebbe. The road to Uganda was not bad, but the 450-kilometer (280 miles) trip took all day to get there. We had visas to enter already, so the border crossing was easy. Entebbe is a lovely city on a peninsula in Lake Victoria with great beaches. We stayed in Lido Beach for almost a week.

We met some locals who assured us they had some really good pot. I thought Dale had forgotten all about his quest to find good pot in Africa. Any pot we had sampled on our trek through Africa hadn't been very good, but this stuff was great, the first we'd had in Africa. We spent time with the guys and saw some of the sights. We took the short bus ride to Kampala, the capital, stayed only a couple of days to prepare for the very long bus journey from Kampala to Nairobi and our flight out.

We flew from Nairobi to Mumbai. We were most interested in spending time in Manali in Himachal Pradesh in the north of India. We took buses and trains via Delia, where we stopped for a few days. It's almost 2000 kilometers (over 1200 miles) from Mumbai to Manali. It was a haven for backpackers and a popular vacation area. The mountains were spectacular, and we found lots of people to party with. For the most part, pot was legal; it grew all around the area. People smoked it in the open.

We got back to Mumbai and flew from there to Colombo, Sri Lanka, at the beginning of July 1988. We had a lovely few weeks traveling around, even though the civil war was in full swing. We took the train through the mountains to the official capital, Kandy. Because of the war, everything was cheap. We got accommodations at amazing places on the beach for only pennies a night. The food was incredible, and we were treated like royalty. Our time there was relaxing. We loved it.

We flew from there to Singapore. The one thing that stands out in my mind was the horrible public fight Dale and I had at the airport. For some reason during the flight, Dale harassed me the whole way. By the time we arrived in Singapore, I was ready to kill him. I wanted to get on the next flight back home and leave him there. He had been pushing my buttons for hours. He would not leave me alone. We got through immigration with no words being exchanged, then on the way to the baggage claim he started again, saying things under his breath that only I could hear, things he knew would make me mad. And they did. We had a big blow out and security was called. They broke us apart, and we managed to settle down before they arrested us both. We made up and stayed a week there, mostly shopping, then flew home, arriving at LAX in August.

Traveling with Dale was always a lot of fun despite our modes of travel. As I said earlier, he was nice, and since no other women were around, he remained faithful and kind. But returning home he reverted to his old habits. Did I know? Did I want to know? Yes and no. I was completely under his spell as I had been in the '70s. He had a way of taking control of my life, and before I knew what was happening, he was the only person in my life except for Amelia.

13

PIRANHAS AND POT

Dale got busy making plans for us to move to Brazil for a year or more. I had no idea what his plans were until they were set and too late to make any changes. Amelia was only fourteen and did not want to leave her friends, so we battled with her, but, as usual, Dale won.

Dale had some friends in Recife. The woman, Carol, was an American and worked at the American school there. Her husband was a farmer, living about a day's drive from Recife. Dale arranged for Amelia to fly from Miami to Recife, where Carol would pick her up. Amelia would start school there. Dale got a property manager to look after the house and rent it out during our absence. We packed up our things and put them into storage. For our trip, Dale purchased a new Toyota Land Cruiser, or at least I thought he had paid for it, and we set off. The vehicle was so loaded, we even had a Zodiac boat tied to the top of it, it was a miracle the three of us fit in it.

We left in January 1989 and had a lovely time along the way. We visited many places as we journeyed. We arrived in Miami on February 6, 1989. We intended to have the Land Cruiser shipped from there to Venezuela, where we would pick it up. But Dale made up some story as to why we had to go back to Atlanta and ship the car from the Port of Atlanta. I later learned that Dale had only made a large down payment on the vehicle, so we did not have a pink slip. The Port of Atlanta did not require one to ship it, but Miami did.

Amelia flew out of Miami and made it safely to Recife where Carol picked her up. She stayed with the family, who had a daughter her age. She was safe and in good hands. Dale and I flew from Atlanta to Caracas, Venezuela. We had to wait a couple of weeks there for our vehicle and belongings. We saw the sights and made some trips to the islands around there while we waited.

Once we retrieved the Land Cruiser, we took off for the Amazon Delta. We had to get to Manaus, Brazil, to get on the Essa boats that would take us to Belem, the end of the river route into Brazil. The road through the jungle to Manaus was a total disaster. It was February and it was wet. This vehicle had four-wheel drive, but it was useless and no match for the muddy roads that went on for miles and miles. We got stuck so many times I lost count, but even on the almost deserted road, there were always big trucks carrying supplies to pull us out. The Army Corps of Engineers saved us more than once. These guys probably thought we were totally out of our minds driving by ourselves through some of the wildest places in the world in a packed vehicle with a Zodiac boat tied to the top of it.

It took a few days to drive the distance, and we found places to stay the nights. In many of them, the cockroaches were the size of rats. I refused to sleep in the rooms, so many nights I slept in the car while Dale stayed in the room. The food options were limited, but we had a lot of canned goods with us. I often ate out of a can while in the vehicle.

After many days we arrived at Manaus, a bustling port city, and got our passage booked on the Essa boat leaving in a day or two. Essa is not the tourist boats you see on the Amazon River, far from it. We had to purchase hammocks to sleep in if we didn't want to sleep on the floor. This was the shipping company that takes the locals and the few backpackers who are brave enough to go; to Belem. It was such a great adventure, and, honestly, I would do it again even now. We slung our hammocks along with everyone else in one big area. The vehicle was driven into the hold of the ship along with other vehicles.

Even though the waters are full of piranhas, which, contrary to popular belief, seldom attack humans, the kids would swim to the side of the boat when we docked at the small villages en route, waving and cheering us on. The local fisherman sold fish to the boat's kitchen. We ate it along with rice and beans as well as beer—lots of beer.

Three days later we landed in Belem and drove through Fortaleza and onto Recife, where we reunited with Amelia. She had made friends and was enjoying herself. The American school there was the best, with only twelve to fifteen kids in each class. They gave Amelia one-on-one instruction to catch her up to the level the others were at. She excelled there.

Dale purchased a cute dune buggy for Amelia and me to drive around.

The north of Brazil is lovely, and I could have been in a much worse place. We found a beautiful apartment right on the ocean. It was furnished and amazing. A young woman lived in the apartment a few floors up from us. She spoke good English, and we became friends. I was learning Portuguese, so it was a learning process for both of us.

Dale finally spilled the beans on why we were there. He'd had this all planned out years in advance. At some point prior to his being arrested in the late '70s, he'd spent time here. It's when he met Carol and her "farmer" husband. He and Carol's husband became partners. The farm was now in danger, losing money, and Carol's husband needed funds to pay off his loans. The economy was horrible. Dale and he decided that pot was more lucrative than whatever he had been growing. So while Amelia and I stayed in Recife, Dale went to the farm, about a twelve-hour drive into the interior of Pernambuco, and started growing pot on the isolated farm.

We had not been getting along for a while, and it was just a matter of time before things blew up between Dale and me. He was gone most of the time, and Amelia and I were having a great time by ourselves on the beach. She had some good friends she hung out with, and I made some friends as well, so life was good for us. Dale was seldom around, so we were happy campers and, for the most part, had a good time. I knew he had a girlfriend out on the farm, but I was happy. My eyes were open, and the love I had for him was gone. When he was in town, we were not intimate, or if we were, it was just out of a sense of his thinking he was fooling me, so I played along. I knew the time was coming when Amelia and I would leave.

I was out one night around the first of July when on a road full of potholes another car and I collided. My dune buggy suffered some damage, so the police impounded it. I hit my head just above my right eye. The other car had one little scratch. The driver was not angry and got me to the hospital where a plastic surgeon was on duty, he did a great job of sewing up my gash. I picked up my vehicle the next day and took it to a repair shop that specialized in fiberglass vehicles. I knew I would be leaving soon, so I told the guy to just patch it up to keep it running for a few more months and to keep the cost down. No way in the world was I going to tell Dale what had happened. As for my cut, I told him that I had fallen in the shower and hit my eye on the faucet. He bought it, and, of course, Amelia kept the secret.

Right after the car got fixed, Dale came back and decided we should drive to Salvador, Bahia, the state right below us, and go to Club Med. Dale always sneaked into these places, and this time was no different. We did our usual thing of paying for one person, me, and then Dale and Amelia would come up the beach in their swimsuits. We were old pros at this. The problem here was that no other Americans were around, only locals. So we stood out, especially since I had a big patch on my eye. But they didn't catch on, and we stayed only a couple of days.

We got back at the end of July. It was then that Dale informed Amelia and me what we were to do next with our lives. When he was up by the farm, he had a metal boat made. He was so proud of his handiwork, he showed us photos. His plan was for his wife and daughter to get on that thing with a Brazilian crew, who would sail it to the States. It would be filled with hash oil. He assured me that he had made plans for us to get to Miami, where we would be met by one of his smuggler friends.

I blew up and told him in no uncertain terms that I might have been that naïve and in love with him in the '70s to put up with his smuggling. Back then he could get me to break the law and lie for him, but for what? What did I get in return but a lying, cheating, and no-good waste of a man! There was no way Amelia and I were going to be a part of his smuggling plans. Not now; not ever. He could get his little girlfriend out on the farm to do his dirty work for him.

I have no idea why he kept up the façade of still wanting us to be his family. Our relationship was not only cold but a Siberian wasteland. Though we wouldn't go along with his latest scheme, he decided that Amelia and I should go back to the US for a short time and then return to Brazil in a few months. We all knew we would not be going back, but we played along as though we would.

Amelia and I packed all the stuff we could carry. We booked our flights and were set to leave on August 12, 1989. The day before, Dale had given me $1000. I was anxious to get as far away from him as possible. I fully realized he had not changed. He was still the controlling con he always had been. But now I could see him for what he was. Yes, it took me long enough to wake up.

He packed that little dune buggy to overflowing; never suspecting it had been in a wreck. We all said goodbye, acting as if we were actually coming back. He took off. Amelia and I breathed a lot easier now that it was over. I was done falling under Dale's spell.

I am grateful that he had come back so that Amelia got to know her dad and decide how she felt about him. He was not worthy of her love. Now she was happy to be away from him. She never lost a moment of sleep leaving him; nor did I.

In the middle of the night at about two in the morning, the phone rang. I picked it up and was not a bit surprised to hear Dale yelling and screaming up a storm! The little buggy fell apart on the jungle road in the middle of nowhere some hours earlier, and he had to walk for miles to get to civilization. I forgot what I said as Amelia and I were laughing so hard we could not catch our breath. I don't even know what he said as I didn't care. Why should I? He hadn't cared for Amelia and I when he had tried to get us on a boat filled with hash oil. What kind of dad-husband does that?

Amelia and I stayed up the rest of the night since our flight out of Recife to Rio was at nine, just a few hours away. We were in a jolly mood by then.

We arrived back in Los Angeles on August 13, 1989. My mom picked us up. To say she was over-the-moon happy would be an understatement. She was giddy! A guy was living in our house, but he would vacate it. Until he found another place a couple of weeks later, we coexisted. The bottom house was rented to the same couple who had rented it when we left.

I was thirty-seven years old and still had my looks and my body, and I was free of the yoke of Dale once again. It's hard to explain, but it was like I was the boss of my own life once again, and it felt great!

I went back to work at a mortgage company. My resume spoke for itself, but I had problems working for someone else. I managed to hang in there for a few months until two of the real estate guys I did most of their loan processing for approached me and offered me a good salary to open a mortgage company for them. It had its pros and cons: it was a two-hour travel time from San Pedro to Rancho Cucamonga, where they lived and wanted the company. I could work the hours I wanted and hire whomever I wanted to assist me.

The guys had a good thing going and sold a lot of properties. The company they worked for had a lot of agents, so the business was there; I did not have to look for it. They would keep me and my assistant very busy. I agreed and started their company at the end of 1989. I received a great salary and bonuses and did not have a dime invested in the company. Some of my old clients heard I was back, and I had my own agents I made a healthy commission on as well.

Anna came back into my life, and we enjoyed some good clean fun. By this time Amelia was fifteen. She had lots of friends and did not need a babysitter. She spent nights with her friends a lot of the weekends, giving me my freedom to party.

At the end of 1989, Christmas came and went. I was thinking that life was great. I was free, and Amelia was doing well and growing up into a beautiful young lady. I was on an even course now, making money, in great health, still looking good with lots of friends, lots of male attention. I pretty much had my mind made up that things would go just fine now. Up was the only way to go, and that's where I was going.

Then the '90s happened.

14

On the Edge

The '90s have haunted me for years. The perfect storm blew in, and it left behind a broken, unrecognizable version of me. In some ways, I am now grateful that I was completely broken, as over the more than twenty five years I have become more than I ever thought I could be. Having to go back and relive it to write about it is very difficult, beyond horrific. If it had not happened to me, and if I did not have the mountain of documentation strewn around me, I don't know if I would believe this actually happened. But it did.

For me, COVID-19 is bad, but it could be worse: it could be the '90s again. I started writing my story in 2007; it is now 2020. I have put off for years writing this portion of my story because I could not face it again. Some parts may be a bit fuzzy because my mind has tried to wipe out many of the horrible parts. But I am going to tell it as it happened, for honesty dictates transparency.

As you read this, please don't think I am attacking the Los Angeles Police Department (LAPD) or the Los Angeles Sherriff's Department (LASD). During the late 1980s and throughout the 1990 decade, these two law enforcement agencies were off the chart corrupt. A quick study of history and a Google search verify this. Examples of corruption are the Rodney King assault case, which happened in 1991. The 1997 Rampart scandal, the worst scandal in the history of the LAPD, identified widespread police corruption in the Rampart Division. The Harbor Division was separate, as they were located by the Port of Los Angeles. With little or no supervision from anyone or any agency, they policed themselves. They could do, and did, whatever they wanted. I pray things have improved since my involvement with them.

At the beginning of 1990, I was on top of the world. My daughter was growing up to be a really good kid (nothing like her mother), and for that I have always been thankful. I was commuting about four hours a day to work with the mortgage company. That was wearing on me. The guys I was working for had also become a challenge. They tried to get me to stop smoking, change the way I dressed (apparently, I revealed too much), and my language and eating habits did not meet with their approval. That I did not eat salads every day and loved a chili cheese dog now and again was offensive to my "perfect" coworkers. Because I did not comply with their desires, they decided that they did not like who I was.

They were getting on my nerves, and the drive was wearing me down. I had a lot of my own clients who had been with me for years, which worked well for the company. But I was working myself to death for them and they were upset because I smoked? The drive was my biggest problem. A couple of times I almost ran off the freeway when I fell asleep at the wheel. It was scary. Anna offered her advice: "Just try a little bit of meth, just to help you stay awake to get home."

She knew a guy I could get it from. What the hell, I thought. I'd been taking drugs on and off for most of my life and never had a problem with addiction. I was smoking a bit of pot on the weekends and that was never a problem. There were several years when I never smoked a joint. And cocaine? I quit all the time. It was never an issue. With that rationalization, I started using meth. That I thought I was above getting addicted shows how great I thought I was! Of course, I would regret that decision for the rest of my life.

Since my return from Brazil, it seemed that the Channel Street property was haunted with bad luck. The tenants Dale and I had rented to were a nice couple, Tammy and Alex, and they were still there when I got back. It wasn't too long after that (around the beginning of 1990) that her body was found in Angeles National Forest. Her stepfather had killed her. It was horrible. Her family moved all their things out. We all felt sick about what happened to her. Then I rented the house to two other guys. They were fine, but they moved out about seven months later. In late 1990, Donna and her husband, Curt, moved in. They were great kids and had a lot of friends who were also young. To my complete surprise, these young guys found me "very hot." I was thirty-eight years old. To say I was flattered was an understatement. I dated a few of the twenty-year-olds. They all knew they were just flings for me. It was great fun to be sought after, especially after my time with Dale, who never treated me as anything but his property.

Around the middle of that year, I'd had enough with the job and decided it was time to part company and go out on my own. But that was easier said than done. I knew the clients I had brought into the company would follow me, and the guys I was working with would try and prevent this. I made arrangements for my exit without their knowledge.

My mom and her current husband were going to come in as partners with funds to get me started in my own business. It took some time, but I got my connections together and found a mortgage company whose owner was a friend of mine from years ago. She agreed to underwrite and fund my loans after I had processed them and they were ready to go. She knew me and that I was good at what I did.

On the day of my choosing, I left the guys' office, with my client files in tow, and never went back. I did not take one of their clients. Any files that I was working on I left with the woman I had trained. She could continue processing their applications. I did not leave them in a lurch but left all of their loans and clients with the company. I spoke to them on the phone and told them the arrangement was not working for me and it was over. Nonetheless, they were upset. They bothered me for some time, but then stopped. And that was that.

I found an office directly across the street from my house. How perfect that I could walk to work. It was, however, still being built and a few months away from completion. I signed a contract with the owner to move in as soon as it was finished. For the time being, I would work out of my house. I flourished.

I was still using meth, but the amount I used stayed the same. My thought was, after all, just a little bit every day—it was not hurting me, and I could quit anytime I wanted. I was not an addict. However, ever so slowly the people around me started to change. I have no idea how it happened or exactly when, but an increasing number of people in my life were doing drugs. Some of them were okay. Some came to me wanting a job or a handout. I helped them, of course. I was still a hippie at heart, wanting to help others. At first, only a few people came to me. Some were friends of my tenants.

At the beginning of 1991, Port Town Financial was officially opened. I bought all new furniture. It was a great office. I could see my house from the window. Amelia was sixteen and doing very well in school. She was driving and living life with her friends. They were all good kids.

Anna came to work for me again. She knew what she was doing because I had trained her years ago. Everything was going very well. Everything, that is, but this little issue I had with meth. I continued to tell myself that it was such a small amount and was hurting no one. Had I only known what this stuff ends up doing to you, I would have run away from it like a mad woman. But I didn't. I thought I had it all under control.

Business was good. Life was good. I still had young boyfriends who came and went. I occasionally gave a few of them jobs if they were out of work, but they never lasted. I was too busy to pay much attention to them, and they got the hint when I was done with them. Cold-hearted? Maybe. But they knew I was not ever going to be a girlfriend or anything like that. Their time with me was brief, so they returned to their age group.

15

Winds of Change

The first rumblings of the storm came in October 1991 when the FBI division out of Atlanta, Georgia, wrote a memo to FBI headquarters in Washington, DC, requesting additional funds for a large-scale investigation into cocaine smuggling in Atlanta and Miami. The lengthy and largely redacted document, which I gained access to years later, goes into detail about a "multi-kilogram distributor" in Atlanta that was a large organization with about twenty individuals involved with distribution in Atlanta and Miami. The document identifies raids and confidential informants who came forward as a result of the raids. The many pages contained a lot of information about this organization. At the very end of the document, it states the following:

> The Atlanta Field Office intends to aggressively pursue all of these avenues of investigation. Drug purchases from [redacted] and Paula Petty anticipated in the next 90 days which will assist in defining the final phases of Atlanta's investigation. To identify all organizational members and to identify the organization's possible Columbian sources of cocaine, the Atlanta division believes that a Title III Intercept investigation is warranted in this matter and will begin coordination of same as the investigative activities outlined above are being accomplished.

I had no idea this was going on. I did not see this document until September 20, 1999, when I received it through the Freedom of Information Privacy Acts release. Had I known about this, I might have been able to take action to prevent the chaos that was going to consume my life. I was not involved in any of this. I knew no one in Atlanta or Miami.

When I first received this document, I read it over and over, reading between the large redacted sections in an attempt to figure out how they got my name. I lived in California. I was a business woman. My life wasn't perfect, but I was not in any way involved in drug dealing. It took some time to finally figure out what had happened. The beginning of the document states that the investigation began in December 1989, a result of information provided by the Miami division of the FBI.

Eventually, I was able to determine that the person who gave the FBI my name was Dale's buddy from jail who lived with us and Dina a few years back, a smuggler from Miami: James, the guy Dale wanted Amelia and me to deliver hash oil to on the boat he wanted us to take to Miami. He was from Miami, and he went back there around the time Dale and I went to Brazil in 1989.

James knew Dale and my history in the '70s, but he knew me only by my maiden name, Petty. I do not doubt that he got busted again. Facing a long prison term, he gave up names, including mine, as part of a deal. When the FBI ran a background check on me, they found the records dating in the '70s, even though I had never been convicted of any felony. Since that time, I had gone straight. The FBI had overlooked my years as a mortgage broker and the fact that I had never been in any trouble regarding drugs. The only trouble I had been in was linked with Dale. If he had never come back after getting out of prison, I would have never scammed any stores. I am not excusing my actions. I did what I did and accept full responsibility. They were minor crimes, and the one time I got caught with Dale, it was dismissed. How did the FBI figure I was part of this major drug operation? They had only the word of a felon who had been caught and was looking for a deal from the FBI. How did they make this leap? I will never know the answer, but they saw what they wanted to see.

This information went from the Miami FBI to the LAPD and then to the local police in San Pedro, who were determined to make a case against me. I lived less than two miles from the Harbor Division Police Department, and I am sure that they would have known if something of this magnitude were going on. But there was nothing.

This misinformation triggered the storm that raged out of control and took me to places I never knew existed. It stole my identity and almost cost me my life. It robbed me of my sanity for years.

16

Storm Warnings

Sometime in early 1992, I needed some work done at the house. A friend gave me the name of a guy who had done work for him. I contacted Ray. He told me upfront that he had been in prison on drug charges, but he was clean and sober. I hired him. He was a good carpenter and continued to do some work for me from time to time.

In hindsight, I should have gotten him out of my life and stopped the meth; instead, I gave the FBI and the police the fuel they needed for this storm to take shape and move forward.

I figured out that I was being watched. From time to time I would notice something or someone, but it did not bother me as I was not doing anything that warranted the police to bother me.

I got more involved with Ray and a couple of his friends. I thought they were okay. They just needed a new start and some help. I didn't realize it at the time, but this thinking was not only stupid but also cost me dearly. One of them, a guy named Joe, had just been released from prison. He had the most amazing long black hair and startling blue eyes. He was twenty-nine and just my type, even if he was an ex-con. Heck, my husband was an ex-con. I thought with my good influence, Joe would stay on the straight and narrow and not go off the deep end. That worked for a while. We did a little meth, I worked all day, and Joe and Ray were painting houses, which was not steady work. I knew Ray had started taking drugs again, but he was always in control. His drug of choice was heroin. Joe was using meth, but I did not know how much either man was using. I did not want to know.

Joe had a friend, Dino, who was still in prison in Folsom. Dino had confessed to killing a man in a drug deal gone badly, so he was in for life. I allowed Joe to give him my phone number, and he started phoning me collect. He told me his story.

As a teenager, he had been under the care of a psychiatrist for mental health issues. When he turned eighteen, his mom's insurance no longer covered him. He went off his meds, compounding his condition. He and another guy were involved in a drug deal in San Diego. Things got out of hand, and the other guy, the son of a border patrol officer, shot and killed the dealer. Dino, only eighteen, was arrested then threatened for hours that he would get the death penalty unless he confessed to the killing.

I was sympathetic. I'd had previous dealing with the police and FBI in the '70s and knew firsthand how they could, and did, manipulate and threaten people into saying things that were not true.

I was so outraged by his situation, that I had him put me on the visitor's list. I flew to Sacramento and then rented a car to get to the prison. It was one of the most shocking experiences I'd had at that point.

Built in 1880, the prison was nothing short of scary, a stone structure right out of a horror movie. Before I could get in to see him, I was forced to change almost all my clothes, including my bra that had under wires, and wear "prison acceptable" clothing, which they provided. I was herded like an animal from one area to another, going through various checkpoints and being frisked along the way. The guards were horrible and talked to me like I was dirt.

Finally, after all the humiliation, I got to see Dino. We sat at a table and talked. I listened to his story. Because of the forced confession, he was never given a trial.

I believed this young man. My heart broke for him.

I got in touch with my old attorney in San Diego, and he promised to look into Dino's case. He finally agreed to take the case, but this was not until Dino was relocated farther south to Corcoran Prison, near Fresno, only a four- or five-hour drive.

I imagine that once the attorney started proceedings on Dino's case, several red flags popped up in the FBI and border police radar, who didn't want this case to go to trial. I can only imagine what the FBI was doing behind the scenes when this big-shot federal criminal attorney started poking around. They could not have been happy.

I visited Dino several times, bringing "care packages" of food and other supplies. I put money in his prison account. Each time I visited, I encounter a bit more difficulties, and the guards treated me harsher. At first I didn't think too much about it, but looking back it is clear that their attitudes shifted as time went by.

In 1992 I had been going to a tanning salon in San Pedro for some time. That summer a woman named Sally often happened to be there when I was. She lived in Torrance, several miles away. Why did she visit this salon in San Pedro instead of one closer to her? I was a trusting soul and did not think much about it at the time. However, she became a nuisance and later a major problem for me.

In mid-1992, I noticed unmarked police vehicles around my home and office. They parked across the street in a lot and even followed me. They were suddenly everywhere. I thought I was losing my mind. I told my mom, and she stayed with me for a week. She saw them too, which shocked her. At least I knew I was not seeing things.

I went to the police station to try to find out what they wanted with me and why they were watching me. All I got was shuffled around, with all of them playing dumb. They said they were not watching me and did not want me for anything.

Then late one afternoon, four or five unmarked cars were in the lot across the street. My house was on a hill, so they could not see the back of the house from where they were. I climbed over the back wall, circled back around, and came up behind them. In one of the unmarked cars sat two agents, looking as though they were reading newspapers…except the papers were upside down. Over the years I'd become skilled at identifying FBI agents. These two were so intent on watching my house and business that they did not even know I was there until I knocked on the window. I took pleasure in startling them. "What the hell are you doing? Do you want something from me? Can I help you?"

They just stared at me through the window and refused to answer. They quickly rolled up the window and drove away, leaving me standing in the middle of the empty lot, wondering what was going on.

I later found out that FBI agents had approached my neighbors to try to let them put up lookout posts on their property so they could see into my house. My neighbors refused to cooperate with them. The agents also spoke to my landlord at my business and told him that I was a meth manufacturer and dealer. My landlord told them that he did not believe I was into drugs and to leave him alone. But still they persisted.

I was irate. I had no idea that befriending a guy in prison and having ex-cons at my house (one of them my boyfriend) were reasons for this constant harassment and police presence.

My renters, Donna and Curt, moved out of the Channel Street house, leaving the rental in a mess. It took me weeks to clean it up. I rented it out to a guy named David, who then proceeded to move in a lot of other people. I tried to convince him to get them out. He did but only for awhile, they always came back. However, he and his friends were the least of my worries.

I had the police on my tail twenty-four/seven. They continued to camp out across the street. I complained, but everyone denied knowing anything. It was like the twilight zone, and I was sinking deeper and deeper into a dark pit. I was starting to believe I was losing my mind.

To cope, I used more meth. All of my life drugs had been my safety net. I could and did escape from reality when reality got to be too harsh and I could not control it. I didn't think I just fell deeper; I was a nervous wreck. But the storm was just building.

In August 1992, Los Angeles Sherriff Deputies Fennell and Booker arrested Ray and took him to Carson Sheriff Station. I don't know why they arrested him, but I imagine it was a trumped-up charge. The only thing they wanted was for him to verify that I was running a meth lab out of my house in San Pedro, that I was a major player in the drug world, and that I had an arsenal of weapons in my house. The police and FBI were watching my house day and night. How was I so clever as to pull off this magic feat under their collective noses? The fumes alone would have carried down the hill to the lot they were watching me from. They had eyes on me twenty-four hours a day. My house was visible for miles around. I would have to be some kind of illusionist to run a drug business while they had me under surveillance.

To get released, Ray promised the police to set me up for a bust before his arraignment on August 28. They released him. When Ray did not fulfill his side of the bargain and was nowhere to be found, law enforcement had to come up with a new plan. And they did.

17

Uninvited Guests

On August 28 at 3 p.m., I was with clients in my office when I saw my daughter coming home. She got out of her car and was immediately stopped by Deputy Sherriff Booker and Deputy Sherriff Fennell, along with Deputy Sherriff Halpin, who forced my daughter go to the tenant's door at 810 Channel Street. While they stood over to the side as not to be seen, they made her first try her house keys to open the door. When her keys did not unlock the door, they made her knock on the door. When the door opened, the deputies rushed in. I ran out of my office, leaving my clients to watch the unfolding drama taking place at my property. By the time I got to the rental unit, the deputies were arresting a young guy named Dave, who was not the tenant. The deputies were looking for the tenant, also named David, but he was not there. I learned that the deputies did not have a search warrant. They pushed aside a young woman, who was visiting, and entered to search the house. Without a search warrant, they found drugs, two handguns, and some cash. During this fiasco, I was yelling at them for using my minor daughter, who had no relationship with the tenants, to gain illegal entry into the property. I was so angry I could not see straight. I told Amelia to go to her boyfriend's house. The deputies took Dave to the Los Angeles Sherriff Department in Carson. The people in my rental unit may have been engaged in illegal activities, but the deputies had no right to coerce a minor child to help them gain entry without a warrant.

They then demanded to search my house for the David they were looking for. They didn't have a warrant, but I had nothing to hide—no meth lab or anything else they hoped to find. I agreed and they marched up the stairs to my home and searched for David. They looked in my underwear drawers and every nook and cranny. I'm not sure how small they thought he was, but it is not likely he was hiding in my silverware drawer or the barbeque! They found nothing in my home. Not one seed, not one chemical, not one weapon. Nothing.

When they finally arrested young Dave, they used my address as the place where the raid happened. The booking sheet states 812, not 810, Channel Street. The two houses were separated by sixty steps. My house, 812 Channel Street, was at the top of the hill. The rental at 810 was not connected in any way to my house. Each house had the address clearly displayed at the side of the front door. They were determined to show that I was the target of the raid.

The police also listed me as the emergency contact for the young man they arrested that day, Dave. I barely knew him. He had not given them this information; they decided that on their own.

Days later a search warrant surfaced, signed by someone named Gail. She had no legal right to be in the property, yet she was identified as having the legal right and authority to be in the property. I had never seen her before the illegal search that had taken place days earlier. She was only a guest at that house. The warrant was manufactured after the fact, and the address they searched and found drugs was the wrong address. The whole thing was illegal and constructed. This was not an honest mistake or clerical error; it was a calculated move to try to get to me, legal or not.

Sometime after this and before my daughter's eighteenth birthday in October 1992, Sergeant McDowell from Los Angeles Police Harbor Division contacted my daughter and told her that I was manufacturing, selling, and using drugs. At the time she was still living in my small two-bedroom, one-bathroom house. Did they think she would not notice if I were producing drugs in her house? He gave her his business card and told her to phone him if she wanted to give him any information.

I was angry and frustrated with all of this. I posted bail for Dave; using my house for collateral. This kid was not the best person in the world, but he was illegally arrested. He was at the wrong place at the wrong time. Things began to move even faster, rolling down the hill gathering speed and power as it went.

Captain Glen Ackermann and Detective III Tom Blake were both assigned to Administrative Vice Detective Headquarters Division and were responsible for the surveillance unit officially named C-5. For the next eight months, they kept me and my home under constant surveillance.

If I did not have the documents supporting this and had not been the object of scrutiny, I would have not have believed this happened. I believe the FBI must have been directing them to move this along to arrest me. After all, according to the FBI, I was part of a major investigation out of Miami.

During this time, I broke up with Joe, and he moved out. He was using an increasing amount of meth, and I'd had enough of his friends.

My mind was messed up and I was paranoid. I kept looking over my shoulder all the time and was barely functioning. I was still working, but it was getting harder and harder to concentrate with cops all over the place. They followed me no matter where I went. And I still had no idea why. I kept asking myself, "What have I done?" Could they possibly be upset with me for visiting Dino in jail?

At the end of 1992, I had to get away, so I took a two-week vacation in Majorca, Spain. I left Hope, a girl I'd known from years earlier, to housesit and keep everyone out. I closed my office for those two weeks. I could not take any meth with me, so I stopped. I had no withdrawal, which reinforced my belief that I was not an addict and could stop anytime I wanted. I continued to tell myself that I used only to keep alert and on top of the police activity. Had I known what was coming and what that drug would do to me, I would have never touched it again.

On the other hand, Sally, from the tanning salon, started getting needier. She was hanging out at my house, telling me that she was being evicted and that she was concerned about her son. She asked if she could stay with me for a few days. I agreed, but after a few days, I told her she had to leave. This went back and forth for some time. She would leave, come back, and then I would ask her to leave again. Meanwhile, Dave, whom I put up bail for, had gone missing.

A friendly cop from LA Harbor Division, Sergeant Steve Wynn, came by one day to inquire about Dave. While we were talking, Sally drove up to my house, unannounced and uninvited. Sergeant Wynn was very nice to me, telling me that if I found out where Dave was, he would pick him up. My bail would then be released. I agreed to let him know if I found out anything. I introduced Sally to Sergeant Wynn, who took me aside and asked if she was single. I told him that I didn't know her that well, but I thought she was. He asked me to give her his pager number so he could ask her out. I was anxious to have Dave found so I could get my house released and figured Sergeant Wynn could help me with this. I gave Sally his number. A short time later I found out where Dave was and contacted Sergeant Wynn. He picked me up, and it just happened that Sally drove up right before we were to leave. Sergeant Wynn asked her to come with us. He had another cruiser come with us to transport Dave. We found Dave, they picked him up, and Sergeant Wynn drove Sally and me back to my house. By then I was sick of Sally and told her to go home or to her mom's. She left. I thought she was just a pain in my butt, and nothing more.

She and Sergeant Wynn continued to meet at my house. He phoned my house a lot asking for her. I kept telling him that she did not live with me and he should phone her at her mom's or wherever she was. She continued to show up at my house, where Sergeant Wynn picked her up in his official police vehicle. I found this a bit strange. I didn't think it was common practice for police to use their official vehicles for dates. I didn't like it, but what could I do? I continued to let them use my house as a meet-up.

Everything about them fell into place when I later found out from Sergeant Steve Wynn's official daily report for September 3, 1993, that Sally was his "reliable confidential informant."

On April 26, 1993, I was inside my residence at 812 Channel Street at about 5:30 in the afternoon when a SWAT team, in full uniform with gear, weapons, and shields, surrounded my property. I could not believe my eyes. To add to my shock, they used a bullhorn to call my name and order me out of my house. Why were they doing this? I think it was at this point my mind snapped—if not all the way, it certainly started to crack. I wondered if this nightmare would ever end. Angry and disbelieving,

I made my way down the stairs. I was quickly brought back to reality when I reached the base of my stairs and Officer Buschke grabbed me by the arm and threw me to the ground. I am a small person and he was a big man, so when he threw me, it hurt badly. He pressed his knee into my back, pulled my arms behind me, and snapped me in handcuffs. Instead of advising me of my Miranda Rights, he told me to "shut up" or I would be taken to Los Angeles Harbor Division Police Station and booked. He did not tell me what I would be booked for. While I was being handcuffed in front of my property and across from my place of business, the police broke into the property at 810, which was vacant. Next, they went into my house, again without a warrant or my consent. Officer Buschke told me that someone had made a phone call from the fuel station stating a gun had been fired in front of 810 Channel Street. The SWAT team blanketed the entire property and detained me for over an hour. After finding nothing, they removed the handcuffs. Without one word, they left.

I don't believe that in any jurisdiction a SWAT team is ever sent to investigate a report of a gunshot fired in front of a residential property. As I understand it, the SWAT team is used for very serious situations like bank robbery, riot, or terrorist threats. Even if what Officer Buschke said was true, the situation did not warrant a full SWAT team response.

About twenty minutes before the SWAT team arrived at my house, a guy I knew had been at my house. He told me later that when he left my place and got to the main intersection of Gaffey and Channel streets, he spotted the SWAT team assembled at the fuel station. The police grabbed him and demanded to know about the narcotic manufacturing and selling that I was doing out of 810 and 812 Channel Street. He told them nothing of the sort was going on at those addresses.

I have often wondered why, if the police were indeed responding to a report of a gunshot, Sergeant Steve Wynn from Harbor Division didn't just call and ask me about it.

Los Angeles Police Harbor Division officers once again canvassed my neighbors, telling them I was manufacturing drugs and had many weapons in my home. It doesn't make sense that they'd persist in this after having searched my home three times and never finding a single weapon or any supplies associated with a meth lab. I didn't know what they were thinking until years later when I got my hands on the FBI report.

Captain Ackermann and Detective III Blake settled their C-5 surveillance unit in the glass company's office across the street from my home. They were so obvious it would have been funny had it not been so horrifyingly real. The nightly high-power spotlights shining into my bedroom in the middle of the night continued, and they took it up a notch by giving a burst of the sirens just to make sure I noticed they were there.

I phoned the LAPD Harbor Division many times to complain and was always connected to Sergeant Ferguson. He recommended that I write down the number of the police vehicles so they could investigate. Why bother? I knew that would never happen.

My life was not mine anymore. My business was on the verge of bankruptcy. Several of my Realtor clients had been stopped and questioned by the police after leaving my office. They were also told of the allegations of weapons and drug manufacturing activities.

I don't recall how or when I first met Russell and his wife. He was an ex-con, but his murder conviction had been overturned, so he was out of prison and out on parole—or so I was told. I felt sorry for them. I was witnessing firsthand what the police were capable of doing. Russell and his wife needed a place to live. She was working, I needed the money, and 810 needed to be rented out. I told them about what I was experiencing with the police, and for whatever reason, they did not care. They also rented the garage that was attached to 810, paying me extra for it.

At about the same time, Rudy came into my life. I didn't know this at the time, but he was Detective III Tom Blake's nephew and confidential informant. Again, I don't recall where he came from or how we met. Prison tattoos covered his body. He with his body art was not my type. If I had been in my right mind, I never would have let this guy into my house, let alone my bed. What was I thinking? Well, that was part of my problem. I wasn't, I couldn't.

Though small compared with other users, I was using an increasing amount of meth. The worse things got with the police, the more I needed to be high so I could block it out. It helped to some degree.

Rudy used a lot of meth, but I never let him keep it in the house. There was a vacant broken-down house in the back and up the hill from my property. It could not be seen from the streets. He would hop over the brick wall and hide both his and my meth over there, bringing over only the amount we needed at any one time. I know this wasn't the right thing to do, but I was a mess. The mess went away when I was high. If you've never been an addict, you cannot understand how this works. If you are a recovering or active addict, you understand. The more meth I used, the farther away from reality I went.

Despite this, I was still lucid enough to keep going to work and continue to try to help Dino. Work was slow, but I still had a job to go to. I was driving up to see Dino regularly, using Rudy's car until he sold it and got me a Dustan Z. He had this scam of getting vehicles with no VINs and somehow getting them registered.

On May 16, 1993, I was with two friends and my cousin at my house when officers from LAPD and the sheriff's department arrived at my front door and demanded to search my house again. They had no warrant. This time I said no. "You guys have searched my home three times already and never found one thing. I am not doing this again." To my surprise, they smiled and left. I thought maybe they were finally figuring out there was nothing to be found at my house. Wrong.

A short time later, my cousin walked down to the corner store at Channel and Gaffey. When she was almost there, she saw an army of police and sheriff vehicles parked at the rear of the parking lot. Before she could turn around, they were on her. They handcuffed her and ran a check on her. She had a minor warrant outstanding for speeding in Nevada. They could have taken her in on this warrant; instead, they phoned me and demanded I walk down to the corner and speak to them or they would run my cousin in.

I left my two friends at the house and met the police at the corner. They told me that if I did not allow them to search my house right now, without a warrant, not only would they arrest my cousin but also put me in one of the police vehicles and get a warrant. To further intimidate me, they said, "It would be a shame if any of the lovely things you have in your house were to accidentally be damaged or destroyed in our search."

I was incensed. I signed the consent form for the search. We went back to my house with the army of police and sheriff vehicles parked in front of my house and spilling into the vacant lot next to my house and down the street. I asked them to let my cousin and two friends go. They did but only as far as my downstairs entry door, where they were searched and questioned about my meth organization. They told the police that there was no meth organization or operation. The police put them in the back of a police vehicle. They were not told about their rights and were interrogated again for over twenty minutes. The police ran checks on them as well but came up empty. These were good people, not drug people. And they were outraged at their treatment and what they witnessed.

The police ordered my cousin to stay in the house with me while they did an in-depth search of everything in my small house, demanding to know where my weapons and drugs were. When they had finished their search of my home, they insisted I go with them to search the garage at 810. They did not want to search the residence, only the garage. I had no idea what the tenants had in the garage. I did not even have a key. I showed the police the rental agreement, but they brushed it off as inconsequential.

They put me in handcuffs again and made me sit on the ground in front of the property for almost two hours. They broke into the garage through the small door on the side. I was not allowed to see what they were doing in the garage. A hazardous material vehicle was called in and they started hauling things out of the garage. I had no idea what they were removing and was told nothing. When they finished, I was not given any information about what they had taken. Apparently, it was nothing or they would have arrested me.

I was left with a broken garage door and my home in a mess. My cousin stayed with me. We were both in shock. This was getting to be too much. I had no idea what I was going to do if the harassment continued.

My business was going under. I was forced to close it down and sell all the equipment and furniture in my office. Almost all of my neighbors had by now witnessed the police raids on my residence. Going to the market, the fuel station, or anyplace public was a nightmare as people stared at me. I was sure they were talking about me. Before this started, I had respect for the police. Now I hated and feared them.

I was running on adrenalin and meth. Rudy saw to it that I had drugs. My use was increasing, but I did not care. As far as I was concerned, my life was over. Being high was the only way I could escape this nightmare. I believed that I had no other choice. I did not understand why they were after me and was powerless to stop the harassment.

One night Rudy and I were going someplace, and for some reason, we were not followed. I have come to understand that a confidential informant can do what they want, as long as they give police the desired information. They can take drugs, commit crimes, and all will be overlooked by the police. This system is wrong.

A few days later, Rudy and I were going someplace in Los Angeles. Without warning, blue and red flashing lights came on behind us. As soon as the siren sounded, Rudy shoved a gun in my hand and told me to say it was mine. Just as the police officers arrived at the doors, I stuck this small handgun in my pants. They pulled Rudy out of the vehicle threw him on the ground, searched the vehicle, and found a shotgun.

These police officers were not from Harbor Division and had no way to know that Rudy was a confidential informant. He was handcuffed. I volunteered that I had a small handgun. I turned it over to them. It was not loaded and no bullets for it were in the car. We were both arrested and taken to Compton Police Station. The following day we were arraigned. I was let out on my own recognizance, but no court case was scheduled.

I continued to visit Dino in prison. I was scheduled to visit him on July 11, 1993. The night before, a friend of Ray's, a heroin addict name Donna, showed up at my house and begged me to let her stay the night as she had no place to go. The next morning, I had to leave early to get to Corcoran Prison, a four- to five-hour drive. I didn't want to leave her at my house because I didn't trust her. So I took her with me. When we got to Corcoran town, I dropped her off at a public park a few miles from the prison and told her to wait till I returned after visiting Dino.

I knew the prison's routine, so I wore the correct clothing and knew what to do. When I got there, however, I was told Dino was in solitary confinement. Of course, I wasn't told why, but I was not allowed to see him. As it turned out, this was my last attempt to visit Dino. To this day I have no idea what became of him.

I left the prison and went back to the park to pick up Donna. To my surprise, she had been arrested for possession of heroin and was sitting in the back of a police vehicle. I started to drive away, but the police stopped me. I had not committed any traffic offense, so they had no reason to pull me over. But they did. They arrested me, searched me, and found nothing in my vehicle or on my person. I was not that stupid to carry anything with me into prison, especially with the police constantly watching me. With no evidence, they arrested me and charged me with possession. I posted bail and got out of jail two days later, July 13. Surprisingly, Donna was released without having to post bail.

For the next few months, Donna and I drove up to Fresno for court appearances. I didn't have money to hire an attorney, so a public defender was appointed to me. My experience taught me that public defenders don't fight for their clients. Mine told me that he didn't get paid enough to defend me, only to make the best deal he could. Innocent or not, I was going to jail; it was just a matter of for how long. How could this be? I had no drugs; no blood tests were done to prove I was high. There was no case.

But with all that had been happening with the police, I felt doomed. My mom and I decided that she would purchase Channel Street from me so I could at least get my possessions out of the house. She would keep the equity I had in the house for me until I finished whatever time I had to do in Fresno. We opened escrow on the first of August to be closed at the beginning of September.

On August 1, 1993, Sally was evicted from her apartment. She and her son had no place to go…at least that is what she told me. As I look back, I wonder if Sergeant Steve Wynn orchestrated this situation. Sally was heavy into meth, but I agreed that she could stay for a few days. She floated in and out of my house and made friends with my renters, whom I was trying to evict for nonpayment of rent (who were also confidential informants).

Sally contacted my daughter and told her lies about me. Naturally, Amelia informed me of this. I kicked Sally out of my home and told her never to return. As she made her exit, she yelled that she would get me for doing this to her.

I began packing up my house in preparation for going to jail. I was still getting drugs and was slamming the crap in my arms. Looking back now, I don't know how I could do such a thing. I just know that I believed my life was over. I didn't know who I was anymore. I had gone down a rabbit hole, and someone else was living my life. Yet I continued to function and didn't look like the meth addict I was.

Toward the end of August, Donna and I drove up to Kings County for another court appearance. My attorney told me that they were again extending the trial date because he had too many cases, so this appearance was just to get another extension. On the way there we had a flat tire that took me almost an hour to change. No one stopped to help. As soon as I changed the tire, we got to the first phone booth to call both the court and my attorney to let them know I'd be a bit late because of the flat tire. When we arrived, I spotted my attorney and overheard him speaking to Donnas' attorney. The gist was that the court was going to revoke my bail and put us both in jail. I couldn't go to jail today! I had to get my stuff out of the house, and escrow, only a couple of weeks away, had to close. I did what any overstressed meth addict whose life had just gone from bad to worse would do: I ran.

I was scared and alone. I had to hide out until the escrow closed. It would be a little while before the bail bondsman started looking for me. I contacted Larry, a good friend, who picked me up. I gave him power of attorney so he could get my belongings. Amelia had my dog. I planned to stay free until escrow closed on the house. Then I would turn myself in and face the music.

I rented a storage unit for my household possessions. I arranged for Amelia to meet the moving company, who would pick up my things on September 3, with Larry there to supervise.

18

STRANGE WORLD

You've heard the saying truth is stranger than fiction. I concur. I lived it.

The first of September, while I was hiding in Orange County with Larry, Sally broke into my house and changed the door locks. With the help of her friends, she removed things from my house and was packing her car. The tenants as bad as they were, objected and tried to stop her. They phoned Larry, who went to the house. He met my daughter there, who was to supervise the movers. Her keys didn't work, nor did the keys I gave Larry.

Sally was in the house yelling out the window at them. Frightened, my daughter left, as did the moving company. Sally phoned Harbor Division and Sergeant Pugel responded. He threatened that anyone having contact with Sally would go to jail. He left and about an hour later Sergeant Wynn showed up. He also threatened the tenants and Larry with arrest. Larry protested and showed Sergeant Wynn the power of attorney. Wynn warned him to leave or he would arrest him. Wynn told everyone to either get back inside 810 Channel Street or leave. They went back inside, except for one of the guys who was working on his vehicle in the front of the property, right beside Sergeant Wynn's police car. He was under the car and could not be seen. He stayed there. He watched as Sergeant Wynn moved to the back of his patrol car, opened the trunk, reached inside, and pulled out a sawed-off rifle. He wrapped it in a yellow police raincoat and tucked it under his arm. Wynn headed toward 812, walking past the open window at 810. Those inside saw the butt of the rifle. He went to the front door of 812 and handed the rifle wrapped in the raincoat to Sally. Sally retreated inside 812, and Sergeant Wynn left.

Later that night, one of the tenants went to my house to ask Sally what she was doing there. He was surprised when she pointed the barrel of the rifle right between his eyes and yelled at him to leave her alone. He got her to calm down and lower the rifle then hustled back inside 810. Everyone was afraid. No one wanted to get shot by the paranoid Sally, who was very high.

The next day, September 4, Sally continued to remove my property from my home with the help of three or four of her friends. They loaded up their station wagon. The tenants again called Larry, who went to the property and attempted to stop her. Sally phoned Sergeant Wynn. This time he arrived with three patrol vehicles. Among the other officers present were Winslow, Buschke, and Penanti. Again, Sergeant Wynn threatened all of the tenants with arrest if they did not leave Sally alone. Larry showed the officers the power of attorney and was told that it was not valid because I no longer owned the property (which was not true as neither the foreclosure nor the escrow had yet gone through). Sally loaded her vehicle and the station wagon and left with the police still there.

When Sally returned later that day, she came in the station wagon. She wanted to get into the garage, but one of the tenants blocked her way, identifying that they had rented the garage and the contents belonged to them. Sally flew into a frenzy. She called the police and screamed that the tenant was protecting all the drug-making chemicals I had stored inside. The police came and made the tenant leave. They broke into the garage again, and again they found nothing but tools and car parts belonging to the tenants. Before the police left, they gave Sally safe passage to load the station wagon with my belongings.

Larry had no choice but to leave. Arriving home, he let me know what had happened. I was beside myself. I tried to escape my reality by getting high.

Sally then invited Sergeant Penanti and Sergeant Winslow into my home, telling them that there was a pipe bomb and a sawed-off rifle in the house. The tenants knew where the rifle had come from, and I suspect that the police had also supplied the bomb. Buschke and Winslow took two statements from Sally. The first one was taken at 5:30 p.m., when she stated that Rudy and I had stolen her car on September 1. These were the same officers who had watched her loading that same vehicle with my belongings for two days—after September 1. That report also stated that I was living there with Rudy and my estranged husband, Dale. Rudy had not been around for quite some time, and Dale had not stepped foot on the property since we left for Brazil in 1989. In fact, he had never returned from Brazil.

The second statement was taken at 6 p.m. that same day and was also taken by Winslow and Buschke. In this statement, she said that Rudy had given her the pipe bomb and rifle on September 1, the same day we supposedly took her car. Her statement indicated that I had escape tunnels running under the property and that my wall safe might be booby-trapped (the *only* items in the safe were tax records and personal documents). I can't imagine anyone believing this story. What "skills" did these detectives possess given that they seemed to have bought into these outlandish stories?

After providing her statements, Sally was allowed to leave the property. The police notified the bomb squad and evacuated the property, as well as some of the neighbors. The bomb squad detonated the planted bomb in the empty lot next to my property. That gave the police full authority to enter my house.

The LAPD officers who were present that day destroyed my home, making it uninhabitable. They knocked holes in the walls of every room, tore an entire wall down in the storage room, pulled the carpet up in the two bedrooms, and tore down all of the mini blinds. They ripped the electrical panel off the wall and broke into the safe, removing all of my daughter's identification papers. All of my papers, including my Social Security card and tax returns, were left scattered over the floor. When they were finished, they left my house wide open, without any locks on the doors.

My tenants went in and helped themselves to what they wanted, including my Social Security card and some other pieces of my identification.

Given this situation, the escrow could not close, and Mom could not move ahead with the purchase. I would lose the property. The Harbor

Division, as well as the other law enforcement agencies, knew about the sale of the property. By their actions, I believed that, come hell or high water, they were intent on destroying me. They had not been able to arrest me for manufacturing or selling meth, so they took a different approach to ruin my life. It took them almost two years to succeed. I was broken.

I fled to Mexico with my dog, Sasha; I am sure that dog saved my life. I was sleeping in a doorway in the middle of Tijuana when a biker group found me, took pity on me, and let me stay in their clubhouse for a few days. I came to grips that this present action was not the answer, so I hitched rides back to Orange County.

On September 6, 1993, Sergeant Rick Angelos with Internal Affairs was assigned to investigate Sergeant Wynn's involvement with Sally as well as the gun that witnesses reported he gave to Sally. Sergeant Bob Nelson from LAPD's Criminal Conspiracy Unit would further investigate it.

Between September 5 and 13, Sergeant Pugle went to 810 Channel Street and picked up two of the four tenants who had witnessed Sergeant Wynn giving the rifle to Sally. They were taken to Harbor Division to give their statements. They were then driven back to Channel Street and told they would get copies of their statements. They never received them.

During the investigation, Angelos was involved in a police cover-up that disposed of witness statements that identified Sergeant Wynn as the one who took the sawed-off rifle into my home. The witness statements were changed, indicating Wynn was carrying a bottle of whiskey, not a rifle.

Bob Nelson filed charges against Rudy for the bomb, but in Nelson's statement, given under oath to my insurance company, he stated, "Rudy was never prosecuted—the complaint was filed. I learned at a later date that they threw out the complaint for whatever reason." Nelson was never asked whom he was referring to when he said "they." No one has ever been prosecuted for either the bomb or the rifle.

I contacted Mom. Because my house was fully insured, we started the claim process with my insurance company. My next nightmare started with the runaround by this large insurance company. My experience taught me never to trust any insurance company again. On September 8, I filed the claim with the Fireman's Fund Insurance Company, which had insured me for many years. In the first inner-office correspondence, dated September 28, 1993, Ginny Davidson, without having interviewed me, stated, "This is a fraudulent claim." She concluded this because the police told her that the house had been a meth lab and I was a meth dealer, a statement made with zero evidence. Fireman's Fund made me bring in documents from the time I bought this property in 1987, including all by bank records and canceled checks from when I ran my first mortgage company and the closing statement from when I sold the 24th Street property. I guess they thought a nut case like me would not have any of these documents, which I had stored in a small unit in Wilmington. While I had to provide years of documentation, the police did not have to provide anything to support their slanderous claims. The insurance company accepted what they said. With no intention of ever paying my claim, the insurance company kept me tied in knots for many years with their team of attorneys. They continued to demand that I provide documents proving I had bought the house. I produced not only these documents but also documents when I purchased most of my furniture. The insurance company did not expect that.

Ginny Davidson called me a liar and stated that if I did not provide the documents they had asked for, the claim would be automatically rejected. I had the copies of the letter, with her boss's stamp and date as having received everything she was still requesting. Over and over she slandered my name in her inner-office memos, calling me a drug addict and stating that I was out of my mind. She had the statements of eyewitnesses and the police reports that were blatant lies. By the end of this mess, I had a mountain of evidence that the police were lying to protect themselves and their buddies. Most of what they did was not legal because they had zero evidence. They had no evidence because what they claimed was not true.

During this time, I moved from one flophouse to another but always staying in touch with Mom. I met some very strange people. They were all drug addicts, the majority of them having warrants on them. I was in a very strange world. I had no idea how I got there or even that this world existed. Something had gone horribly wrong in my life. Of course, the meth did not help me to understand anything. It only served to numb reality.

Sergeant Skipper was a notoriously corrupt officer out of the Redondo Beach Police Department. He had no business in San Pedro, but on September 13, 1993, he arrested one of the tenants at 810. Russell was in his car in front of the Channel Street property when he was caught with two ounces of meth and weapons of some kind. He was taken to the Redondo Beach police station. Rick Angelos, who is the Internal Affairs Officer involved in the investigation of Sergeant Wynn, was called to the Redondo Beach police station to interview Russell, I have no idea who decided Internal Affairs had any business interfering with a civilian for a drug bust. Russell was eager to give statements against me in exchange for being released without any charges. Of course, he was already a confidential informant for the police. But Russell could not supply any solid evidence since none existed. I was not even close to the property at the time.

On September 14, I called Angelos in response to a message relayed to me regarding questions he had about Sergeant Wynn's involvement with Sally. I answered his questions then questioned him about his involvement with the incident at my property on September 3 and 4. Even in my fog, I knew there was something wrong with all this. He told me to call Sergeant Skipper.

"Why? He had nothing to do with anything; he was in Redondo Beach," I said.

"Just call Sergeant Skipper," Angelos said.

A few days later I phoned Sergeant Skipper, who believed I was a heavy hitter in the drug scene. He demanded I go to work for him undercover. I tried to reason with him and to explain that I was not part of the drug scene. Sergeant Skipper told me that if I did not do as he wished, he would see to it I was charged and convicted for both the bomb and the rifle found at my house.

I was on the verge of hysterics. Crying, I told him I was innocent. He did not listen to me and kept insisting I work for him. I argued that I could not help him as I didn't know any drug kingpins. Then he said, "I know you are innocent, but that doesn't matter."

I knew this man's reputation, and I was even more out of my mind with worry now that he was involved. I did the only thing I knew to do: I ran all the faster.

On October 15, Sergeant Angelos contacted my insurance company and provided them with false information. He told them that I was manufacturing drugs and making bombs in my house at 812 Channel Street. The insurance company accepted this without any evidence to support his accusations. Sergeant Angelos is with Internal Affairs and should have had nothing to do with giving anyone information because his job was to investigate Sergeant Wynn.

I had my first deposition with Ginny Davidson on October 26, 1993. My mom came with me. I was lucid and stayed in control. Naïve as I was at the time, I thought the insurance company was on my side. After all, I was their insured. Little did I know that they had already made their decision based on what the police had told them; of course, I knew nothing about this at this time. Ginny started asking the most ridiculous questions: "How did you purchase the property in 1987? Where did you get the money from?"

I answered all of her questions, again providing documentation. But it was an exercise in futility.

On November 4, I was riding in a car with a guy in Orange County when he got stopped. They checked us both and discovered a warrant on me. Very happily they took me in and jailed me at Carson police station. Within a day, I was transferred to Sybil Brand Jail in Los Angeles, where I spent the next three days on the concealed gun misdemeanor charge. Then I was transferred to Kings County, where the bogus drug charge was waiting for me. By this time, I had no hope of release because I had jumped bail. I worried about my precious dog, the only thing I loved and cherished at that time. My mom had given her to me years ago. She was unique and fiercely loyal to me; she had been with me all this time and was in the vehicle when I got arrested.

I made collect phone calls to my mom and daughter to let them know what had happened. I told them not to come to see me. There was no way I wanted my child to see me in the orange prison clothes. Both my mom and Amelia sent money so I could purchase from the jail commissary personal items like toothpaste and snacks. I agonized over my beloved dog. I imagined the worst-case scenarios. The guy I had been with could not keep her at his place. Life had no meaning to me. It was over. I had lost everything, including my mind.

I did not go to court on the minor charge until December 22, 1993. The only court papers I received was the sentencing report, and nothing in that report identified the charges. But the sentence was 120 days. I had already served fifty-two days and had twenty-six days of conduct credits. Because I was a good prisoner, they also credited me a few more days for good behavior. I also had to pay a fine of $790. I had nothing, so this amount was a fortune. Fifty dollars of that was for a laboratory test I was never given. I also received probation for three years. All of this because I wanted to help a guy in jail?

The so-called trial did not state what I was convicted of. I guess jumping bail was enough. I was never charged for manufacturing meth or weapon possession. None of it was connected to what had happened at Channel Street.

My time in jail was one of the bleakest periods of my life. Once I was sentenced, I worked in the laundry. I spent the days reading and thinking about my mom, my daughter, and my dog. One good result was that I was off the meth. I got along with the other inmates. This was a city jail, not a state prison, so the other inmates were all low-level criminals like me. Christmas came and went.

I got out of jail at the beginning of January 1994. I had just enough money to take the bus back to Los Angeles. Friends I had made while incarcerated, who had been released before me, lived in the area. They picked me up. They were meth heads like me, and I was back using that very night. During my entire time in jail, I longed for the release from reality that meth provided.

The next morning I phoned a friend who would let me stay at his place. I took the bus from Fresno to Los Angeles, where Alan picked me up. A nice guy who used a little meth had a job and an apartment. Best of all, he knew where my dog was! My dog was the single ray of light in my life. Alan took me to get her. She was safe, though very dirty. Our reunion was glorious!

Right after I got out, I contacted the insurance company and was advised that they did not have a police report on file for the damages to my residence that occurred on September 3 and 4. On three separate occasions, I went to Harbor Division Police Department to try to get the report. Walking into that building was beyond horrible. I felt like everyone was watching me. Their hostility and hatred of me were apparent. They had no right to hate me; I was the victim. I was such a mess, and I felt lower than dirt. The first two times I tried to file the report, I was shuffled from one desk to another, and all the while I heard their whispers and snickers. Finally, after about two weeks, they took the report.

The police told me to itemize my loss. I had already done this for the Fireman's Fund, and the list was very long. My house had items from all over the world, unique and one-of-a-kind things. I had a silk rug from China and a twelve-piece setting of china from China. I could go on and on. The police would not accept the list that I had already completed for the insurance company, so I had to use their forms and do it all over again, each time being reminded of all I had lost. These items held many memories; each one had a story behind it. It was painful to have to relist it all. I calculated the total amount of the loss at $69,000. That was a low estimate and did not include the equity I had lost in my home when the escrow fell through because of the major damage done to the property.

The police gave the insurance company another report that did not have my signature on it. In that report, they listed only a television and stereo. That didn't make sense. I had given the television to my daughter and had never claimed it or anything else I had given to her or that I was able to remove myself.

Despite the police report and the pages of documentation I supplied, the insurance company believed I was lying to them. Why didn't they believe me? I am sure that the company had no intention of paying this claim.

I moved out of Alan's place in early January since he couldn't have a dog where he lived. I was back in San Pedro with no place to stay.

This part of my story is blurry. Though I have documents of aspects that give me some perspective, my personal life was in shambles. I cared only about getting drugs, my dog, finding dog food, and making my monthly payment to the probation department in Kings County ($15 a month toward $790). I had no job and was a heavy meth user, injecting it into my arms by this time. I started doing jobs for drug dealers to buy my drugs and dog food. Mostly, I transported money or drugs from one place to another. I had to walk or hitchhike to do my "jobs." Most days, my dog and I wandered the streets; at nights I either wandered or did my "job." Never in my life could I imagine a life like this existed. This was the underbelly of society. I kept asking myself, "How the hell did I end up here?" At times, if I was high enough, I would forget how I ended up where I was. Then it did not matter because it was not me in this situation; it was someone else. Someone else had my body and soul, and she was living my life.

At one point I ended up with a group of sex workers who were drug addicts as well. They let me stay at their house with my dog. They were good to me, and they were doing pretty good out on the street. I figured I had nothing to lose and decided to give prostitution a try. I was a washed-up meth head with no dignity, no morals, and no nothing. One night the girls told me how to let a "John" know you were a working girl. They also warned me to watch out for one cop whose only job was to bust working girls. They knew him by sight and described him, but everyone looked the same to me. So I went "to work."

I got into a vehicle and we drove to a back alley. Before we even got to the subject of money, I start balling my eyes out and told the guy I couldn't go through with it. It turns out that he was the cop the girls had warned me about. He could have busted me, but it was pretty obvious that this was not my normal line of work. He let me go. A cop just gave me a break, something that did not happen in my life! I got out of his car and ran back to the house. I was sure the officer was coming back for me, so I hid in a thorny rose bush. All night, the girls tried to get me to come out, but nothing would budge me out of my hiding place…until morning when I needed some dope. My dog, Sasha, did not leave my side all night. Looking back, she saved my life. At this point, I did not care if I lived or died, ate or starved. But I cared for Sasha, and she needed me to take care of her. That alone kept me going.

The girls decided that it would be better if I just worked for them. I cleaned the house, cooked for them, did their laundry, and took care of them. In return they took care of me: gave me dope and paid for my dog's food. I did this for some time.

I was still dealing with the insurance company. On February 3, 1994, I sent them a letter asking about the status of my claim.

On February 18, 1994, months after I no longer owned the Channel Street property, Deputy Fennell from the Los Angeles Sherriff Department obtained a search warrant with my name on it for 812 Channel Street, stating that I was involved with the people who were squatting on the property. He claimed that I was the girlfriend of the man selling narcotics from there. I had never met the people who lived there and had not been anywhere near the property. Would this nightmare never end?

19

The Blue Code

One night I ended up in San Pedro with a girl, doing dope on a small sailboat that belonged to a friend of hers. Sasha was at the hookers' house in Harbor City. As we talked to this guy, I shared that I was homeless; and he offered to give me his boat. The one condition was that he owed a lot of back dock fees that I would have to pay. He told me that the manager was a real battle-ax and to stay clear of her. He signed the boat over to me the next day. This amazing opportunity ended my being homeless.

It felt like I had been homeless for years, but it lasted less than three months, from late January until March 1994.

At the marina, I was immediately befriended by an older man, Bob, who lived in the marina not far from my new home. Bob was a true friend. He helped me in many ways, and I could never repay him. In the morning he would pick up Sasha and me in his little runaround skiff to hide me from the office and the manager. He would drop me off on the rock jetty and keep my dog for me during the day. The manager left the docks around 5 p.m. every day. I would sneak back in, get Sasha, and return to my boat. Bob fed me and my dog, and he gave me money for drugs.

I had to find a way to get money to pay for the dock fees and the fine I owed Kings County. I hitched rides to the welfare department to apply for welfare payments. This took several trips. After my first interview, I told the worker that I had no money for bus fare and had to hitchhike there. I don't think she believed me at first, but then she saw me hitchhiking right outside their office. She came out and gave me the tokens for the bus. As I write this, it strikes me funny that she warned me against hitchhiking, saying it was dangerous. I had been on the streets for months; hitching a ride in broad daylight was not dangerous in comparison. I did not tell her that, but she did note that I was having significant issues. She arranged for me to see some kind of shrink doctor, who gave me antidepressants. I never took them after reading about the side effects. I did not need any other drugs in me. I had way too many as it was.

Eventually, my application for welfare was approved and I started receiving welfare checks as well as food stamps. I went to see the manager and told her I was going to pay off the slip fees if she would only give me some time. I offered to make a payment every other week. To my surprise, she was kind and accepted this arrangement. I was then free to come and go as I pleased. I needed to find a job. Bob was still caring for Sasha most of the time. He loved her, and being the amazing dog she was, she loved him right back.

I got a job in Manhattan Beach. I had a job! I was working at a travel company that specialized in African safaris. They agreed to pay me under the table as they were not paying me much. I started work around the first of April 1994. I must have been good at hiding my addiction because they had no idea I was on drugs or just how bad my addiction was. I was a tweaker (a meth addict), but I did my job. I answered the phone, got coffee, and attended to whatever other tasks they assigned me. At one point I rearranged their storage area, which was a big mess, so I was of some value to the company. I still had a shred of decency in me, and I never, in all that time, stole anything from anyone.

I had not been in contact with my daughter for months. I did not want her to see me in my condition as a homeless person. I spoke to my mom quite often. She worried about me and offered to help me, but I would not let her. She had done enough. Besides, I was ashamed of who I had become. I would not let her see me. Now that I had a job and some money to buy decent clothes at a thrift store, I felt it was okay to contact my daughter.

She was happy to hear from me and offered to pick me up in the mornings on her way to work and take me to the bus station, where

I'd take the bus to work. Because I was ashamed of what I had become, it was difficult to be around my daughter. She had lost respect for me. Who could blame her? She did, however, still love me. She had kept some of my clothes she had managed to get out of Channel Street. I now had a few pieces of good clothing.

The battle with Fireman's Fund Insurance Company continued, with letters going back and forth for months. They had photos of all my things that had been taken through the years at my home at 24th Street and Channel Street. The insurance company still required me to submit documents showing items similar to what had been stolen. I had to go all over Los Angeles to exotic stores to find and photograph these things as well as get the cost of each piece. It took a long time. Thankfully, Bob drove me around.

On March 3, 1994, Fireman's Fund Insurance took Sally's deposition. It was full of holes, discrepancies—basically, a pack of lies. On April 6, 1994, they took my daughter's statement, trying to put words in her mouth. Most of her answers were, "I don't know," "I don't remember," or, "I have no idea." She refused to let them manipulate her. At one point in the interview, they asked her if she had ever been known by another name. Of course, she answered, "Yes."

They could not figure out how my daughter's name had changed three times, and Amelia could give limited information since she didn't have all the facts regarding the name changes. Ms. Crumpler, the interviewer, repeatedly said, "The only way you can get your name changed is through the court."

"No, we did not go to court," Amelia said and showed her two Social Security cards with the two different last names on them, as well as her current driver's license.

In the end, they had no choice but to let it go. They got no useful information out of her.

I eventually paid the dock fees and traded in the small sailboat for a thirty-five-foot cabin cruiser. It had no engine in it, but it was much bigger and more comfortable.

On September 1, 1994, Officer Jeff Hamilton of the LAPD Harbor Division led an eviction raid on 810 Channel Street. Four people were arrested for trespassing. Upon their release, they were told to retrieve their belongings and never return, which they did. The problem was that they had witnessed Sergeant Wynn give the rifle to Sally as well as all of the events of September 3 and 4, 1993, and were to testify at Sergeant Wynn's Internal Affairs hearing on September 13. When they asked about the hearing and told Hamilton they were to testify, he told them to contact the Harbor Division in a month or so, and they would be told the court date. Hamilton knew the court date had already been set for September 13, less than two weeks away. He had effectively gotten rid of the witnesses.

Officer Hamilton and Sergeant Jaurequi provided the story of the eviction to the local newspaper *Newspilot*. The story had details about the drugs that were found, but no arrests had been made. That didn't make any sense because had there been drugs, the police would have arrested someone. Hamilton and Jaurequi told the paper, "The former owner of the house apparently is homeless and may be wandering the streets of San Pedro. There were unconfirmed reports that she was kicked out after becoming hooked on methamphetamine and she befriended her tenants." It was apparent they were not done with me, and for whatever reason, they were still trying to hurt me. Of course, I was not homeless then. I was working, and I had absolutely nothing to do with the Channel Street property.

Sergeant Jaurequi had been recalled to Harbor Division only a few months earlier as part of Internal Affairs to handle my complaint against Sergeant Steve Wynn. His involvements in the eviction raid were a clear conflict of interest because he couldn't be engaged with the raid and still conduct a fair and impartial investigation. I now know that it was a waste of time to file a complaint through Internal Affairs against any police officer. Law enforcement will stand behind the Blue Code and do their best to protect one another and keep one another out of trouble. It is no wonder that policing is in such a mess and that so many people do not trust the police.

Harbor Division knew where I lived and had a phone number for me, yet they never advised me of the date of Sergeant Wynn's court date, which speaks volumes for the integrity of LAPD at the time. I found out about it from the newspaper reporter when I contacted him about the untrue story about me and the eviction raid he had written in the paper.

I called Internal Affairs and spoke to Sergeant Crowsley, who had taken over for Angelos. He had the nerve to ask me if I wanted to testify at the hearing on September 13. To add insult to injury, he told me that the Harbor Division did not know where I was. Another lie. I had told them where to contact me, and they were watching me. The reporter, Mark, agreed to give me a ride to the hearing. He wanted to write a follow-up story because he believed he had been given misleading information.

The night of September 12, a black-and-white patrol parked at the marina with the lights off. Several times during the night they shone their high-powered light into my boat. I reported this to Internal Affairs the next day, but nothing was ever done about it.

Also on September 12, Mark, who was at the newspaper office next door to the LAPD's Community Center of Harbor Division, was paid a visit by Officer Jeff Hamilton, who tried to convince Mark that it was a waste of time to go to the hearing. Mark didn't buy it. Hamilton threatened Mark that if he gave me a ride and attended the hearing, Mark would not have a job much longer. Mark did give me a ride and stayed for the duration of the hearing. He wrote a follow-up story, but his supervisors restricted what he could write. Strangely, Mark disappeared and was no longer at the paper. I never learned what happened to him.

The day of the hearing, a few seconds before I was to testify, the officer who was defending Sergeant Wynn whispered to me, "Your daughter is doing okay, and she said to tell you hi." He had phoned my daughter at her place of employment. This was intimidation, but I had grown used to their tactics.

The court and the three captains who presided over Sergeant Wynn's hearing were a joke. Because Officer Hamilton ensured that the witnesses who had seen Wynn with the rifle would not be attending the proceedings, there was no one to contradict Wynn's testimony. There were so many holes in Wynn's story, you could drive a truck through it. My testimony contradicted much of what Wynn said. In the end, however, they convicted him of bad behavior and suspended him for fifteen days without pay.

When I finally got a copy of the Board of Rights Rationale, it stated that this was not Wynn's first time being in trouble it went on to say:

And throughout, as we discussed, we were concerned with that supervisory failure theme that we seem to see in a number of these complaints.

I have no idea what happened regarding these other complaints, but it was obvious that Wynne was abusing his authority and not doing his job. Even the police agreed with that—Internal Affairs at its finest.

Meanwhile, the investigation into the Rampart scandal of the LAPD Hollywood Division was just beginning. Many police officers connected with the Rampart CRASH unit were implicated in some form of misconduct, making it one of the most widespread cases of documented police corruption in the history of the United States. The police were responsible for a long list of offenses, including unprovoked shootings, beatings, planting of false evidence, stealing and dealing narcotics, bank robbery, perjury, and the covering up of evidence of these activities. Much of the Rampart investigation was based on statements of admitted corrupt CRASH officer Rafael Pérez, whose statements implicated over seventy officers of wrongdoing. Of those officers, fifty-eight went before an internal administrative board. Twenty-four were found to have committed wrong doing. Twelve were given suspensions, seven were forced to resign or retire, and five were terminated. As a result of the probe into falsified evidence and police perjury, 106 prior criminal convictions were overturned. The scandal resulted in more than 140 civil lawsuits against the city of Los Angeles, California, costing the city an estimated $125,000,000 in settlements. The full extent of the Rampart corruption is not known, and several rape, homicide, and robbery investigations involving the Rampart officers remain unsolved.

I suspect many cases were like mine, in which witnesses were harassed, evidence corrupted or lost, police informant statements based on what police wanted to hear rather than what was true, and police officers blatantly lying to protect one another. Concepts of justice and fairness were absent from police work.

This scandal of the LAPD in the '90s was an accumulation of years of corruption and cover-ups. I got caught in the middle of it all. Complicating my case was the FBI wanting me arrested for the drug dealing they thought I was involved in. To say that things got out of hand is an understatement.

Shortly after the hearing, my mom's husband became quite ill. He had been sick for some time, but his condition worsened. He wasn't well enough to drive, so he and Mom let me have his car until he was well and could again drive. I got my driver's license back and got insurance. I could easily move around again. I also lightened up on my drug use. I wanted to stop, but I did not know how. Addiction takes over your life—you think you are in control, but drugs control the user.

I was still dealing with the insurance company, complying with their ongoing demands for unnecessary documents. They kept stringing me along. Often, they refused to take my phone calls. I spent a lot of time running around and sending them documents they already had.

Even with the Rampart scandal blowing up, the police harassment did not stop. They were still following me at times, and I was a nervous wreck. In January 1995, I was at the Laundromat getting my clothes out of the car when a police cruiser pulled in behind me, shined its high-powered light in my face, and laughed as they blared "BOO" over the loudspeaker before driving away. It may sound like a small thing, but with all of the harassment, lies, and false accusations I had endured, it upset me terribly. These incidents left me shaking. People at the Laundromat witnessed this, so I picked up the laundry I had dropped, got back into my car, and went to another Laundromat to do my washing—all the time looking over my shoulder. I would be looking over my shoulder for years and years to come.

Early in March 1995, I attempted to obtain documentation from the police department regarding the 1993 police activity at Channel Street. What they gave me was a report for someone's stolen car in Harbor City. I spent days going back and forth to the Harbor Division, and each time I felt like crap. It seemed like everyone in the station stopped and stared at me. But I sucked it up and demanded the paperwork. One time Sergeant Pugel and I got into an argument when he said that Sally had every right to be in my house because my mom had given her permission. I knew that wasn't true because I had the notarized document that Mom had submitted to the insurance company stating that she *never* gave Sally permission to enter the house. But he wouldn't look at it and brushed me off. I picked up his business card and left. Mom was furious. She phoned him many times, but he would never take her phone calls. He was either "not available" or he had "just gone out." It was no surprise that he never returned her calls. I finally told her to let it go.

In March 1995, I hired an attorney to deal with the insurance company. A cousin was a lawyer, and he agreed to have his associate handle my case, even though they were personal injury attorneys. They were leery about this at first as they knew my past and had read the false but incriminating documentation from the police. They did their best to defend me.

The safari company fired me in June 1995. I don't know why. Perhaps they figured out I was on drugs. I still had food stamps and welfare.

Since I had cleaned up and my meth usage was low, I was able to get a good job at a mortgage company. I still knew how to do that job—the one I had been doing for years until LAPD put an end to it in 1993. I started my new job in June 1995 and went off of welfare. Finally, I could support myself.

On August 23, 1995, Fireman's Fund took the under-oath statements of Sergeant Angelos and Detective III Bob Nelson. Neither of these men had much to do with the events at my home. Why didn't they call on Wynn, Buschke, Winslow, or any number of law enforcement officers who were there? When I went through their sworn statements, it took my breath away. I could not believe these officers would perjure themselves to the degree they did. Angelos went so far as to say, "Paula was a no-good drug dealer and bomb maker." Their statements were filled with lies, and they contradicted themselves and each other. Most of what they swore to was hearsay, as neither of them had any firsthand knowledge because they were not present at the events they were swearing to.

In late September 1995, my mom's husband was diagnosed with a brain tumor, inoperable cancer. On October 6, I quit my job and moved into her house in Las Vegas to help her care for him as long as we were able. We moved him into a hospice care center, where he died in March of 1996. Between October and March, I was driving back and forth from Las Vegas to LA for interviews with Fireman's Fund.

Mom started spending time with me on the boat after her husband passed away. I went to work for another mortgage company and started to get my broken life back together. I was still using, but I was trying to keep it down.

It was just luck that my mom was with me the March morning when two guys in suits jumped onto my boat and, before I knew what was happening, had me in handcuffs. They identified themselves as FBI and advised me that I was being taken in for crimes I'd committed in Tennessee, Kentucky, and Kansas over the last two years. What the…? They were extraditing me to Kansas for "interstate flight to avoid prosecution." They escorted me, handcuffed and in my pajamas and slippers, through the marina. Of course, I had an audience. My mom and I were protesting at the top of our lungs as the agents continued to spout that I had committed crimes in those states. I could prove I had not left California except to go to Las Vegas to help my mom.

I finally convinced them to explain what they were talking about. A woman with my name and my Social Security number had committed crimes in those states. Her description was female, 5' 8", with brown hair. "Look at me! I'm five-foot-two with red hair." I told them of my Social Security card and other personal identification being stolen and that there was a police report on all this. Check with the LAPD; they knew where I was during the time these crimes were committed. A group had gathered around us, and all of them were saying that I had been in this marina for a long time.

At first, the agents did not seem interested in any of our arguments, but my mom, bless her heart, was a fireball. She'd had enough of all this crap with law enforcement destroying her daughter's life. At seventy-eight, she yelled at the agents and blocked their car with her body, prohibiting them from getting me into the vehicle. Naturally, they resorted to threats, which didn't faze her. "You will have to take me in with her. I will not allow you to do this."

They finally phoned their superiors, who advised them that the girl they were looking for had been arrested the day before in Tennessee.

I was frantic. How much can one person take? I was shaking so badly that I could hardly stand up when they took the cuffs off and released me. I was embarrassed, but the good folks at the marina who had witnessed this felt bad for me and were hostile toward the agents, who left without apologizing or making any conciliatory comments.

20

Mom

At the end of 1996, Mom decided to sell her home in Las Vegas and move in with me. She was in the early stages of Alzheimer's disease. There was never any discussion on where she would go and who would take care of her. She would stay with me, and I would take care of her. We also decided to move the boat from this marina to another, still in Wilmington, but in the Port of Los Angeles. It was a much nicer marina and had a laundry facility. However, to dock there, boats had to move under their own power. Mine didn't have an engine. That posed a problem.

I knew a nice guy, Doug. He was a druggie like me, but he was honest and kind. We had become good friends. He had an idea for moving my boat that involved putting his little electric motor on the back of my boat, on the swim step, and then he would guide it into the slip at the new marina. The little electric motor pushed my thirty-five-foot cabin cruiser around to the other marina and got it into the slip without anyone knowing that my boat had no engine.

Doug introduced me to Tom, who became my first boyfriend in years. There had been many men in and out of my life over the years but none I cared about, and none who stayed for longer than it took to have sex once or twice. If they had dope, I slept with them. Meth made sex more intense. I had no self-respect left, but by 1996 I stopped having random sex and saw only a few guys I liked. That didn't happen often and never when my mom was around.

My fight with Fireman's Fund Insurance was ongoing. We had various court dates and everyone showed up, including Sergeant Wynn as he had been subpoenaed by my attorney. The police were not happy about this and were hostile, as usual, to me. On March 26, 1997, we were again scheduled for a court date. My mom was with me. I was outside the courtroom speaking with Sergeant Pesanti. It was not a cordial conversation as he continued to try to intimidate me. Sergeant Wynn was there as well, and if looks could kill, I would have been dead as dead could be. Once again, the case was postponed. While we were at court, Detective III Ginelli of Harbor Division Narcotics raided my boat with guns drawn and no warrant. A friend of mine was there. They manhandled her and threatened that unless she showed them where my drugs were, she was going to jail. They detained her and tossed my boat. They threw everything around looking for nonexistent drugs and left it in a horrible state.

This was the final straw! When I saw what they had done to my home—again—I saw red. I marched into the Harbor Division and demanded to see Ginelli. I was yelling so loud that he was forced to come out. I gave him hell. I told him I was going after Wynn, and I would come after him as well. This had gone too far. I had been harassed by the police from 1992 to 1997, and I was not going to take it anymore. I demanded that he send the officers who had destroyed my home to go back and put it back the way they found it. To my total shock, he did just that. The officers put everything back then left.

Mom and I had a long talk and concluded that the insurance company was going to drag its feet forever. We would never know what was going on with them unless we fired the attorney, who would then have to turn over all the discovery documents. It is from those documents that we were able to piece together the whole horrible story. We had boxes of files: all of the documents from the attorney as well as all of the documents Harbor Division had to give me over the years. Mom and I had a lot of anxiety when we considered the volume of information we possessed and what some of these documents exposed—especially considering the Rampart scandal that was coming to light. We were a bit paranoid, so we rented a hotel room for a couple of nights and spent the time organizing the information into binders. We made copies of everything, rented a small storage unit in Mom's name, and hid everything there.

Not long after, Mom's eyesight started failing. She needed me more than before. Her mind was still sharp, but we knew what was coming. She made me power of attorney and completed a health directive as well. I quit my job to care for her.

Mom encouraged me to go after the police with the proof I had; she would pay our living expenses while I pursued the case.

Tom bought a boat, and I moved on it with him in the slip next to my boat, where Mom stayed. He supplied all the drugs he and I were using. I never looked like I was high. No one who did not know me well knew that I was an addict. I was ashamed of what I was doing and wanted to stop, but I just could not do it. I was frightened I would not be able to function. I had a fight ahead of me, and my mom would require a lot more care. Quitting would have to wait.

Now that I had all the documents organized, I was shocked at the extent of what the police had done. I felt ready to fight, and I had proof. My timing, however, could not have been worse. The Rampart scandal was in full swing. The LAPD, City Attorney, Internal Affairs, LA Sherriff's Department, and other elected officials at the time could not tolerate additional scandal. But I tried it anyway.

In June 1997, I met with Lieutenant Ramm with Internal Affairs in Los Angeles. I handed him a binder containing all the evidence that had taken almost four years to gather. The lieutenant lied and said he had never heard anything about me, Sergeant Angelos, or Fireman's Fund Insurance Company. I had documentation from Fireman's Fund that proved he had spoken to investigators with the insurance company on several occasions regarding my claim and Sergeant Angelos. Lieutenant Ramm did not investigate and avoided my phone calls.

I sent identical binders, with cover letters, to the chief of police, mayor, and my city council member. The only one I heard from was the city council member. He wrote a letter on my behalf to the LAPD. In December 1997, I also filed a complaint to the FBI and sent them a copy of the binder. This was before I received documents through the Freedom of Information Privacy Release Act, which showed the storm began with the FBI. I wonder how quickly they shredded the documents I had sent them.

I tried to get someone in authority to look at my documentation and to file a case against those responsible, but it was just a never-ending list of captains and lieutenants. None did anything but lie to me about how my case would be investigated then passed me to another captain. I kept getting the runaround. The same song and dance happened with my complaints to the LAPD headquarters.

In July 1999, I contacted Lois Lar, who was with the American Civil Liberties Union South Bay Chapter. She accompanied me to Parker Center, where we met with the assistant to Inspector General, Sergeant Carlos Velez. I turned over a binder with all of the documents showing the actions of LAPD and LASD. After repeated phone calls with nothing happening, I started to think that I had heard his name before. I went back over the thousands of pages of documents and found that Sergeant Carlos Velez was the partner of Sergeant Rick Angelos in 1993. He was directly involved in the incident at Channel Street, and he also took one of the statements from Sally on September 6, 1993. It seems to have all come full circle—same cops in different roles, all doing everything in their power to brush their dirt under the rug and get rid of me.

On September 30, 1999, Detective Richard Ginelli, who had raided my boat in March 1997, was busted for heroin possession. The police played it down and told the media it was not related to the Rampart investigation. They also stated that it was a small amount for his "personal use." I found out later that it was actually a couple of pounds, far more than personal use. Everyone knew he had been dealing, but with the Rampart scandal, that was kept quiet. The police did not want another scandal like Rampart. Ginelli got away with it. He had to go to rehab for sixty days and then he got his job back! I have asked over and over, "How is that possible?"

I was working part-time as an extra for television and movies. I could choose when I worked. It wasn't long before I realized that I could not fight LAPD and take care of my mom, so I walked away from the LAPD fight. I put all of the documents in a storage unit and devoted myself to taking care of my mom for the remainder of her life.

I had my dog Sasha, who had been through so much with me, and Salty, the dog I got for Tom. We settled into a somewhat normal routine. My mom was not getting any better, and the Alzheimer's was affecting her memory. She could still get around on her own.

Harbor Division stopped bothering me as I think they wanted me out of their lives. Then, for no apparent reason, an officer from the Port Police (still LAPD but much smaller in scope) started to bother me. At first I thought it was my imagination. Then when I was at the market, my mom became confused and called 911. The Port Police responded. When I arrived back at the boat, they were there and prepared to arrest me for elder abuse. Mom apparently had told them she wanted to go home and that I would not let her. As soon as she saw me, she realized her mistake. She told the police she was confused and that she was home. I pulled out the medical papers and the official documents to prove I was not lying to them. Since they knew I was her caregiver, I said that I would appreciate it if they would help by not confusing her anymore.

Time and time again the one officer (whose name I have forgotten) stopped me for nothing as I was coming into the marina parking lot. He searched me and detained me several times. It caused me a lot of embarrassment. I got to the point that I did not care anymore. "Hey, do your worst. I am doing nothing wrong."

I went to the Port Police Office in San Pedro and took copies of the documents from my mom's doctor, the power of attorney, and the health directive so that they would have a record of my mom's condition. She had a terminal illness and had signed papers before the illness had affected her ability to think, identifying that she wanted to die in peace with me on our boat, not in the hospital.

Mom's eyesight was going, so we went to the Braille Institute in Los Angeles and enrolled her for services. They were amazing. They picked her up at the marina, took her to the facility, and taught her how to deal with her failing eyesight. They gave us many amazing things like movies that were narrated so she could hear what was taking place on the screen and audio books. This worked out well for a while, and she loved going there. As her condition worsened, she had to stop going to Braille. I had to stay with her all of the time.

Unfortunately, I was still an addict. I wanted to stop but could not see a way to go to rehab with my mom needing me. It would have to wait.

Tom and I brought in the new millennium together, but shortly after that, we split up. He left his dog, Salty, with me.

Times were difficult, knowing that Mom would die soon. It was particularly hard when she no longer recognized my daughter.

Alice, a good friend who lived at the marina, came by to help me from time to time. My mom was a small woman. I could lift her and take her out onto the deck for fresh air and sunlight. We spent many days talking about everything. Her long-term memory was still sharp. She told me about her life, things I had wondered about, like her life with my dad and before my dad. She left nothing out. She said I deserved to know, and I was grateful. Things that did not make sense to me all my life now fell into place.

Within a short time, she went from walking on her own, to needing a walker, to being bedridden. She could eat only baby food and wore adult diapers. She wanted to sleep a lot. One day she said, "I am dying. Why should I be awake any more than I have to be?"

I could not argue with that, so her doctors gave me the pills to help her sleep and to control the blood clots. She refused to go to the doctor anymore, so they came to the boat a few times. Then she requested that they stop and begged me to make them leave her alone. We respected her wishes.

To better accommodate my mom, I tore out the sitting area in the main cabin of the boat and put a feather mattress in there. A friend put a board across the front of it that prevented her from falling out. For about nine months this was our life. I watched her die a little bit every day. I no longer wanted to be apart from her, even if she was sleeping, so I slept on the floor with the dogs next to her bed. The only people I saw were Alice, who stayed with Mom so I could go to the market, and the guy who brought me my dope.

No one in the marina, except the few people who did drugs, knew I was an addict. It was my dirty little secret. I would use only on my boat, never on my mom's. The guilt I felt was overwhelming, but it was not the time to quit.

It was an honor for me to be able to take care of my mom in her final days. It hurt like nothing else I had experienced, yet it also made me happy. She had done much for me throughout my life, and this was the least I could do for her. My love for her was everything. She was an amazing woman who was always by my side. She defended my right to be wrong. She was my best friend. No matter what crap I did, she never stopped loving me and believing in me.

She knew of my passion to one day move to Africa and told me she wanted me to take her ashes there if possible. If that wasn't possible, she told me to scatter her ashes where I saw fit.

Those long years and months were the most of everything. Most every human emotion: great love, horrible sorrow, and amazing gratitude.

21

LETTING GO

I have no idea why the various law enforcement agencies did what they did to me, other than to try to destroy me. Before any of this started, I had respect for law enforcement. This ordeal forever changed how I looked at every officer. I realize now, almost thirty years later, that some of them are decent people, but when I have to go through Los Angeles, I am very careful not to get pulled over. If I see a law enforcement vehicle anywhere around me, I break out in a sweat and feel sick to my stomach.

Did I hate the LAPD and the LASD? Did I wish them harm? With every fiber in my being, I wanted them to hurt. I wanted them punished for their actions against me and what they had taken from me. Fireman's Fund Insurance Company was also on my "hate list." They treated me unfairly, believed every lie they were told, and did not look at any documents I provided them. My hatred toward these people was strong and all-consuming, and it would stay burning inside of me for many years.

As I look back, I realize that I could have acted differently. I could have said no to the drugs and to the people I allowed into my home and my life as friends. My attempts to help Dino were a major contributor to my troubles—but in my mind, I was just trying to help this poor kid get a fair trial. All of this contributed to the storm that raged in my life for almost ten years.

I was not a follower of Jesus then. Now that I am, He has helped me to realize that evil is in the world. Sometimes it touches our lives and other times it grabs us by the throat. But He promises His children that

He will go with us through the storm and deliver us safely on the other side.

22

Freedom

Mom's condition continued its downward spiral on September 11, 2000. She was going to leave me very soon. She was so tightly curled into a fetal position that I could not lay her down flat. I tried to turn her over to make her as comfortable as possible, but her body was stiff. Her eyes were open, and when she looked at me, I could tell that she knew me. We both knew that her suffering would soon be over.

I measured time by her breathing. With each breath she took, I held mine, waiting for her to take another breath. I watched her for hours and talked to her about all the good times we'd had together. I told her how much I loved her and how sorry I was for all the bad things I had done and the pain I had caused her. I have no idea if she understood me or even heard me.

Morning gave way to the afternoon with no change. When night came, I made my bed on the floor next to her as I had so many nights before. I cuddled with my dogs, Sasha and Salty.

When I awoke the following morning, my mom's eyes were open and staring at me. I wanted her suffering to end, but I did not want her to go. She was my rock, my love, my mom. Oh, God, what was I going to do without her? She looked straight at me, and although she could not speak, her eyes told me everything.

I spoke to her, telling her that I would be okay, that I would make it to Africa. I would never forget all she had done for me, and my memory of her would never die.

I yelled to God, "Take my mom home; take her to heaven."

At that moment, Mom looked at me and took her last breath. She was gone.

Stunned, I sat with her in my arms. Her eyes were open, but there was no life in them. I gently closed her eyes.

Alone with the woman who had given me life, many thoughts ran through my mind. I kept hearing her say, "Paula, I love you," in the loving voice she always used when she said this.

At that moment, I believed I would beat the meth addiction and that I would make it to Africa. I thought a bit about God, but only that my mom was with Him. I was grateful that He had taken her home. I did not believe that He was with me. Why would He want to be near a sinner like me?

I was all alone. I had fulfilled my promise to my mom: I had taken care of her the best I knew how and had not put her in a home. She died where and how she wanted to, with just the two of us. Finally, the ambulance came to take her to the funeral home where she was to be cremated.

I phoned Amelia. She took our loss hard, but we all knew it was coming. She had no respect for me, but she loved me because I was her mom. She and Brent, her husband, knew I was on drugs, but they did not know the extent of my addiction. My daughter did not push me away. On the contrary, she wanted me to come to her house and asked if I was okay to drive. I was not because I could not stop crying.

I finally closed and locked my mom's boat. I spent the rest of the day on my boat, holding my dogs close, loving them as they loved me as only a faithful dog can. The following day I drove to my daughter's, and we mourned and cried together. She arranged the memorial and got me through it.

I wanted so intensely not to be a drug addict. I wanted to be normal, whatever that felt like—I had no idea since it was a distant memory. I had no idea how I was going to quit this addiction. I just knew that I had to get myself together.

I had already taken most of my mom's stuff to Amelia's when Mom came to live with me. All that was left were her clothes and photos, which were in storage at the marina, along with my photos and documents.

Almost immediately, I had a buyer for the boat, so with all of that done and the memorial behind me, it was time to get a job.

I did not look for a job in the mortgage business because my self-confidence and self-respect were at an all-time low. My life was in shambles. I found a job handling clients at a call center for executive travel.

To say I worked in a cubicle was generous. My space was more like a cubbyhole. The work environment was not great. The upside was that no one knew me or anything about my life. No one knew I was an addict as I functioned well, did a good job, and minded my own business.

I got my drugs from the same people I had for years. I was barely surviving. I went to work, scored my dope, went home, played with my dogs, went to bed, and then did it all over again day after day.

I firmly believed that I would go to Africa. I had no idea how or when, but the burning desire had become an inferno. It was all I thought about, all I cared about besides my dope and my dogs.

I hated that I was still on meth. I wanted so badly to quit, but I did not know how I could function without my dope. It had been a long time since I was clean. An addict forgets how to live without the stuff.

After a year of working at the travel call center, a ridiculously low fare of $350 was offered for travel consultants for a round-trip flight between Los Angeles to Johannesburg. I grabbed that opportunity but was not able to go until February of the following year, 2002.

I faced a decision: either I quit the dope altogether or not go to Africa. Well, the dope lost and Africa won. I made my plans. Quitting a long-running addiction is not to be taken lightly, but there was no way I could go to rehab. It was up to me and me alone to make it happen.

On Thanksgiving Day 2001, I ate the traditional dinner at Brent's mom and stepdad's in San Pedro. I had that day off plus Friday. I would need at least three more days off for my strategy to work. I planned to phone in the day after Thanksgiving and say I was sick.

After dinner I went back to my boat and did my last shot of meth. I grabbed the rest of it, as well as my needles and syringes, and threw everything into the ocean. I had bought plenty of Vicadin as well as Soma days before, so I was ready to do this.

Before my last fix wore off, I told my neighbor that I thought I was coming down with the flu. I asked if he would look in on me and the dogs the following morning. I took a couple of the pills and then crashed. I pretty much stayed that way for three days. Every time I started to wake up, I dosed myself again and went back to sleep. I managed to phone work. I was so sick it was not hard to pull off convincing them I was. On day four, I had only one more sick day off. It was time to start waking up.

That day I took fewer drugs and started coming around as the "downers" left my system. The more awake I was, the more okay I felt. Hour by hour I was not shaking, and I started feeling better. And my craving for the meth was gone! Holy molly! Was I really rid of this addiction?

As the day wore on and I was coming more fully awake, I kept worrying that this was a dream, and I would wake up with a needle stuck in my arm and a bag of meth next to me. But, no, it was true. I was awake and I was fine. Had I done it? Was I off meth after all those years? Yes! And I was never going back. Never.

I thought I had done it all by myself, but I later realized that God was holding my hand. It was He who held me together because there is no way a stone-cold addict like me could have ever kicked a meth addiction alone.

Now I could make plans for my trip to Africa. My old friend Doug, who was also on meth, wanted to go with me. His mother had died not too long before, and he had inherited a tidy sum of money. But I told him if he was to go, he had to quit the meth. Sure enough, he did! We were both clean.

We made our arrangements. I knew what to expect even though the last time I had set foot on African soil had been in 1988. Finally, the day arrived for us to leave. My neighbor took us to LAX. I was so excited I could hardly stand still. Airports still had smoking sections at the time, and Doug and I stayed in one, puffing away until our flight was called.

We arrived in New York for a layover. It was only when I was buckled in that flight and we took off that it hit me that the next time my feet touched the ground, I would be in Africa. I felt incredible freedom. I was on cloud nine.

We arrived in Johannesburg and got a connecting flight to Nairobi. It is a big busy city, and I felt like I had finally come home. Before my mom had gotten so ill, one thing we had talked about was Craig, who had truly cared for me so many years ago. She had loved him. I had severe guilt about the way I had treated him. I always knew that I loved him. I knew he was in Africa, but I had no idea where or how to get in touch with him. Mom had made me promise that I would try to find him and let him know how much he had meant to her. One day I would find him, deliver my mom's message, and apologize for what I did to him.

It had been about thirty-one years since I'd had any contact with Craig. The chances of finding him were incredibly slim because Africa is huge! All I knew was that he was a pilot for someone and that he lived in Arusha, Tanzania. This would be my starting point. On our second day in Africa, Doug and I boarded a bus early in the morning that would take us from Nairobi to Arusha. It wasn't too far, and we traveled on a good tar road. We arrived early afternoon and found a decent place to stay that had a nice restaurant and bar. We dropped our stuff, went to the middle of town, and found a travel agency.

If Craig was flying for someone, maybe they would know. I realized the probability was next to nothing, but I had to start someplace. I asked the owner of the agency if he knew Craig.

"Oh, yeah, I know him well!"

You could have blown me over with a feather. I repeated my question just to make sure we were talking about the same person. "I haven't seen Craig in over thirty years. Would you give me his phone number?" I asked.

He gave me two cell numbers and a home number for Craig.

Now what do I do?

Doug and I went back to the hotel, had a beer, and then asked the manager if I could make a call. He placed the phone in front of me. Okay, wait. I had to have another two beers before making the call. What do I say? I was not mentally prepared to have found Craig so soon.

After three beers I felt ready. I phoned the first cell number, a local Tanzania number. When I heard Craig's voice, my knees got weak. He

sounded just as he had the last time I'd heard his voice. Time stood still.
"Is this Craig?" I said.
"Yes, who is this?"
"You will never guess in a million years... It's Paula."
Dead silence.
"Are you there?" I said.
Still nothing.
"Craig, do you remember me?" I was quickly getting concerned that I'd made a horrible mistake.
Finally, he found his voice. "Yes! I remember you. Where are you?"
"Here. Arusha."
Silence again. Then he spoke. "Where?"
I gave him the name of the hotel, which, of course, he knew where it was.
"I'm on my way back from Nairobi. I'll be there in about two hours."
We agreed to meet him and his wife, Lola, at the hotel bar.

Those two hours felt like two years. I didn't know what to expect. I had treated him so poorly and hurt him so badly. He had every right to come in and tell me to get lost. But I was determined to fulfill the promise to my mom. I had come this far, and the ease in which I found him told me it was to be.

When he stepped through the door, I immediately knew it was him. When he saw me, a big grin spread over his face. I knew then everything was going to be okay. Lola came in behind him. I was shocked. She looked so much like me: red hair and the same type of mouth.

Craig and I hugged, and then we all sat down. We made introductions all around. It was a bit awkward at first. We ordered gin and tonics and then we loosened up. I told Craig about my mom and that one of her final wishes was that I find him and tell him how much she had loved him. It was so hard to keep the tears from streaming down my face, and it took me a while to compose myself as I told Craig what had happened to my mom.

We talked about lots of stuff. I apologized for all the horrible things I had done. He told me it was okay. It was long ago and all was forgiven. Lola was kind to me, but I sensed she was not happy that I had found her husband. Thankfully, Craig had told her about me.

We exchanged email addresses, and I told them I would stay in touch. I was in Africa for just about a month and was leaving for Ngorongoro Crater the following morning by bus. It was an amazing visit just to see him and learn that he was very happily married. I was thrilled for them, that he had found a new love, and that I was just a memory. I had done what my mom asked me to do, and I had also shed a lot of guilt I had been carrying around for years.

Doug and I traveled to the same places as Dale and I had years before, only in the opposite direction. We had a fantastic time. When it came time to board our plane back home, I was very sad to leave Africa. I longed to remain, but I was positive that I would be back soon. I would somehow live in Africa, my little voice said. What was this little voice anyway? It was not the drugs, for I was clean. It was not my imagination, but it was there in my head, and it was getting stronger and louder.

We arrived back in Los Angeles, but my heart and soul had stayed in Africa. My neighbor picked us up at the airport. I was over the moon to see my beloved Sasha; however, something was not right with her. My neighbor told me that Sasha had started walking funny and had a cough. My heart sank. *Oh, God, no. Don't let me lose her not her. Not now.* But in the back of my mind, I knew she was getting old, and it was just a matter of time.

Life back in the States resumed its routine. I only existed: I exercised in the morning, went to work, went home, worked on the boat on my days off, or I drove down to see my daughter, son-in-law, and granddaughter. I don't know if Amelia knew I was off of drugs or not; we never talked about it.

In the meantime, Sasha was getting sicker. I was at the vet's office with her every week. She had arthritis and had trouble walking. I started taking both my dogs to work with me. Salty was about six, but Sasha was almost thirteen. I would take them for walks during my breaks and lunchtime. One of the gals I worked with fell in love with Salty. This would later prove to be a lifesaver.

My fiftieth birthday in April came and went with no fanfare. I was home alone on my boat drinking black cherry soda and cheap white wine. I longed for Africa. It was all I could think about—all I wanted to think about, all I wanted to do. The voice grew louder still.

Sasha was getting very sick and was on so much medication that my heart was breaking. My "Road Dog," who had been through so much with me, was going to have to be put down soon. I was not ready, but the vet discovered that Sasha had cancer of the throat. I could not put it off any longer. I loved her too much to let her suffer.

Sasha had been through so much with me in the horrible '90s. If not for her, I don't think I would have had the will to live. It was for her I kept going: to feed her and take care of her. She was my whole life. I held her close and spoke to her while the vet gave her the shots. I felt her relax as life flowed out of her. They had to pry my arms from around her to get me to give up her dead body. The vet cremated her for me and put her ashes in a little gold box I kept.

After the grief softened, that little voice was not so little. The urge to go to Africa became intense; it was like a fire burning in my soul. Before, I never would have considered leaving Sasha and going to Africa, but now that she was gone, I had to ask myself, "What am I doing here?"

I made plans to leave, but in November 2002, the Rolling Stones were playing in Anaheim. No way was I was going to miss that concert. The Stones were also playing in LA on February 6. I went to both concerts; I thought that these were the last concerts I'd ever get to see my beloved Stones play.

Once I arrived in Africa, I had no plans of ever returning to the USA except for occasional visits. After attending the most wonderful Stones shows ever, nothing was holding me back from executing my plan. I gave Salty to my coworker who had loved her for so long. I spent my last Christmas with my family. Amelia gave me a big coffee table book by Bill Wyman called *Rolling with the Stones*, along with the Stones' CD *40 Licks*. When I packed my backpack, those went in it. As heavy as that book was, there was no way I would leave it behind. On February 7, 2003, I boarded my flight and arrived in South Africa two days later.

I had no idea what I was going to do or how I was going to do it, but I would make Africa my home.

23

BABOONS AND ME

I had arranged to volunteer for a month at a baboon orphanage near a small town in Northern South Africa called Phalaborwa. These were my only plans. I'd figure out what I'd do next later.

I loved working with the baboons. The babies stole my heart. They are so cute and smart—amazing animals. My time there was one of the best experiences of my life.

Working with them, I naturally came into contact with field guides and people who worked in the bush. I thought it sounded like an interesting job. After speaking to some of them who were as old as I was, I learned about an organization with a good reputation that offered affordable training. I could earn a certificate, and they would even help me find a job as a guide.

With that all set, I still had to wait for the course to begin in about two more months. Once my time with the baboons was over, I wanted to travel around a bit through Botswana and into Zambia to see the chimpanzees in northern Zambia. I took trains and buses, and I hitchhiked out of South Africa and through Botswana. I stayed in northern Botswana at an overland truck camping stop since I had my tent and sleeping bag. The owners let me do a bit of work for them. After two weeks, I entered Zambia.

I hitched a ride from the border to Livingstone and made my way to a backpacker's camp, where I put my tent up and settled in. I planned to stay for only a few days, but then I meet a Swiss girl named Sylvie. We hit it off.

Sylvie had about a week until she was going to join an overland truck and travel with them to Kenya. I had time to spare, so we looked at the map to see where we could go that was cheap and had camping areas.

We hitched a ride to the lower part of Lake Kariba, a very small village. We ended up getting there late at night. The camping area had closed its gates, so we went to one of the bars/restaurants and asked if we could put up our tent in front of the place. They took one look at us, two women with our backpacks and tent, and said that we could stay in the staff quarters.

The following morning they took us to the only camping area. It had three nice big chalets right on the lake. They had a restaurant and a bar…and cold beer. It was lovely, so we set up my small tent.

While looking out over the lake, without a care in the world, Sylvie and I were enjoying our fourth or fifth beer. Suddenly, we heard two vehicles coming in: big Toyota Land Cruisers decked out with World Food and IFRC (International Federation of Red Cross) stickers all over them. We took one look and said to each other, "Who are these two yahoos?!" We watched as two guys were each shown to separate chalets. Then they showed up with their beers and started circling Sylvie and me. They took more than one good look at our lovely little tent. They must have walked past us a dozen times before the older one, Dan, finally asked, "What are you doing here? You alone?"

"Yes, that's our tent. We are traveling together."

The two guys exchanged amazed looks, clearly not believing that two women were in the middle of nowhere with no vehicle and just a small tent to sleep in.

We chatted for a while, and then they invited us to their chalets for dinner, where the cook was already at work. They insisted we move our tent at least closer to the chalets. We had put up the tent in front of a pool with ugly water covering the bottom of it—a mosquito breeding ground. We readily agreed to their invitation. A free meal and all the beer we could drink and a lot fewer mosquitos. As the night wore on, Dan talked us into sharing their chalets with them. Since Dan and I both smoked and were about the same age, and the other two did not smoke, we decided I would share Dan's chalet, and Sylvie would share the other one.

The chalets were large and each had two double beds. I made it clear there would be no funny business. As we talked more, we learned that they both worked for the UN on the emergency food aid program. They were based in Choma, about two hours from where we were and about two hours north of Livingstone. Both of the guys were what are called European Africans: native Africans but they were white.

The guys were hitting the booze, but it was getting late. Sylvie and I wanted to go to bed. They told us to go ahead and make ourselves comfortable, promising not to wake us when they went to go to bed. I took a shower and put on my conservative pajamas. I was tucked into my bed with the mosquito net secured around the bed and reading. Dan came in. I could not believe after all he had drunk that he was still standing up and holding a glass of whiskey.

He started talking and talking, and he kept drinking and trying to get me to drink whiskey. I declined and repeatedly told him that he should get some sleep because they had to be back in Choma the following morning for work. They were going to give Sylvie and me a ride that far, and then we were going to catch the bus back to Livingstone.

He tried kissing me, but I pushed him away. "Hey, look buddy; I'll just go sleep in my tent. I am not going to have sex with you or even kiss you. I made that very clear from the beginning."

He relented and plopped onto his bed, still talking, trying to tell me how lovely I was. I told him he was just drunk and to go to bed. At four in the morning, he finally went to sleep. They had to be on the road in just four hours. At 7 o'clock his alarm went off. He got up, fresh as a daisy. I could not believe it. All the booze he drank and not one bit of a hangover.

Dan was good-looking, big-boned, broad-shouldered, wavy brown hair, and big brown eyes—a very sweet kind guy. I rode with him, down the mountain to Choma, and Sylvie rode with his friend. Dan was lonely and wanted someone other than another guy to talk to. He said he would be in Livingstone the following night and asked if he could take me to dinner. I agreed and reminded him not to get too excited as I wanted only to be friends, nothing more. He accepted that and said he'd pick me up at the backpacker's camp at about seven the following evening. As it turned out, he stood me up. I was a bit pissed off, but no big loss since I was not interested in him.

The following morning I was in my tent when all of a sudden Dan poked his head in, a big grin on his face. Before I could say a word, he apologized. He had gotten stuck in Choma and could not get out till this morning. Since I did not have a phone, he had no way of contacting me. He asked me to have dinner with him that night. I couldn't refuse. He handed me money for a taxi to meet him at a very small camp/lodge on the outskirts of Livingstone. It was a cozy little place with a few chalets, a bar, a restaurant, and a big camping area with some large safari tents. The cook was preparing our dinner and had set up a table in front of Dan's chalet.

We had time before dinner would be ready, so we went to the small bar; nothing but a few chairs and a pool. When Dan asked me what I wanted to drink, I looked up and spotted a bottle of Kahlua. This was Zambia and not in a tourist resort. In all the times I had been in Africa, I had never once seen a bottle of it. My mom and I had been big White Russian drinkers. Before Mom got sick, she always drank it the same way: two parts Kahlua, one part vodka, and a bit of milk. I asked the bartender if I could have a Kahlua and milk. What happened next made every hair on my body stand on end. He said, "Madam, would you not rather have a White Russian?"

I stared at him in disbelief. Not only had I never seen a bottle of Kahlua while in Africa, I had never heard anyone ask for or get a White Russian. I nodded, unable to speak. And then when he made the drink *exactly* as my mom would have, I freaked out a bit. I had three more, all made as if Mom were making them. I had no idea what to make of it.

Dinner was served at the chalet. Dan was on his eighth whiskey and showed no sign of being drunk. I had a pretty nice buzz going on by this time while still being freaked out over this whole White Russian thing. We ate dinner, but Dan said he was not feeling well. *No wonder, you idiot. You've had eight double whiskeys with a tad of water. What do you expect?* Little did I know at the time that eight whiskeys were nothing to him. But he did look a bit odd.

Dan begged me to stay in the chalet. He feared he was coming down with malaria. There were two beds in the chalet, so I agreed to stay to be sure he was okay. Again I made it clear that he was not to think of doing anything funny or I would immediately leave. He promised. I felt his head and noted that he was running a fever. Maybe he was sick. He went straight to bed.

The following morning he looked really bad and was burning up. I took him to the doctor. Sure enough, he did have malaria. He asked me to stay with him for a couple of days until he recovered. After three days he was much better, and we had plenty of time to talk. He begged me to stay in Livingstone and would pay for my accommodation and food and even buy me a phone so he could call me from Choma. What did I have to lose? He had not tried anything with me, so I agreed. He took me back to the backpackers' place and paid for a week. He gave me enough money to cover my meals nicely!

So it began: every Friday night he would drive in from Choma and we would stay in a nice place. After about three weeks, we became intimate. I moved from my tent to an available camper. Dan came on the weekends, and we would either camp at the Waterfront in his rooftop tent or get a room. Then he drove drive back to Choma on Monday mornings for work.

When he was in Choma, he phoned me every day at least four times and sometimes more. Dan drank a lot on those weekends, and I thought it was because he worked hard during the week and needed to relax and have a good time on his days off. In the beginning, I tried to keep up with him. Big mistake! The first night I tried, I was sicker than a dog and stayed sick with one of the worst hangovers of my life that lasted two full days.

This routine lasted for about three months until he finally rented a house for us in Choma. The owners of the backpackers' place did not want Pepper, the little floppy-eared big-eyed cuddly dog that had belonged to the original owner and had been my constant companion during my stay at the backpackers', so they told me to take her. The town was small with not much for me to do; Dan was gone a lot in the bush working, so I had nothing to do but read, clean house, and cook dinner.

If not for that little dog, I would have gone crazy. But I had grown to love Dan and felt that I was meant to be there.

I did get to experience much of what Africa was about. Having been born and raised there, Dan was full of stories. We often went camping at a little-known national park called Lockinvar that was only about a three-hour drive from Choma. Dan's uncle had run the place after Hubert Smith, father of the famous African author Wilber Smith, passed away. Dan had grown up visiting it when it was a cattle ranch. It was wide open, the plains stretching forever and supported a lot of wild game. We camped in our roof-top tent and cooked over the open fire. We were usually the only people there. It was amazing.

One night we were awakened by a soft beating on the front of the tent. Neither of us was stupid enough to check it out, but the next morning we looked. We saw where a leopard had jumped onto the bonnet of the vehicle and had laid on the roof right outside our tent. It was exciting, a bit scary, but also a wonderful experience.

In June 2004, Dan's contract with the UN ended, so we decided to go back to South Africa, pick up his vehicle, and then figure out what to do. Dan had never traveled without a vehicle, so he was at a loss as to how to get where we needed to go. For me, it was nothing to get around Africa, or anyplace, with no vehicle. I got us sorted, and we packed, leaving Pepper with the garden boy, who loved her. The house rent was paid up for two months, so we left everything there and took only the stuff we thought we would need.

Zimbabwe was going down the tubes fast, but it was still safe to travel there. The problem was that inflation was so high, you had to have foreign currency to change on the black market, or else to buy anything would cost about a hundred times more. We made our way to Victoria Falls right over the border from Zambia and caught a bus to Bulawayo. There we ran into trouble because we had US dollars, but in Zimbabwe, they wanted South African rand, of which we had none, but we did manage to change a bit to get us going.

We found a bus of sorts to take us to the South African border post of Beit Bridge, about sixteen kilometers from the nearest South African town of Messina. For some reason, the bus stopped by a large fuel station–truck stop about ten kilometers from the border. The drivers unhooked the trailer with everyone's stuff in it. Then the drivers hopped onto the bus and told us they would be back soon. We waited and waited. It was getting later and later. We were in the middle of nowhere with all of our stuff and no bus. I took matters into my own hands. I told Dan to get our belongings out of the trailer while I walked over to the fuel station. After a short time, I found a nice guy who was going across the border and had agreed to take us. The guy had to leave us at the bottom of a steep hill because he had goods he was exporting from Zimbabwe to South Africa and had to clear customs. So our ride ended about seven hundred meters from the immigration post.

By the time we got up the hill, hauling our stuff, we were huffing and puffing and red in the face. Immigration and customs wanted us out of there before we passed out on their side of the border, so they checked none of our bags and stamped us out. We had to do the whole process again on the South African side. We were on South African soil, but we again had run out of Rand, and it was getting late. I left Dan sitting with our belongings and searched for a solution. There were no banks to exchange money, and we had no way to get to Messina. I spoke to several mini-bus drivers until I finally found one who would take our US dollars for bus fare. Those sixteen kilometers took forever as the bus had only two gears: first and second. It chugged up the hills and coasted down the other side. We did manage to get to town and found a reasonable hotel that took Dan's passport for security for the room until we could get to a bank the following morning and change dollars for South African rand.

We took the train to Pretoria the following afternoon, arriving at about four in the morning. We had to remain in the station because no one is allowed out of the gate till about 6 a.m. It's just too dangerous. We were in the middle of a very cold South African winter; sitting in the very cold breezy station waiting for the gates to open so we could go to the backpackers' camp I had booked.

We had to get to Pietermaritzburg, where Dan's 4X4 Toyota Hilux was stored at his attorney's office. We boarded a comfortable South African bus. I had already booked a hostel that had en suite double rooms and a lovely garden. Dan visited his two children and grandkids while I stayed at the hostel. Dan hadn't told anyone about me, and I was not ready to meet his family.

The time arrived to head back up to Zambia and pick up Pepper as well as the belongings we had left there. We drove back through Zimbabwe, still so beautiful in 2004. We had bought a good tent, sleeping bags, and all the camping equipment we needed for the two of us. We camped along the way and had a lovely trip. Dan taught me more about Africa along the way. Pepper was waiting for us in Choma. We did not spend any time in Zambia but just loaded up and started back.

In those days it was not easy to transport a dog across the border into South Africa. We had to smuggle Pepper over the Zimbabwe–South Africa border. Originally, Pepper, who was at this time an old dog, had been brought from Nigeria in an overland truck. She was a real trooper, so when we got to the South Africa border, I said, "Border," and she lay down on the floor, quiet as a mouse. Driving through the gate where they check you, Dan was a wreck. He had no experience with smuggling. Pepper and I were fine. They asked Dan to get out of the vehicle and open the trailer. He went white. Pepper was under my long skirt and never made a sound, but Dan almost blew it. His hands were shaking, and he fumbled with and dropped the keys. I don't know how the customs officer did not know something was wrong, but he let us through.

We had no idea what we were going to do with ourselves. Dan had saved quite a bit of his UN salary. We decided to go to Phalaborwa and see if we could volunteer at the baboon facility. The woman who ran it was surprised to see me and welcomed both of us. We began our four-month stay in a small camper she had on the property, next to one of the large cages of young baboons. I loved it there; many of them who had been my babies when I had left in 2003 still remembered me. I worked with the babies, and since I knew the routine, I was allowed to play with them as well as be with the older ones.

Four months later, Dan and I grew tired of the mud, the dirt, and the daily feeding of the big wild baboons that lived in the area around the facility. So we packed up and set up camp at a place in Phalaborwa. After a while, I grew tired of camping. We rented a tiny one-bedroom house in town. When I had been there in 2003, I had met a nice family.

Dan and I spent time with them occasionally during our time with the baboons. We spent that Christmas of 2004 as well as New Year's with our friends.

One day we were moving a bed around and somehow my foot caught on something. I fell hard onto the cement floor. Dan was sure I had broken my arm, but I said it was just bruised and would be okay. He insisted he heard a bone crack. I put ice on it, and after about two hours, it started turning all kinds of colors and the pain became unbearable. He took me to the hospital. Yes, it was broken, but it was a clean break and did not require anything but a sling and pain pills. My arm healed in eight weeks. I removed the sling and slowly regained strength in my arm.

Dan and I were getting restless, and we needed to do something to earn money. Dan suggested that we contact a woman we both knew up in Zambia who was starting an Orphans and Vulnerable Children's Center at a mission in a small village in Western Zambia, not far from Livingstone. I emailed her, asking about bringing in outside temporary volunteers up to help out. She wrote back telling us that she could use the help and to come on up.

I created a program with an itinerary that included information about the mission, how volunteers could help, and also a bit about the three-country tour on the way up to Zambia. Volunteers could not only help in and around the mission but also see a bit of Africa. I sent the information out to volunteer organizations that looked like they might be interested in this program. An organization contacted me, said they liked it, and added us on their website.

This was an unusual program with lots of appeal for volunteers, and no one was doing this type of thing. The volunteers would arrive in South Africa and take the bus to Phalaborwa, where we would pick them up and transport them to a campground for two nights. Then we would drive up to Zambia, camping the whole way. We'd spend nine nights in the village helping out at the OVC (Orphans and Vulnerable Children's Center), the mission grounds, or any place in the area that needed help. From there we would take the volunteers to Livingstone for three nights to see Victoria Falls and have some fun. Then we would drive back to Phalaborwa, a four-day trek, and stay two more nights before taking the volunteers on a safari in Kruger National Park. The following day we would put them on the bus to Johannesburg, making the whole tour in twenty-six days.

At the end of February 2005, Dan and I traveled to Johannesburg to purchase tents and basic camping equipment we'd need to implement this program: tents, tables, metal plates, a small propane tank with a cooker top for it, and various other things we needed. We were running low on funds by this time. If this did idea did not work, we had no plan B.

But it did work! In March five volunteers booked to go on the very first mission tour in April 2005. Honestly, we were not fully prepared. We had only a double cab Toyota pickup and a trailer. We had made some friends in Phalaborwa and paid one of them to make a basic safari body for the back of the pickup. It had canvas sides and plastic windows that could be rolled up and secured.

The first group of five arrived on April 4. We did not know what we were doing, but we had a plan and forged ahead. The trip worked out very well. Dan was our driver; at each overnight stop, we would camp African style. It was an adventure, and the volunteers loved it. We would unload everything and the volunteers put up their tents. Dan took them around, showing them the sights and telling them stories about Africa and his growing up there. I prepared dinner. I was used to cooking on the propane tank with the cooker on it, but the meals were basic because there was a limit to what I could do on one cooker. We carried all the food, pots, pans, dishes, and tables…everything we needed in the trailer. It was most of our worldly goods.

On the first trip down, we learned of a great new campground in the bush in Botswana called Elephant Sands. We decided to give it a try. It was pure heaven in unspoiled wild Africa. The first time we drove in, elephants were everywhere. This place was right on our way both going up and coming back. Though very basic, it was the perfect camping place. We were the second guests ever to stay there. We met the owners, a jolly guy named Ben and his wife, Marie. They were amazing and the same age as Dan and me. We became fast friends. Since it was difficult to cook there, Ben cooked dinner for us at a reasonable price. The volunteers loved it there—we all did—and I did not have to cook!

We knew the dates we would be there each month, so we established a standing reservation.

I had no idea what I was getting into with this first group, but it was very successful. This one trip went on to become a once-a-month adventure. It began what has become my life's work.

When working at the OVC and Mission, we camped on the mission grounds. As time went by, we met a lot of the people from the church, and since we were always there on a Sunday, we took the volunteers to the church service. The first time I walked in, I thought, *I wonder if this building is going to burst into flames with my coming in.*

I have no idea the exact date my mind started wandering in this direction, but I found myself thinking about God. I often talked to the ladies from the church. Listening to them and watching them daily, I couldn't help wonder why they were happy all the time. They were really poor people and had so little, yet they were joyful. They had something I did not have and never had: peace. How did they get that? Little by little the voice in my head started to make sense, and at some point, I knew it was God speaking to me. I was dumbfounded. How did that happen?

My daughter and I had been emailing each other, and by the end of 2005, we both noticed a difference in what we were saying. She asked me, "Have you found God?" I told her I thought so. She then told me that she had also started on her walk with God and had found an amazing church. The whole family was attending every Sunday. A new relationship bloomed between my daughter and me.

Our volunteer program was in full swing. Dan and I worked with groups of volunteers every month except February as it was just too wet. Since I had not been back to the US for three years, and we had a little bit of money saved up, we decided it was time for me to go back in 2006 to see my family, whom I missed horribly. When I left, my relationship with them was shaky. I wanted desperately to mend things, especially with my only child.

When I arrived in California, I was warmly welcomed, and she wrapped me in her loving arms. She and Brent had missed me. This trip began the healing of my relationship with my daughter and family. We talked about God and how He was changing our lives. I went with them to church and loved it! This was not a traditional church with everyone wearing their Sunday best; rather, it was a teaching ministry, and most attendees wore jeans and flip-flops. They were real people you could relate to. What the pastors taught hit so many buttons inside me. Thoughts I'd had about God and my life started to make sense.

My daughter and I had some issues to work through. The '90s haunted me. Amelia had bad memories and no idea what had happened during that time. And other issues regarding the life Dale and I had lived had to be addressed. The church had a counseling department, so Amelia made an appointment for us. The counselor helped us to get things into the open. I cried a lot, but we were on the road to recovery. My heart was full of joy.

That voice that had spoken to me for so long now had a name: God. And He was doing things in me, changing me in good ways.

I met one of the pastors, an amazing teacher who made sense of the Bible, bringing it alive. I discovered that the Bible was about God and me. The words spoke to my heart and mind. The pastors and teachers were good to me and provided a great learning experience for me. They gave me hundreds of sermons on CDs so I could listen to them at home in Africa.

When it came time to return to Africa, I was very sad and couldn't stop crying. I had to go back, but I now had a wonderful relationship with my family, especially my daughter. I was torn about leaving; my heart was breaking. I had no idea when I would be able to come back. But I heard God—I was learning to listen to Him—telling me, *Go back. Africa is where I want you. This is just the beginning of a new life.*

I felt so different upon my return. I saw Zambia as my new home, and I felt something inside me that had not been there before.

As soon as I got back, we had too many volunteers booked for March. We had to get a second vehicle. Dan's credit was good, so we purchased a new 4X4 Mahindra that could seat four plus the driver. It had an enclosed back so we could load a lot more equipment. While I was in the US, I had gotten my driver's license renewed since it had expired while I was in Africa. Now both Dan and I were driving with eight to nine volunteers at a time. However, I was so tired after driving it was getting too much for me to cook at every stop along the way. Over time we had developed relationships with the campsite managers we stayed at, so we arranged with them to cook dinner for us.

As the number of volunteers kept increasing, it wasn't long before we had to trade in the Toyota for a new Land Rover Defender 110 that could seat eight plus the driver. With it, we towed a trailer. With that and the Mahindra, we could carry everything and everyone.

The tours were very successful. The volunteers loved traveling through three countries, seeing a little of Africa. But the strain of constant travel was wearing out Dan and me. We had made good friends with people at the local church as well as the village chief. They wanted us to stay in the village and spend more time with volunteers working at the OVC and mission.

By this time I was starting my journey with God. I was like a sponge, wanting to know more and more about Him and my relationship with Him. I listened to the CDs Amelia's church had sent with me. I attended the local church, but I could not understand the sermons. They were for the local population, of course, and the speakers' accents were so strong that I couldn't catch everything. But I loved the fellowship with the people, and the singing was powerful. I felt good inside worshipping with them.

I wanted God in my life, turned my life over to Him completely, and got baptized. This was not easy to do, but I did not doubt that God had been with me, protecting me, for all of my life. There was just no other reason why I was still alive, in good health, and not rotting in a South American prison. It took me fifty-four years to pay attention and make the right turn. I couldn't have done that without God working in my life.

A lot happened in 2006. In June, a volunteer arrived. Matt was an electrician and very handy. He was the only volunteer we'd ever had who did not have an email address. He was rather quiet during his time with us. When he left, I figured we would never hear from him again.

We changed the volunteer program in July 2006, to have the volunteers fly directly to Livingstone. Now the volunteers would be at our campsite at the mission for two weeks, cross over to Botswana, make the five- to six-hour drive down to Elephant Sands and stay there for two nights, drive back up to Chobe National Park, just over the border from Zambia, for two nights, cross back over the border and stay at the village for five more nights. They would spend three nights in Livingstone to see Victoria Falls, have some fun downtime, and then fly out of Livingstone to return to their homes.

24

WHAT TREE

We made a quick trip to South Africa and purchased four big canvas safari tents, as well as a big circus-type tent for use as a kitchen, along with a better three-burner propane cooker and other equipment to make camping a bit easier and more comfortable.

We hired a night watchman and a helper to do the cooking. I got busy training her how to cook Western food. She was eager to learn and I was happy to teach her because I was tired of cooking.

Volunteers arrived. With the new tents and equipment, the accommodations were much nicer. You could stand up in the tents and they slept four. We had purchased two-inch foam mattresses for the volunteers to sleep on. We were still camping, but it was more comfortable.

Dan and I decided to get married in August 2006. At that time we were staying in the house that was for the doctors, but with no doctor, the house was vacant. I did very little planning for our wedding. The women at the church, along with the missionaries from the UK, organized it all.

The volunteers who were there were invited to the ceremony. About a week before the wedding, they gave me a "kitchen party," which is part of the African wedding celebration. We got married in the church, officiated by a reverend. It was a real church wedding and reception, so very different from the four ceremonies with Dale or his proxy. This was my first real wedding and celebration. The choir sang and we had dancing. A lot of people attended many I knew but some I did not.

Everyone wore the traditional dress of the tribe we lived with including me and the wedding party. It was very colorful and so much fun. The whole thing—food, wages for the women who cooked it, dresses for the wedding party, beverages—cost about $2000. A merry time was had by all; however, I do think half the village had a hangover the next day.

Soon enough the mission hospital hired a doctor, so Dan and I moved out of the house and back into the tents.

Later that year I got a surprise: an email from Matt! He had gone back to the UK and was very unhappy. He wanted to know if he could come back and work for us. He knew we could not pay him much, but he said that he had property in the UK that he rented out, so he had income. Well, yes! We could use the help. In time I came to realize that this man was, and still is, a gift from God.

In January 2007, Matt arrived. The church was able to process Dan's and my work permits. That was a scary time because there had been a miscommunication between us and the person who had been working on our permits. By the time the church applied, we had overstayed our time in the country by about fifty days. Immigration told the church that we would have to get out of the country *immediately*!

Dan and I began making arrangements to travel to South Africa. I was going to wash my passport in a machine and then get a new one that had no days in Zambia stamped in it. The Immigration Department was not computerized back then, so this would have worked. I don't remember what we were going to do with Dan's, other than he would have to stay in South Africa until a new passport could be issued for him there. Americans can get a new passport in just a few days but not South Africans.

I have no idea how the church was able to convince immigration to let us stay *and* issue our work permits, but in a few days, the problem was sorted. I know this was an act of God because we really should have been thrown out. The church did us a big favor and made us mission partner's—missionaries. I have no idea why they would do that for us. We did not have a sister church that they were partners with to allow us to be mission partners, but we were, and Dan was not even a Christian.

The mission ground was crowded and it had only one bathroom. So Dan I moved back to the campground we had stayed at when we had first arrived. The owner was more than happy to have us as permanent residents and charged us no more than we had been paying the mission. It was a nice place with power and two separate toilets and showers. The lovely location was right on the river.

Pepper was still with us, but we wanted another bigger dog, so the night watchman found us a lovely dog. I named her Salty. She was part Rhodesian Ridgeback and part village mutt. She was lovely with her "Mohawk" that ran down her back. She reminded me of my Sasha.

We wanted to do more to help the villagers, but we did not know how to go about offering aid or what to do. One day we were in our camp waiting for the next group of eight volunteers to arrive, and an elderly man on crutches approached us, boldly saying, "I am an elderly man taking care of my orphaned grandchildren. We have no place to live."

We could hardly believe what we'd heard. Although we had been in the village for some time, we never really *saw* the village, just some vendor stalls we purchased items from. We had no idea what was going on in the village or its size. And we certainly had no idea how bad the living conditions were.

We drove the old man to his shack, an accurate description of his living space. It was nothing more than a few pieces of old wood wrapped in black plastic and a cardboard "roof." It was tiny, and in it sat his very elderly wife with three young kids running around. How had we been there for this long and never knew people were living like this?

Now we had a project that needed our help. This man needed a home. Since almost all of the homes in the village were, and still are, traditional "termite mound mud" made, the nicer ones had wood poles supporting them. We decided to study several of them to find out how they were constructed.

We drove around and talked to people who lived in nicer homes. Some even had iron sheets for the roof. Matt pretty much figured out how these were constructed. Now we had a basic design to work with.

The frame came first. We dug holes and then secured large poles in them. We took tree branches, stripped them of their foliage, and tied them onto both the inside and outside of the frame, creating a cavity. Next, the mud-balling stage. We ordered from a local man loads of termite dirt to be delivered to the location. We mixed it with water to make mud balls and filled the cavity with them. Next, we "threw" the mud onto the structure, covering up all the small poles (branches) on both sides. The sun is strong, so this all dries in a very short time. Then we created another mud mixture, but this time the dirt to water ratio is more water than dirt, so the mud is not as thick, allowing us to smooth it over to make an even layer and fill in all the cracks. We decided not to roof it with thatch because there's not proper thatch available, only dried grass that does not last long and allows the rain to eventually run down the walls, destroying the structure. Matt designed a wood frame to attach to the poles so we could nail metal roof sheets to the frame. These huts are cool in the summer and warm in the winter, and the metal roof protects the structure. These have been around for ages, and they work well. The ones we put up last for about fifteen years.

The first one we built using volunteer labor had several minor issues as Matt was just learning to do this. It took two months to get it up and get it right. The volunteers loved doing this work. They got a look at African life and came to know the people they were helping. It was a big success for all involved.

Before we finished the first one, we had requests for four houses. So we started a list. Time went on and the list grew longer and longer. About four months and three huts later, we had a long list. Then I thought that I should ask the chief if he approves of this. No one else was building for families who had no place to live to take care of their suddenly growing families.

I should point out that this village is steeped in very strong traditions, and their culture is unique. They strive to keep it alive and pure and do not allow orphanages anywhere in this province. The orphaned children are taken care of by extended family members. The families are tight-knit, as it has always been. But due to the devastation of HIV/AIDS, many elderly people found themselves having to care for their grandchildren after their adult children have passed away. This village had a serious problem as the elderly did not have suitable places for these kids to live in.

I made an appointment to see the chief, an amazing God-fearing man whom we all love and deeply respect. But I couldn't just knock on his door; I had to go through channels. For some reason, he liked me. We did not know him that well at the time, but he agreed to see me. I explained to him what we had been doing and how the list of people wanting us to build homes for them was getting longer and longer. I asked him what he thought about it and if it was okay to continue.

He was delighted and told me that he had hoped we would help his people in this way. I wondered about this. We had been here for over two years, and I had seen him on other occasions, so why hadn't he advised me that this was what he wanted us to do? As I said, it's a very different culture, sometimes confusing, one you learn by living here. And one thing I learned is that for him to ask us or even tell us what he wants us to do is just not done.

He assigned one of his counselors as our advisor to help us determine who was eligible to get a home. The people in need would go to him and give him a copy of their National Registration Cards. He would then give us a letter stating this person was on the list. Matt began meeting with him regularly to plan who would be next on the list.

In this part of the country, the land belongs to the chiefs and cannot be purchased. He gives it. We requested from the chief a piece of land for us to build our house so we could put down roots. We had no idea if he would agree. We were not Zambian and not from the tribe. Who were we to have land? But the chief granted us a big parcel of land. A few years later, when I knew him a lot better and was with him at one of our meetings, I asked him why he had given us a big parcel of land when he barely knew us. What he said I will never forget. "I had thought about it, but I have no idea why God put that thought in my mind long before you requested the land. God told me to keep you in this village, so I just listened."

I will forever be grateful that our chief listened to what God told him. This village is my home now.

We went with his minister of lands to the parcel we had been given, which was outside of the village and covered with big trees and bush. It was not exactly what we had in mind. It wasn't near anything and it was big. They pointed to a tree in the distance and said the land went back to "that tree." What tree? There was nothing but trees. I had no idea what tree he was referring to, but Dan and Matt thought they had some idea.

The first thing we had to do was clear the land, which was going to take some time. Our night watchman had a brother who needed work. He also had no place to live and nothing to eat. Perfect! Along with the watchman's brother, we cleared a patch of bush and gave him one of our old nylon tents. He now had a place to stay and a job. He came into our campsite once a day to get food to last until the following morning. Every so often he came to our campsite and showered. We hired another guy a few months later to help him, but this one skinny guy did the majority of the work. Digging one big tree stump out of the ground by hand is extremely hard work. And we had to remove dozens of them.

In the meantime, we stayed in the campground, keeping busy with welcoming volunteers every month and building huts. I had been using the internet hookup at the mission, a great inconvenience. I had to drive over to the mission, plug my laptop into the cigarette lighter adaptor, and work in the hot cramped car. A phone company had just put up a tower, so we had the use of our cell phones—before this, we had to drive for about an hour to get a signal. With that tower, we could use a dongle that we plugged into our laptop, for which we had to buy data, and we could connect to the internet. The village was slowly coming into this century with cell phones and interest access. I had power at the campsite, so I was set. My office and bed (foam mat on the floor) were in the tent, but Dan had a desk made for me. It had become necessary to now have internet access as we were getting many more volunteers. This was a good situation, but it created a lot more office work.

It took almost eight months for our land to be cleared enough for us to even think about moving onto it. Even then it was barely livable, but our minds were made up for us when the guy who owned the campground informed us of a significant increase in our rent. He gave us three weeks' notice. So I gave Matt and our guys (we now had four guys working for us) two and a half weeks to make it happen. The property was far out of town, and it had no water or power. In fact, there was no water company. Our options were to go to a public pump or hauling water from the river. Power was not planned for this area for years.

Dan and I were pretty good friends with the people who owned a chain of stores in Zambia that sold lots of things, one of them being generators. They had visited the area often on vacation with their boat and knew how we lived. I guess they took pity on us as they sold us a generator for half the price. Elephant Sands gave us one of their old propane refrigerators. Matt and Dan cleaned it up. It worked somewhat; at least it would keep the butter from melting.

All the guys we had working for us, plus a couple of other young guys we hired for the two weeks, got busy digging deep holes for long drop toilets as well as clearing more of the land so we'd have even ground to pitch the sleeping and kitchen tents. Matt and Dan got busy hooking up outside showers. The construction of these things is complicated to explain, but they were very basic. We used three large metal drums that hold two hundred liters of water each. We rigged up our supply water on a gravity feed. Under one of them, they built what is called in Africa an "embola," under which you built a fire. Voila! A primitive water heater.

We had a one-week break between departing and arriving groups of volunteers. So the middle of September 2007, we moved onto our own land that would be our home for as long as we lived. It was primitive, but it was ours.

To get water, the volunteers went down to the croc-infested river with buckets, and two of our guys waded into the river. They made an assembly line to get the water to the Mahindra that we had removed the canopy and made it a pickup. In the back of the vehicle, we had two big plastic drums, also holding two hundred liters each. Once they were full, we drove back to camp, about four kilometers from the river. We had a tiny pump that we installed in an old cooler box. The volunteers and the staff would bucket water from the plastic drums into this, and the tiny pump slowly pumped the water up to the big metal drums to supply us with both hot and cold water.

The two showers had plastic buckets in them. We turned on the water just long enough to get wet and fill the buckets, soap up, and then rinse off using the buckets. Hair washing was quick and basic. We got our drinking water from the reverend's house. His water came from the mission, which had sand filtration and was good drinking water.

The volunteers loved this setup! They thought this was the real Africa that they had signed up for. Volunteers kept coming and our work went on. With no power, I still had to sit in the hot car and work on the computer, but at least I could stay home and do it. We ran the very small loud generator for two hours in the night.

The night sky was a constant delight, for the stars were so bright and the skies clear—very little light pollution.

Our night watchman made a big fire each night, lighting the way to the toilets at night. Every night we made a campfire for the volunteers to sit around until bedtime. It amazed me how much they loved this type of "vacation."

We were still running the Botswana safari four nights each month. Matt stayed at the camp when Dan and I took the volunteers on safari. It was a real treat to have running water at the campsites when on safari. Elephant Sands was still an adventure. We still took our old, nylon tents and camped, but they had a much better water system. Although it was salty water, there was a lot of it. We also went on "bush camps" out of Elephant Sands, taking the volunteers out to the wild bush. It was amazing to see and be close to so much wild game. In the evenings, we sat around the campfire eating dinner and listening to Ben and Dan's stories about life in Africa in the "good old days." We were in the middle of nowhere. We listened to the sounds of the bush and the many animals all around us. It really was an African adventure—now my life.

It soon became apparent that we needed the tent Dan and I were living in for the volunteers. The canvas kitchen tent was fast falling apart, so Dan got busy building two structures. When you live in an area that has termite mounds up to twenty feet tall, *do not build with wood*! I, of course, did not realize this, California city girl that I was, but Dan should have known better since he was born here. If you've ever encountered termites, you know how destructive they can be. Well, our termites are on steroids.

It took some time, but we hired extra guys to build a kitchen and a living area for us; Dan used a lot of wood as support. He used bricks for the walls and put our living space in the middle of the camp. This turned out to be less than ideal as we had no privacy. He put up the kitchen very near to it. I ended up living in a bug-infested, crawling-with-ants barn-like structure with no ventilation. And remember: we had no power so no fans. In the summer, it was hotter than anything you can imagine; and in the winter, it was colder than living in the Rocky Mountains in a tent in January. I never thought I would say this, but I longed for my tent! I would live in that for years.

The year 2009 was a big year but also a hard year. Money was tight. Our Land Rover had been seriously overheating, so we took it to the dealer in Lusaka to get it fixed. Halfway home we realized it was not fixed but we had no choice but to drive it back, praying it would make it and stopping often to let it rest and put more water in. Since they did not fix it, they picked it up and brought us a loaner vehicle, a mini-bus, so we could continue with our work and the Botswana safaris. The guy who was towing our vehicle drove off a mountainside and totaled the Land Rover. Thankfully, the driver was okay. Their insurance would pay $20,000, but a new Land Rover cost $35,000. We applied the insurance money to a new Land Rover and the dealer carried the paper for the balance. I had to pay it off in installments of $1000 per month. Thank God they did not charge us interest because the rates were about 30 to 40 percent.

Two amazing volunteers came back to us in 2009. One was from the UK and the other from Australia. Both stayed for a couple of years. The church took care of obtaining their work permits as well as Matt's. The woman from Australia also donated funds for building huts—a lifesaver.

I quit smoking after forty-three years, one of the most difficult things I have ever done. Seriously, it was so hard. African cigarettes are cheap and many people smoke, including Dan. But I had to quit because I was coughing my lungs out every time I got a sniffle. Any cold I caught went straight into my lungs. I was on antibiotics for months, puffing, coughing, and convincing myself and anyone else who would listen that it was not the cigarettes making me cough. The mind is a powerful thing, but in the end, I had to stop lying to myself.

The Australian woman was so very kind and generous, she offered to pay my fare to go back to see my family. It was so amazing to see my loved ones. My son-in-law is a Rotarian and knew about our water problem in Africa. He had me speak at his club. This was something new to me, so my presentation was crude but from my heart. His club, as well as another club along with a private donor, raised $16,000 for us to dig a borehole! I was beside myself. I could not believe we were going to have water.

It had been three years since I had seen my daughter, but we had kept in touch over the internet. Our relationship was growing by leaps and bounds; we were drawing closer together than I ever imagined. My grandkids and I were getting to know each other. My grandson was too little to remember me from my previous visit, but my granddaughter remembered me.

We went to the amazing church every Sunday, and I again met the pastor I loved so much. This time instead of giving me CDs to take back with me, they gave me DVDs. They taught me so much. I had never experienced a church like this one. I became a member, so now I had a home church!

The visit was good for me. The bond I now had with my family, especially my daughter, was solid. God had done this. He brought us together in ways I never thought possible. It was truly a miracle. My daughter finally respected and loved me, a gift that meant everything to me.

Leaving again for Africa was horrible. I cried and cried, again not knowing when I would be able to go back. But it was time for me to go home.

25

Long Drops

The $16,000 the Rotarians had raised for the borehole was transferred to me. I found the Rotary Club in Livingstone, which I joined. Imagine me a Rotarian! So every Friday I drove into Livingstone for supplies and attended the Rotary meeting. There I met Margaret, a most amazing woman who became a dear friend and my mentor. She put me in touch with several companies who did this kind of work. One of them was willing to come out to the village.

We got water, lovely flowing water! It was not drinkable due to our sandy soil, but we could use it for everything else. No more hauling it from the river. We had to purchase another generator to pump the water as we still had no power. We got it at half the cost, and the Rotary money paid for it as well.

A whole new world opened up for me now that I now had friends in Livingstone. I love Rotary and everything about it. I made friends and worked my way up first as secretary, a role I held for two years. Then, amazing as it sounds, they made me president for the Rotary year 2013–14.

Our work with volunteers continued to grow. In 2009, large school groups came in, which became our staple. These groups did so much for the village as well as help us to survive. We built a makeshift campground in the back of our property for them. They brought their tents and did all of their own cooking. Every year they would come, the numbers grew, increasing not only our income but also what we could do in the village. We built them a better campsite in the front portion of the property and dug for them long drop toilets. It was perfect. Another company came in as well, with lots of students eager to experience Africa and to help the people in the village. We owe much to these groups. They not only helped us but also built homes for the villagers and bought many of their supplies from our local vendors.

The village was growing out our way. Suddenly we had neighbors, and electricity was now within our reach. A former volunteer from the UK donated the funds for the electric company to hook us up. Being an electrician, Matt wired everything. By the end of 2010, we had water and power. A couple of Rotarians from the USA came the month when we had gotten power and purchased our first electric refrigerator. We could now store food, and our menus for the volunteers got a whole lot better. We also purchased a freezer.

The volunteer numbers increased. Life was so much better. We could have fans and finally got a real stove. Up until now, our cooks cooked everything on a BBQ that Dan built. If the food had to be baked, they heaped coals on top of the baking dish. They were quite creative, and the volunteers could not believe what these gals could do without a stove or an oven. Matt and I even cooked a turkey one Thanksgiving in this makeshift oven. But now we thought we were on easy street with an oven, refrigerator, and freezer! Of course, we still had long drop toilets and outside showers, and the volunteers were still in tents. But we were blessed.

I watched my DVDs from the US church all the time and kept learning about and growing in Christ.

In 2011, the International Rotary Convention was held in New Orleans. Our club had an ongoing shirt project. Former sex workers who wanted to get out of the business were selected through the Catholic Church. We paid for their tailoring classes, and at the end of the course, we gave each one a sewing machine. They sewed shirts with the Rotary logo on them, and we sold many of them at these conventions. My club paid for half of my airfare plus most of the convention expenses in 2011. After the three-day convention ended, I went on to California to see my family again.

My grandson was old enough for me to get to know, and my relationship with my granddaughter bloomed. I had missed most of their short lives, and for that I was sorry, but my daughter had explained to them that it was God who wanted me in Africa; I was doing good things. Having been raised as Christians, they understood somewhat why they never saw me. I did send them videos of my life in Africa, including lots of wild game I was able to be so close to on safari over the years.

I went to church with them; saw my favorite pastor, who, once again, sent me back with three years of sermons on DVDs. I watched them all at home. They taught me how to live and love as a Christian. Everything they said made sense. The Bible was not just a boring book I could not understand. With them walking me through it, it became the living Word.

My daughter trusted me with driving her vehicle, and I would do chores for her and take my grandson to and from school. My family was truly my family. I was in awe of what God had done for us all. Leaving was again very sad because I never knew when I would be able to get back. But God told me, *It's time to go.*

Life went on. The Mahindra died, so we took it to the dealer in Namibia, just over the border, and gave it back to them. We needed another vehicle. We bought a Toyota Hilux double cab. We had saved enough money to purchase it from a private party.

In 2012, I received a donation of $5000 from a woman who had been here volunteering at one time. It was to help me build a real home in the back of the property, away from the main camp. Our staff built it with two other guys from the village. This was the first time I got involved in building in Africa. No way was Dan going to design or build my home. No wood, only cement blocks and metal window and door frames. Matt helped a lot. It is not a complicated design and nothing fancy but functional. It has a bathtub, a flushing toilet, one bedroom, a living room (that would be my bedroom), a kitchen area (but no appliances or sink), my office, and a laundry room. My staff could not understand why I wanted them to put "small" rooms in the house. It took some explaining for them to understand that they were not rooms but closets and one pantry. They had never seen anything like this before.

We had a big group come in from Canada the day we moved into the house and the day before I was to take them all to Botswana. I was so tired I thought I would die, but we were in the house, though it was not completed. We'd finish building it around us.

At that same time, a friend of mine was moving to a much smaller home in Livingstone and was selling most of her furniture. Lucky for me and great timing because we had very little. I bought a futon, TV, assorted tables, lamps, and a few other things. By this time we had a double bed. It went into the bedroom for Dan; I slept in the living room on the futon.

Dan's drinking had worsened. Although I hate to include this segment, it was a big part of my life and my walk with God. While I knew Dan loved me very much and depended on me for everything, he often was abusive. When drunk, he called me horrible names. At times he threw things at me (but always missed). I was frightened at times, but mostly I was stressed. Often he apologized in the morning. He was always very kind and sweet to the volunteers; it was only me he would abuse. This drew me closer to God. I prayed for strength to get through it and to help Dan. I had married Dan for better or worse. No matter how bad the situation got, he needed me. Someone had to take care of him. I was his wife and knew he could not help himself.

He started falling asleep when driving, and he sometimes walked sideways even when sober. He knew he was sick and something was very wrong. He got so bad I finally told him he had to go to the doctor. As much as he hated to, he went to see him. He had a brain disease caused by alcoholism. He stayed in the surgery at the doctor's office for five nights and was warned that if he did not stop drinking, it would eventually destroy his mind and kill him. Alcoholism is a disease and not just an addiction. He just could not stop drinking. I do think he wanted to, but it was not going to happen.

In 2013, a couple from my son-in-law's Rotary Club, whom I knew well, came over and brought all of my photos, which were in big albums. I had dated them and included where they had been taken and who was in them. They were my life and history. To have them was a precious gift.

The most amazing volunteers started coming in, including large groups from universities in the UK, Canada, and the USA, and many former volunteers came back and brought their friends or families.

And we had many new people volunteering. They did a lot of work in the village, which was appreciated and needed. They built homes and purchased goods in the growing village. Their support through the years was truly amazing. Almost all of our volunteers were great, loving, caring people. We appreciate everything they did for us and this village.

Many of these volunteers sponsored children's school fees, allowing us to send over thirty-five children through high school. After a while, we decided that because the high school fees were low and most of the villagers could afford them, instead of continuing this program, we'd start a college sponsorship program. With many generous donors, we have sent, and continue to send, many students through college. Without our many donors, we would not have been able to do this.

I have always been a paper pusher, a skill that came in handy as every donated dollar, whether for building huts, sponsoring children through school, or any designated gifts, is documented.

In 2014, with so many volunteers coming, we had saved enough money to build two chalets with en suites. One has four beds in it; the other is a dorm that sleeps ten in five bunk beds. These rooms opened up the way for older volunteers or those wanting better accommodations to come.

A very good friend, Paul, came to us in 2006. He lives in Northern California and had always helped us with sponsoring school children as well as donating funds for whatever we needed. He had met my family one year when I was in the USA. He had flown in and spent a couple of days with us in Southern California. A dedicated Christian man, he is one of the finest human beings I have ever met. In 2014 he found out I had used all of his donations for the village and had not been back to see my daughter since 2011. This got his knickers in a knot and he told me I was to use part of the funds he sent me to pay for my airfare back to the USA every year.

In 2014 I did go back and have been every year. I was so blessed to visit my family every year. My relationship with my family, including my cousins and my only niece, continued to flourish. I got to know them all again.

While visiting in 2014, I found Rick, my old friend from 1969, and his son, Darrell, who had grown up with Amelia. I was overjoyed as those were some of the best times of my life. Through Rick I reconnected with other old friends and started getting to know them again. It had been many, many years since I'd seen any of them. Because I was able to go back to the US every year, my friendship with many of them grew. We shared many memories. My life was getting better and better. What had I done to deserve so much joy? Nothing! God just showered His grace on me, and all I had to do was to remain in Him.

In 2015, we parted company with the church by mutual agreement. We became a nonprofit nongovernment organization: Home for Aids Orphans was born. I will always be grateful to the church for all they had done for us through the years. Without them we would not have been able to stay in Zambia and grow; we owe them so much. Though it was not always easy, it was time we stood on our own. I had to learn how the government here worked and how to comply with the rules and regulations in an African country, as well as get our work permits. It was hard and scary. What if I failed in some way or did something incorrectly and got us all thrown out of the country? With the help of a very good attorney, I got it right and registered with every appropriate agency, including putting all of our employees on the pension plan, registering with the federal government, and fulfilling every requirement to run a nonprofit in this country.

In time we built up the camp site and installed a toilet block for the volunteers as well as a storage room with a refrigerator for their food and supplies. We also built a six-foot-high brick wall around the entire property. It took years to complete, but it created security, making the volunteers feel safe.

The groups came in increasing numbers. Every single volunteer who has come, and will come, holds a special place in our hearts. Without them, we could do nothing. Their help and continued support are above anything I had ever dreamed of. Many lifelong friendships have come from our amazing volunteers.

26

LIFE WORTH LIVING

Right after Christmas 2015, I was sitting in my bedroom when Matt phoned me and told me to put the dogs away. He and Dan were bringing me something. *Oh no. Not another dog.* I had five and, please, no cats. We had tried that before and it did not work out well for the cats. I was not going to do that again. Matt assured me it was neither.

You could have blown me over with a feather when Dan handed me a tiny baby Vervet monkey! Oh my! But what was I going to do with a monkey? Well, I didn't have much of a choice. If I did not take it and care for it, it would die. Period. It was love at first sight. Once she wrapped her tiny hands around my neck I was hooked. I phoned friends in town who had raised monkeys and got a quick lesson on what to feed her and how to care for her. I rushed to town the following day for baby formula and bottles. My staff made a cage for her. So began my "mothering" of baby Vervets.

A wonderful organization in Zambia takes the babies after they are weaned, rehabs them, and puts them with their own kind. They are eventually released back into the wild. They were so helpful in walking me through the process of raising these tiny amazing creatures I loved so very much.

DJ was my first, and when she turned six months old and was on solid food, it was time to give her to this organization. I cried for days, but she was ready to go onto her next adventure and a new life in the wild. The parting was painful. I was her mom, and she loved me as her mom. It's hard to describe the love and affection she gave me, but it's very real. Then to my surprise, DJ was not my only "baby." I raised three more in the next four years. I am expecting to raise more in the coming years. It is an amazing experience, and each baby has been special with its distinct personality. I believe God sends me these babies because He knows how much they need me and I need them. The organization and I have a great relationship, and they call me when they have an orphan.

How did I ever get so lucky to live my life in Africa, to be able to have a life worth living, doing something that made a difference to someone other than me, and loving it so very much? And to also get to raise baby monkeys, to love and take care of them, and to receive so much love back from them? I have no idea why God choose me, of all people, to give so much too, to make my life a good one. If anyone was undeserving it was certainly me.

The more I learned to walk with God, and the more I watched the sermons from the church in the USA, the more I understood about God and His great love for me, the more I wanted to know. Jesus is now a big part of my life. I know that *no one* deserves His love and forgiveness. He died on the cross for all of us; we only have to come to Him and ask for forgiveness.

In 2016 Dan's drinking and his condition were in a downward spiral. I had to help him...or try to help. With threats and begging, I finally got him to agree to go to a sixty-day rehab in South Africa. I can't say that Dan was happy, but I gave him an ultimatum: "Go into rehab or I am leaving you. I just can't take it anymore." So he went. But within ten days of coming home, he started drinking again.

I had stopped drinking and would not allow anyone to drink in his presence, but it did no good. I tried praying with him and had him watch the sermons with me. Despite everything, he could not stop. I never gave up praying for him, but his drinking jumped to a whole new level. It was not his fault; he was a good and loving man, but the alcohol would not let him go. He was always great with the volunteers, and they all loved him. But when he drank, his treatment of me was horrible. Too often during these moments, I wanted to kill him just to shut him up and stop him from yelling at me. Of course, I felt awful and asked God to forgive me. I asked Him to get me through this time and to show me how I could help Dan.

Early in 2017, we built a third chalet that sleeps six people in three bunk beds. We can now house twenty people. We took down two of the tents. For the two that are still usable, we laid a slab and kept two beds in each. They come in handy when we are busy and need extra beds.

My granddaughter, Ariel, her friend, and my son-in-law, Brent, came out in 2017. Ariel spent her eighteenth birthday with me in Africa. One gal who had been here before brought her parents, a South African girl was still with us, another young former volunteer came, and a seventy-three-year-old Australian woman came, who was the hit of the party. It was one of the best groups ever. Matt and Dan went to Botswana with us. It was so amazing to be able to show my family where I lived and what I did, as well as all the amazing game we saw on safari. Ariel stayed with me for two months, but Brent went home after Botswana. Other volunteers came and went when Ariel was here, so she got to know a lot of people around her age from all over the world. I was so proud of her. She took to Africa and worked hard alongside all the other volunteers. Ariel left in August. It was sad to see her go, but I would see her in October.

Dan's grandson came out in 2018 for a month. I had not seen him since he was a little boy. He was a delight to have with us. We got to know each other much better. Dan's daughter has been out two times, in 2012 and 2014, and we have a close relationship.

My yearly visits to the USA are great! I get to clean up, wear nice clothes, put on jewelry, and be a girl—so different from the world I live in.

I started speaking to Rotary Clubs. My speaking skills have greatly improved, and my presentations are much better than my first one. Many clubs have helped and are still helping to build a community school.

In February 2019, Dan was drinking more and barely eating. His sleeping times had been erratic for years, but they got more so. He slept for hours and hours, got up, and drank until he passed out. So went the cycle. At times he slept for days, then get up refreshed and got on with it.

I did not think anything was different on February 10 when he slept almost the entire day. Late that afternoon, he was in his room drinking when I heard a crash followed by moaning. I rushed into his room and found him on the floor, unable to get up. This had happened before, but something different was in his eyes. They were turned partway up into his head. His color was sickly. Something was very wrong. Dan was a big man and too heavy for me to lift by myself. I phoned Matt, who hurried over. We got Dan onto the bed in a sitting position, but he kept falling over. He was in bad shape.

Matt held him up while I grabbed a thick foam mattress out of the storeroom. We had virtually no furniture in the kitchen area, so Matt and I laid the mattress on the floor. We managed to get Dan into the kitchen and onto the mattress.

I knew in my heart that he was close to the end. He seemed to know it as well. All that day he drifted in and out of conciseness. When awake he begged me not to take him to the hospital. Truth be told, there was nothing they could do for him, not here. We have no life support equipment, and Dan would not have wanted it anyway.

He wanted to smoke, so I lifted his upper body and sat behind him to support him, lit a cigarette, and held it to his mouth.

We had volunteers with us, so Matt had to explain to them that Dan was very sick and I was with him. They were great girls and understood the situation. They had seen Dan only a couple of times since they had been with us and it was obvious to them that he was not well.

The day wore on. At times he convulsed, his eyes rolled back, and he went weak in my arms and passed out. Then when he woke up, he wanted another cigarette. This went on through the night. When he was awake and lucid, I talked to him about God and how he still had time to ask God for forgiveness and turn his life over to Jesus. To my surprise and joy, he did! I have to believe he meant the words he spoke. I believe God gives you until your dying breath to come to Him.

While Dan was in the process of dying, I also had to care for my third baby monkey. Matt came back to my house at times to check on Dan, but I needed him to be with the volunteers. I was more or less okay. I had been through this before with my mom, but it was a stressful night for all of us.

I kept Dan's brow wiped and turned him as best I could, trying to keep him comfortable. At one point he looked at me with so much love and trust in his eyes. "Paula, please forgive me. You are the great love of my life. I know you will stay with me until the end."

I told him I loved him as well, and I did. I would never have left him, and I surely would not leave him now. Late on that same afternoon, a gal who came to see us from time to time arrived. Matt told her what was happening, that I was fine, but to leave me alone for now. I would need her help in just a short time.

Dan lived through the night, but his time was very short. I phoned my daughter for moral support. Talking to her helped me. I prayed for God to take Dan as peacefully as possible. Dan had been in a lot of pain for a long time, both physically and mentally.

At 11 a.m. on February 11, Dan took his last breath while I held him in my arms.

I phoned Matt. He and Crystal, the German gal who had arrived the night before, came to the house. We have no morticians here, so it was up to me and Crystal to clean Dan and dress him in his burial clothes. Sadness filled me but also relief that Dan was finally at peace. After preparing his body, we rolled him into a blanket.

I had to go to the hospital and tell the doctors what had happened and get a permission form to use the mortuary. That done, I returned home. With the help of my staff, we carried Dan's body to the Land Rover, placed him in the back, and took him to the mortuary building. The doctor had to come to the building and pronounce him dead.

I had phoned his family the day before when I knew he was not going to live. I phoned them again. His daughter, Tania, made arrangements to fly up from South Africa for his burial on the fifteenth. I drove into Livingstone on the fourteenth to purchase a coffin and to pick up Ryan, the son of one of my girlfriends in the US, who was scheduled to arrive to volunteer with us. He had been here before and knew Dan.

The news spread throughout the village like wildfire. The customs here are very different from the West. When someone passes, the people in the village assemble at the "funeral home," the home of the deceased. The men gather outside, the women inside. They all mourn until the day of the funeral, staying all day and all night. The ladies cook for everyone. This would not do well for me because I needed to be alone. A few of our very good friends advised the people who were planning to mourn with me that this was not our custom. Everyone understood and left me alone.

The day of the funeral was wet with drizzly rain. Our close friends went out early in the morning to dig the hole for the burial, as is the custom. The missionaries from the UK were amazing. They drove down from Lusaka. Due to their intervention, we were able to bury Dan in the private small graveyard across from the hospital, as well as use the little chapel for his service. One of the missionaries gave the eulogy. It was comforting to know God was there with me. Tania stayed for a few days, as did Crystal. My husband was laid to rest; his burial site is close, so I go over often just to say hi to him.

Epilogue

In 2019 we received enough donations, including the Rotary Clubs', not only to build on to a small building but also to open up a community preschool, kindergarten, and first grade. I have no idea why God put this in my life because I don't do well with small children! But I know He wanted me to do this. The children of this community needed this school because the only other primary school in this village was built in the 1950s for a student body of about 350, but they have over a thousand students.

In 2019 a group from Scotland came. They had raised funds for a second grade, which opened in 2020. We then got a donation from a woman whose Rotary Club had earlier funded a first grade and one of the toilet blocks. Now they wanted to build the office and storeroom. My family, as well as my niece and her husband, had also donated funds for the second toilet block we needed. Two other school groups raised funds for the third grade, which has been completed. Two Rotary Clubs in the US have donated funds for an additional two-toilet block.

I am constantly amazed by God and what He is doing here in Africa. Why has He chosen me for this task? That's a question I always ask. I am an old woman who finally found what I had been looking for in all the wrong places all my life. I found God, and with Him, I found peace and forgiveness of all my numerous past and future sins. I am in the earthly home until He calls me to my eternal one. This is where God wants me. He uses me in ways I never imagined, and at times I don't understand. I sometimes try to get out of what He has planned, thinking that I have a better plan. But His voice in my head and heart is persistent. I try to listen closely and pray that I am walking the way He wants me to. Yes, I still sin, and I will always sin, for I am human. I had too many years of doing life my way. God is much better at it than I am. He is on the throne of my heart, directing my life now.

The Beginning

Acknowledgments

My daughter, Amelia McFarland, for her support financially, emotionally, and spiritually and for her unwavering love.

Brent McFarland, my son-in-law, who never gave up on me or this project.

Ariel Kempf, Debbie Price, Paul Greenberg, Robyn Greenberg, Ramona Alt, Margaret Whitehead for reading the initial draft and pointing out my many mistakes.

Paul Kupras for his spiritual support and for reading the early draft and giving me much needed feedback.

Dorrie Ball for correcting part of the original manuscript so many years ago in my office in Africa and Amanda May for her moral support.

Erin Brown for editing. Lynnette Bonner for designing the front cover. Richard Gregory for editing, reading, and the shoulder to cry on. Taylor Durick for creating the back cover artwork.

Desmond Hitchins for opening his house to me in Livingstone and lending his ear.

And last but certainly not least, Matthew Jon Burditt my business partner, who's been like both brother and son, and has put up with me and this story since 2007.

About the Author

Paula Van Zyl lives most of the time in her village in Zambia welcoming volunteers and showing them the beauty of this part of Africa. She enjoys escorting visitors on safari to Botswana to experience the majesty of the African bush and its wild game. Paula nurtures infant vervet monkeys so they can be rehabilitated and sent back to the wild.

She continues to raise funds to build a village school and awareness in the USA to bring to light the plight of the children in the village who desperately need a start in life and an education. Her time in the USA is spent with her family including the newest member, the first great grandchild.

This book is the story of her life experiences from one extreme to the other and her conversion to Christianity late in life in Zambia.